G000113683

Educational Innovation in Economics and Business VI

Educational Innovation in Economics and Business

Volume 6

The titles published in this series are listed at the end of this volume.

Educational Innovation in Economics and Business VI

Teaching Today the Knowledge of Tomorrow

Edited by

Tor A. Johannessen
*Norwegian School of Economics and Business Administration,
Bergen, Norway*

Ansgar Pedersen
*Norwegian School of Economics and Business Administration,
Bergen, Norway*

and

Kurt Petersen
*Norwegian School of Economics and Business Administration,
Bergen, Norway*

KLUWER ACADEMIC PUBLISHERS
DORDRECHT / BOSTON / LONDON

A C.I.P. Catalogue record for this book is available from the Library of Congress.

ISBN 1-4020-0478-8

Published by Kluwer Academic Publishers,
P.O. Box 17, 3300 AA Dordrecht, The Netherlands.

Sold and distributed in North, Central and South America
by Kluwer Academic Publishers,
101 Philip Drive, Norwell, MA 02061, U.S.A.

In all other countries, sold and distributed
by Kluwer Academic Publishers,
P.O. Box 322, 3300 AH Dordrecht, The Netherlands.

Printed on acid-free paper

Printed in the Netherlands.

Contents

Contributors

Biscaccianti, Alessandro, *Group ESC, Dijon, France.* *abiscaccianti@escdijon.com*

Carey, Catherine, *Western Kentucky University & Northeastern University, USA.* *cathy.carey@wku.edu*

Corbitt, Gail, *California State University, Chico, California, USA.*

Costea, Bogdan, *Lancaster University, Bailrigg, Lancaster, UK.* *b.costae@lancaster.ac.uk*

Christensen, Gunnar, *Norwegian School of Economics and Business Administration, Bergen, Norway.* *gunnar.Christensen@nhh.no*

Crump, Norman, *Lancaster University, Bailrigg, Lancaster, UK*

Courvisanos, Jerry, *School of Economics, University of Tasmania, Locked Bag 1 – 315, Launceston, Tasmania 7250, Australia.* *jerry.courvisanos@utas.edu.au*

Dalglish, Carol, *Brisbane Graduate School of Business, Queensland University of Technology, Australia.* *c.dalglish@qut.edu.au*

Estenstad, Nils A., *Trondheim Business school (TØH), Sør-Trøndelag College, Norway.* *nils.estenstad@aoa.hist.no*

Feron, Michel, Head of Strategy, *HRM and Organisation Department, Reims Management School, 59, Rue Pierre Taittinger, 51100 Reims, France. michel.feron@reims-ms.fr*

Forsythe, Frank P., *University of Ulster at Jordanstown, Northern Ireland. fp.forsythe@ulst.ac.uk*

Frederick, Jenifer, *Queensland Audit Office, Brisbane, Australia.*

Gütl, Brigitte, *Business Education and Evaluation Research, University of Innsbruck, Innsbruck, Austria, Brigitte.guetl@uibk.ac.at*

Haaken, Stefan, *D2 Vodafone, Düsseldorf,* Germany, *stefan.haaken@d2vodafone.de*

Hubbard, Graham, *Monash Mount Eliza School of Business, Mount Eliza, Australia.*

Kelly, Martin, *The University of Waikato, Waikato, New Zealand. Kelly@mngt.waikato.ac.nz*

Koch, Adam J., *School of Business, Swinburne University of Technology, Hawthorn, Australia. ajukkoch@netscape.net*

Lassk, Felicia, *Western Kentucky University & Northeastern University, Bowling Green, KY, USA. f.lassk@neu.edu*

Maes, Rik, *Department of Information Management, University of Amsterdam, The Netherlands. maestro@fee.uva.nl*

Malik, S.D., *New Paradigms Consulting Group, 30 Lake Lacoma Drive, Pittsford, NY 14534, USA.*

Martz, Ben, *University of Colorado at Colorado Springs, Colorado Springs, Colorado, USA. wmartz@brain.uccs.edu*

McCuddy, Michael, *College of Business Adminstration, Valparaiso, Indiana, USA. mike.mccuddy@valpo.edu (mike.mccuddy@sbinet.com)*

Morse, Ken, *Waikato Management School, University of Waikato, Hamilton, New Zealand. kmorse@mngt.waikato.az.nz*

Murray, Lynn, *School of Computing and Information Technology, University of Western Sydney, Australia.* *l.murray@uws.edu.au*

Neil, Thomas C., *Clark Atlanta University, Atlanta, Georgia, USA.* *penguin@mindspring.com*

Pirie, Wendy, *College of Business Adminstration, Valparaiso, Indiana, USA.* *wendy.pirie@valpo.edu*

Ravn, Jakob, *CBS Learning Lab, Copenhagen Business School, Copenhagen, Denmark.* *ravn@cbs.dk*

Schroeder, David L., *College of Business Adminstration, Valparaiso, Indiana, USA.* *dave.Schroeder@valpo.edu*

Semeijn, Judith H., *University Maastricht Research Centre for Education and the Labour Market (ROA), Maastricht, the Netherlands.* *JH.Semeijn@ROA.Unimaas.nl*

Solberg, Svein Linge, *Trondheim Business School (TØH), Sør-Trøndelag, Norway.* *svein.solberg@aoa.hist.no*

Strasser, Sandra E., *College of Business Adminstration, Valparaiso, Indiana, USA.*

Thijssen, Thomas J.P., *Anton Dreesmann Institute for Infopreneurship, Amsterdam, The Netherlands.* *adi@fee.uva.nl*

Thompson, Herb, *Murdoch University, Murdoch, Australia.* *hthompso@central.murdoch.edu.au*

Van der Velden, Rolf, *University Maastricht Research Centre for Education and the Labour Market (ROA), Maastricht, the Netherlands.* *R.vanderVelden@ROA.Unimaas.nl*

Vernooij, Fons T.J., *Graduate School of Teaching, University of Amsterdam, Amsterdam, the Netherlands.* *mail@fons-vernooij.nl*

Welte, Heike, *Business Education and Evaluation Research, University of Innsbruck, Innsbruck, Austria.* *Heike.Welte@uibk.ac.at*

Acknowledgements

The editors would like to express their gratitude to those who have made this book possible: first of all the EDINEB Network and the Norwegian School of Economics and Business Administration, Bergen, Norway, and in particular the administrative staff at the school of their generous sup-port before, during and after the conference.

Our warmest thanks to Ellen Nelissen (office manager of the EDINEB Network) and Bob Janssen Steenberg (graduate student International Business at Maastricht University) for all the background work making this book possible. Ellen Nelissen, whose excellent assistance in planning the conference as well as with the conference management greatly contributed to a successful conference. Bob Janssen Steenberg wrestled the words through the computer and delivered excellent work by producing this book. Henny Dankers conducted the final manuscript checks. Finally, we thank the authors for sharing their reflections and experiences with "Teaching Tomorrow's Knowledge Today".

Tor Aase Johannessen
Ansgar Pedersen
Kurt Petersen

The Editors

Tor Aase Johannessen is assistant professor at the Department of strategy and management at the Norwegian School of Economics and Business Administration (NHH). He is a graduate from the school, and holds an MBA from Johnson Graduate School of Management, Cornell University, USA. After several years in managerial positions within marketing abroad and in Norway, joined NHH in 1988. He has been a consultant to clients in the service industry, with emphasis on customer handling and expectations. Since 1994, he has been in the teacher-training program at the school. Tor Aase Johannessen has done research on evaluation of teachers in Europe, and is now a member of the National Council for Education of Teachers in Norway.

Ansgar J. Pedersen was associate professor of marketing at the Norwegian School of Economics and Business Administration until he retired a few years ago. For several years, he was Head of the Department of Marketing at NHH. Ansgar Pedersen is a graduate in Economics from the University of Oslo, and has completed the International Teachers´ Program at Harvard Business School. His main interest both for research as well as teaching has been the development and the competition in the distributive trade. Ansgar Pedersen has been a member of the board of the Research Centre of the Wholesale Association, and of the board of the Norwegian Retailers´ Institution for Education and Research.

Kurt Petersen is Director of studies at the Norwegian School of Economics and Business Administration. He is a graduate from the school and has had various administrative positions dealing with educational issues. Kurt Petersen has been chairman of the Student Affairs Committee initiated by the National council of Universities and has served as a member of various committees set up by the Norwegian Ministry of Education. He is now a member of the National Council for Education in Economics and Business Administration in Norway.

Preface

In the world today, change itself is said to be the only constant. Knowledge travels fast, through a variety of distribution channels, many of which were unknown only a few years ago. Therefore, knowledge can be a highly perishable commodity An important objective of the dissemination of knowledge will always be to ensure that it arrives fresh after the shortest possible route.

Academic research within the areas of business administration and economics has often been criticized by the business community, which claims that much of it is mainly directed at the establishment of researchers themselves, who reply to and discuss it within the establishment instead of distributing it to the business community. It may seem that many universities and other research institutions have turned into mere "know- ledge manufacturers", where the emphasis is more on the output volume than on quality or relevance, with little or no consideration for the end users. This further enlarges the gap between the research institutions and the business community, and paves the road for a variety of consulting firms, with hourly costs to the clients where only "the sky is the limit". To all responsible and serious researchers within the field of business administration and economics, this is not a desirable situation.

In addition, students may often wonder whether they are studying yester-day's knowledge, instead of being continuously updated on current and relevant research. The proliferation of learning opportunities today makes learning for tomorrow even more complicated. In our global society, success or failure in business frequently depends on which party has the most current knowledge of the issues and facts involved.

As universities and corporations attempt to prepare management to be alert to future changes, improved, and even brand new teaching methodologies are required. The main focus of the sixth EDINEB conference was on the distribution and selection of new knowledge. How can business educators deliver new knowledge to students and the business community more rapidly than before? How should we define the core business curriculum when new knowledge becomes old knowledge?

Through these articles presented at the conference and selected for presentation in this book, the editors feel that the many dilemmas involved have been well analyzed and discussed.

Tor Aase Johannessen
Ansgar Pedersen
Kurt Petersen

PART I

TEACHING AND LEARNING METHODS

Focusing on Capabilities Development to Reduce Knowledge and Skills Obsolescence

Alessandro Biscaccianti[1] & Michel Feron[2]
[1]*Groupe ESC Dijon, France,* [2]*HRM and Organization Department Reims Management School, France*

1. INTRODUCTION

The purpose of our article is to discuss the issue of obsolescence of knowledge in order to link *what* is learned and *how* it is learned.
We believe that:
1. learning is an exchange process amongst three main stakeholders: the students, the professors, the practitioners[1];
2. teaching and learning cannot be separated: each stakeholder holds the responsibility for the continuous improvement of the competencies of the others;
3. fundamental rethinking of pedagogical relationships amongst the stakeholders is necessary to avoid the obsolescence of competencies. This implies the definition of a new blueprint for the transmission and the validation of competencies.

The observation that, in French, the meaning of the verb apprendre can be to teach and to learn depending on the context of the sentence, has been the starting point of our thought

Our first objective will be to analyze how knowledge and competencies are linked, and why focusing on knowledge is misleading.

---

[1]With the word "practitioners", we make reference to both consultants and operational managers in companies.

3

T.A. Johannessen, A. Pedersen and K. Petersen (eds.),
Educational Innovation in Economics and Business VI, 3-17.
© 2002 *Kluwer Academic Publishers. Printed in the Netherlands.*

Second, we propose an enlarged pedagogical approach integrating all the dimensions of the development of competencies.

Third, we will show how this approach can be used to avoid the problem of obsolescence and how to evaluate all the dimensions of progress of the learner.

To conclude, we shall give an overview of two examples of what we implement in our school, and we shall situate our proposals in an historical context.

2.   OBSOLESCENCE OF COMPETENCIES IN CLASSICAL PEDAGOGICAL APPROACH

2.1   A few words about competencies

For the word *competencies*, French scholars and practitioners refer to three main components: *savoir, savoir-faire* and *savoir-être* (Klarsfeld & de Saint-Giniez, 1999; Grimand, 1995; Le Boterf, 1994; Aubret, 1993; Minet, Parlier & de Witte, 1994). The word *savoir* is related to the theoretical knowledge acquired by studying, *savoir-faire* to the skills acquired by doing, *savoir-être* to attitudes and behaviors.

Savoir-être can be dissociated from neither knowledge nor skills. It is the spring that creates the never-ending interaction between them, which is necessary to keep competencies up-to-date.

We translate *savoir-être* into English as **capabilities**, from the Latin *capere*, 'to take in or understand'. Moreover, the word capability includes the concepts of power and ability; which are at the basis of personal mastery (Senge, 1996.)

2.2   The priority of knowledge and the consequences on educational processes

As shown in Figure 1, it is possible to find close links between each specific dimension of competencies and educational methods. The transmission of *knowledge* is based on *teaching*, the acquisition of *skills* is based on *learning by doing* and the development of *capabilities* is based on *coaching*.

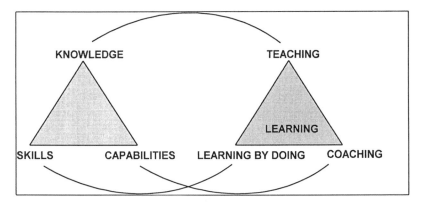

Figure 1: Competencies and Educational Methods.

This vision seems rational and encourages one to think that this might be an equilibrium between the three main pedagogical methods used to develop competencies. But, when we look at actual practices in Western countries, it seems clear that one approach is clearly put ahead, that of knowledge.

The consequence is that teaching is the most widespread pedagogical method, as shown in Figure 2.

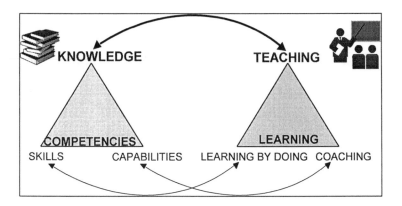

Figure 2: Priority of Knowledge in Classical Learning Processes.

2.3   The French context

An overview of the French educational system is useful to understand why our learning approach is truly innovative.

The French pedagogical approach is in its core similar to the one prevalent in Western societies. Nevertheless, a particular feature of higher education in management provides a chance to temper the priority of knowledge.

There are two main actors at play in the French context:

- The University System, focused primarily on creating and transmitting knowledge, even though some recent developments begin to integrate skills in pedagogical objectives;
- The *Grandes Ecoles de Commerce* (Business Schools), focused on making skills explicit and putting them into practice. Theoretical knowledge is considered as a preliminary basic requirement. Tenured professors are usually in charge of teaching the *knowledge*, while practitioners are recruited as visiting professors to transfer *skills*.

The University System focuses on checking students' theoretical knowledge while *Grandes Ecoles de Commerce* focus on checking students' ability to adapt and replicate operational skills.

Although in *Grandes Ecoles de Commerce* the practice of case studies and internship is highly developed, skills are often tackled by using teaching as the pedagogical method, instead of letting students learn by doing (see Figure 3). The reason for this preference can be attributed to the belief, typical of the French educational system, that knowledge and expertise are mainly properties of the individual that can be developed through formalization and rationalization (Baumard, 1996).

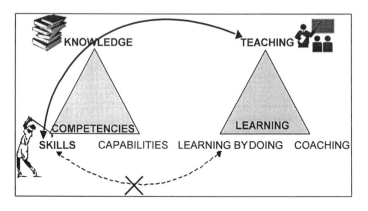

Figure 3: Competencies – Educational Methods Relationship in French Business Schools.

In systems, universities or business schools, we observe a subconscious and/or a critical preference for a mono-directional relationship instead of a bi-directional one between the professor (*the one who knows*) and the student (*the one who learns*). Some nuances can arise when working with small groups, where interaction between professors and students is easier.

2.4　　The ancient Greek theatre and the traditional French teaching

In ancient Greece, the theatre techniques were based on the unity of time, place and action. In the same way, despite the many innovative methods developed in the last ten years, still the most widespread teaching method seems to obey three rules: one time to learn, the youth; one place to learn, the School; one way of learning, the teaching (see Figure 4).

Even when students undertake a long internship in company, or enroll in a post-graduate program after some working experiences, the educational institution still remains the focus for acquiring formalized knowledge.

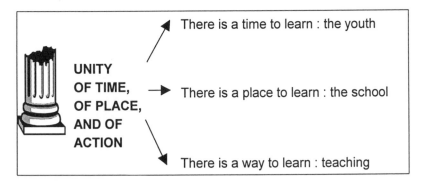

Figure 4: Greek Theatre and the Classical French Educational Teaching.

3.　　AN ALTERNATIVE PEDAGOGICAL DESIGN

Traditionally, the problem of obsolete knowledge is tackled by focusing on the determination of the right kind of knowledge and skills to be transmitted. Instead, we believe, the discussion should focus on pedagogical processes and tools, in order to let students master the processes of creating and internalizing their own competencies. We argue that with this alternative approach students develop a higher ability in making their competencies evolve with the tasks that they are assigned.

In our approach, we consider that learning has two types of results: the "product competencies" and the "process competencies" (Wolfs, 1998). Product competencies are what the individual is able to do facing a particular situation. Process competencies have to do with how individuals reach product competencies, i.e. the combination of learning strategy and learning skills.

The fundamental task of the teacher is to favor the development of process competencies. When teachers create a pedagogical approach, they must always consider how students will improve their process competencies when using it.

To reach these objectives, it is necessary to simultaneously introduce as often as possible double loop learning between the three main stakeholders (students, professors and practitioners).

As shown in Figure 5, when designing a course we always preserve the continuous internal and external interaction between the system of competencies and pedagogical methods. Therefore, all of the three dimensions of competencies (*knowledge, skills, capabilities*) are developed through the use of each pedagogical methods (*teaching, learning by doing, coaching*).

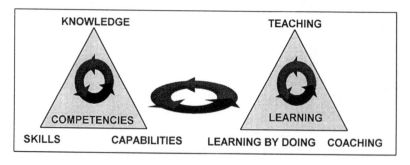

Figure 5: An Interactive Approach to Pedagogical Processes.

4.   CONSEQUENCES ON THE RELEVANCE OF DEVELOPED COMPETENCIES

The traditional learning process can be described as following (see Figure 6):
1. Professor observes and studies the practices of the company.
2. Professor creates the theoretical knowledge from this observation and study.
3. Professor transmits knowledge to students.
4. Professor checks the fit between his/her knowledge and the students' one.
5. Students use the acquired knowledge in the company when working.

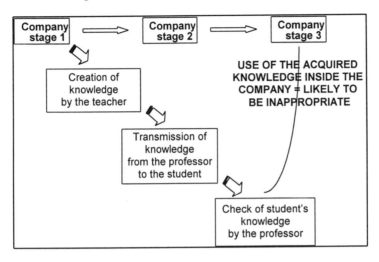

Figure 6: The Obsolescence Mechanism.

During the duration of this process the company and the environment evolve. Because of this, it may happen that the knowledge becomes obsolete. The longer the process of creating/transmitting/assimilating the knowledge, the higher the risk of unfitted knowledge. The approach described above can simply avoid the obsolescence of product competencies.

The risk of preserving useless competencies is considerably limited by introducing systematic interactive links between all partners. As shown in Figure 7, the professor and the practitioner carry out the development of the pedagogical design simultaneously, and every steps of emergence of competencies is validated by confrontation with an up-to-date state of the reference company. This is the approach we use when designing our courses.

To give students a realistic view of what happens in the business world, the professor must also be directly involved in what is changing in companies. Generally, consulting simultaneously with teaching is the most suitable way. But the best situation is to be a part-time manager in a company, either during sabbatical periods or by creating one's own company. For practitioners, it is necessary to take charge of different pedagogical aspects, from setting up the pedagogical design to meeting with students.

Finally, students have to be placed in professional situations to present their work to practitioners or to work as junior consultants.

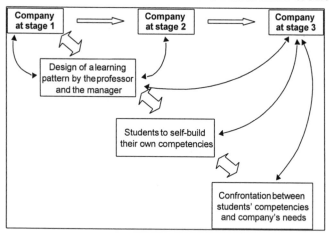

Figure 7: Permanent interactive adjustment of the learning process.

5.   AN INNOVATIVE APPROACH TO COURSES DESIGN

Our approach to learning processes development has four main pedagogical dimensions:

1. **Dialogue to build *learning processes***: we design our courses to maximize the opportunity of interaction between all stakeholders (students, practitioners, professors) involved in the process. We think that learning is the result of the exchange between all the actors, and our experience shows that students learn the most when professors and practitioners have an interest in learning from students.

2. **Students' freedom in choosing learning objectives and implementing learning processes *to stimulate appropriate intellectual challenges***: we invite students to focus on experience instead of performance by avoiding premature or preconceived judgment and by exploring as many ways as they can. We encourage them to defend their arguments, especially when they are different from those proposed by the professors or the practitioners.

3. **Professors' and practitioners' co-design of Problem Based Learning (PBL) cases to develop customized actions which can create *real added value for companies***: we encourage managers to detect in their day-to-day operational activities some critical issues to be developed in a real life case study. Students are therefore provided with a relevant company problem to be identified through the analysis of a company's

data and documents. Their report must provide the manager with significant insights for finding operational solutions to the issues.

4. **Professors' and students' involvement in customized consulting missions to keep** *the sense of reality* **and to encourage** *stepping back* **and** *constant questioning*: when possible, students and professors develop a consulting mission inside the company to make an analysis of the situation and to implement operational solutions based on state of the art best practices and theories.

The first example is the design of the learning process we use in our Change Management and Consulting course (the detailed design for this courses appears in Appendix A):

1. Professor and company manager discuss and analyze the practices of the company;
2. Professor and company manager create a PBL case study based on existing business issues and described exclusively by actual company documents (no case solutions are proposed by the professor);
3. Students work individually and in teams to make a diagnosis and set up recommendations submitted in a written report and an oral presentation to the company manager and to the professor;
4. Company manager to evaluate students' work and to present his/her own approach to the case;
5. Professor to teach related theory by making reference to company case study and students approach;
6. Students, company manager and professor to develop in-company consulting mission.

A second example concerns the course on Human Management Resources and Consulting (the detailed design for this courses appears in Appendix B):

- Professor, consultant and company manager choose a consulting mission currently running;
- Consultant gives students the initial question that began the mission;
- Students work in teams to make a first diagnosis with some recommendations. This work is submitted in a written report and an oral presentation to the consultant and to the professor;
- Consultant evaluates students' work and presents a first outline of his/her own approach to the case;
- Students work again in teams to set up a proposal for the consulting mission. This work is submitted in a written report and an oral presentation to the manager and to the professor;
- Manager evaluates students' analysis and explains why he/she accepts or refuses their recommendations.

6.   OPPORTUNITIES FOR MUTUAL LEARNING AMONGST STAKEHOLDERS

It is our belief that learning is first of all a matter of exchange between all the stakeholders (professors, practitioners and students) involved in the process. Each actor has a responsibility to help the others' learning. At the same time, each stakeholder can find in the relationship an opportunity to learn.

Instead of focusing on teaching techniques or providing information that is often fixed, inflexible or obsolete, our courses are designed to promote the creation and transfer of competencies through socialization between all the actors of the learning process. Moreover, our aim is to facilitate the development of the capability of articulating and leveraging competencies. (Baumard, 1996; Nonaka & Takeuchi, 1995).

In Table 1 we show the main learning outcomes we observe in our courses. In the rows we put the actor of the learning relationship; in the columns the recipient:

Table 1: Mutual learning relationships amongst stakeholders.

<table>
<thead>
<tr><th rowspan="2"></th><th rowspan="2"></th><th colspan="3">To (recipient)</th></tr>
<tr><th>professors</th><th>practitioners</th><th>students</th></tr>
</thead>
<tbody>
<tr><td rowspan="9">From (source)</td><td>professors</td><td>A
permits team-taught courses</td><td>B
stepping back from day-to-day business approach</td><td>C
building personal cognitive processes</td></tr>
<tr><td>practitioners</td><td>D
fitting to reality in constructing conceptual frameworks</td><td>E
senior practitioners can train more junior practitioners</td><td>F
acquiring intelligence about the situation</td></tr>
<tr><td>students</td><td>G
feed-back on transferability</td><td>H
developing mentorship</td><td>I
students' mutual learning and teaching</td></tr>
</tbody>
</table>

To successfully design and run such a course, professors need to keep a close professional relationship with companies. The continuous interaction with practitioners helps professors to keep close to reality and to develop a pragmatic approach to business while working on defining theoretical and conceptual frameworks (Cell D).

To properly design the case study, the practitioners must closely cooperate with the professors to analyze the situation and chose those elements that are relevant to the issue and need to be proposed to the students to allow them to find and understand key issues. This provides effort to step back from the day-to-day business life and to take into account a professor's perspective and contributions (Cell B).

The activity of coaching the students over the short period of time of the consulting mission allows the practitioner to develop some of those pedagogical competencies that are more and more required today for operational managers: positive attitude in interpersonal communication, awareness of subordinates' development needs, delegation and control. Students are therefore invited to give feedback to the practitioner on these subjects and on any other thing they think should be told to the practitioner (Cell H).

We ask students to use the same approach towards professors, in order to get feed-back not only on the clarity and consistency of the knowledge they transfer, but as well on their competencies in sustaining students personal development and self-learning (Cell G).

The enhancement of learning is promoted as well by the mutual learning provoked by the exchange between the same class of stakeholders. Thanks to this pedagogical design:

- professors are encouraged to develop team-taught courses and to put across interdisciplinary competencies (cell A);
- practitioners are given the opportunity to train more junior practitioners (cell E);
- students are stimulated to foster a cooperative approach in mutual learning and teaching (cell I).

Our experience shows that this type of pedagogical design helps students to feel empowered with their learning and committed to their own personal and professional development.

As a result, we observe that for each hour of direct class lecture or case discussion (coaching sessions included), students work individually or in groups up to 2.5 hours. That is an exceptionally high ratio. The main benefit that students claim to get from the interaction with professors is the development of personal cognitive processes and the capability of building their own approach to the creation of knowledge from information and phenomena (Cell B).

From continuous interaction with practitioners, students acquire intelligence about the situation and the capability of understanding those elements that are often invisible to an external observer. Nonaka & Takeuchi identify this as the socialization necessary to acquire tacit knowledge.

The final evaluation of the course is consistent with our belief in mutual interdependence of the stakeholders:

- 1/3 of the final grade is given by professors, who evaluate students on their learning and ability to create a conceptual framework for the given topics. Students are considered as junior lecturers;

- 1/3 of the final grade is given by practitioners, who evaluate students on their professionalism, efficiency and effectiveness in delivering operational analysis, diagnosis and recommendations for the given company issues. Students are considered as subordinates or junior consultants;
- 1/3 of the final grade is given by students, who self-evaluate themselves on:
1. their professionalism in relationships with their peers, professors and practitioners
2. knowledge, skills and capabilities they acquired during the course
3. actions and means they will put in place to improve their competencies and develop a consistent professional project in management and consulting.

7.   AN HISTORICAL POINT OF VIEW

To go a step further, we think that the concept of competence as the result of *savoir, savoir-faire* and *savoir-être* should be completed by making reference to the ancient Greek concept of *Mètis*, the conjectural intelligence.

In Table 2 we briefly describe the main features of the four different types of erudition identified by the ancient Greeks: *Episteme (savoir), Techne savoir-faire), Phronesis (savoir-être), Mètis*[2].

Table 2: Ancient Greeks types of erudition (adapted from Baumard, 1996).

	Episteme(Knowledge)	Techne(Skills)	Phronesis(Capabilities)
Definition	Theoretical Generalization	Ability for Task Accomplishment	Social Wisdom
Goal	Truth	Method	Wisdom
Approach	Abstraction	Observing and making	Socialization
Field	Universal	Systems	People
	Episteme(Knowledge)	Techne(Skills)	Phronesis(Capabilities)

When we design a course, our key learning objective is the development of *Mètis*, that is intelligent understanding of phenomena and use of all competencies to successfully solve problems and achieve results. An individual who has developed *Mètis* is able to progress even if he/she does not have all the cognitive or experiential elements that, in a traditional approach of competencies, would be necessary to take a decision.

---

[2] For a much wider description on these four categories, and particularly on *Mètis*, see Baumard, 1996 and Dètienne & Vernant, 1974

8. CONCLUSION

We believe that those who develop today capabilities to stimulate the learning process will create the knowledge of tomorrow.

When an individual uses all available tangible and intangible resources to modify his/her existing competencies and to create new ones, this individual is better able to manage the complexity of the environment. To do so, the individual needs to leverage his/her potential and motivation to perform successfully. In this way, the obsolescence of competencies is minimized.

Instead of focusing on which knowledge and skills need to be transmitted, we think that the issue of the obsolescence of knowledge should be treated at the level of pedagogical process and tools, in order to let students master the process of creating and internalizing their own competencies. We conclude that students passing through such a process become skilled at acquiring these evolving competencies.

The pre-requisite and challenge of this approach is that it implies a change in the image we have of the role of professors, students and managers.

To reduce obsolescence issues, it is not enough to update knowledge and skills. It is the person himself/herself who must first change and update.

Professors, students and practitioners must think of themselves as permanent learners while taking into account all dimensions of competencies and using any interactive situation as a learning opportunity.

This means that they must not be specialized only in one approach of a situation, but they have to give again an important place to *Métis*. Learning is a multidimensional process, and it is by crossing all these dimensions that we obtain the best results for all stakeholders.

APPENDIX A – DETAILED DESIGN OF CHANGE MANAGEMENT AND CONSULTING COURSE

Amongst the consulting missions developed there are the following:
- the change of the opening hours of the entire regional network of CIC - Banque SNVB, a major regional bank in France, based on a survey of customer needs, Human Resource constraints and Trade Unions stakes (manager involved: the Regional Director);
- the organizational design of business processes in "Institut Œnologique de Champagne" following the acquisition of a minor competitor (manager involved: the President and CEO);
- the audit of the working procedures of the sales force of Fiat Auto Reims and the implementation of the new quality standards issued by Fiat Auto France (manager involved: the Director of Sales);

Course features		Day[3]		
		Mon	Tue	Fri

week 0	Activity	Team Building Seminar	Team Building Seminar	Consulting Methodology
	Pedagogical Method	Gaming & Playing	Gaming & Playing	Interactive Simulation
	Trainer	School Professor	School Professor	Consultant
	Pedagogical Focus	Skills & Capabilities	Skills & Capabilities	Skills & Capabilities

week 1	Activity	Company 1 Case Study	Company 1 Case Study	Communication Techniques
	Pedagogical Method	PBL	Teaching	Coaching
	Trainer	Company 1 Manager	School Professor	Consultant
	Pedagogical Focus	Skills	Knowledge	Skills & Capabilities

week 2	Activity	Company 2 Case Study	Company 2 Case Study	Consulting Methodology
	Pedagogical method	PBL	Teaching	Interactive Simulation
	Trainer	Company 2 Manager	School Professor	Consultant
	Pedagogical Focus	Skills	Knowledge	Skills & Capabilities

week 3	Activity	Company 3 Case Study	Company 3 Case Study	Personal Professional Project
	Pedagogical Method	PBL	Teaching	Coaching
	Trainer	Company 3 Manager	School Professor	Consultant
	Pedagogical Focus	Skills	Knowledge	Skills & Capabilities

week 4	Activity	Company 4 Case Study	Company 4 Case Study	Consulting Methodology
	Pedagogical method	PBL	Teaching	Interactive Simulation
	Trainer	Company 4 Manager	School Professor	Consultant
	Pedagogical Focus	Skills	Knowledge	Skills & Capabilities

week 5 to 8	Activity	In-Company Consulting Mission *		
	Pedagogical method	Learning by Doing Coaching		
	Trainer	Company Manager School Professor		
	Pedagogical Focus	Knowledge, Skills, Capabilities		

[3] Wednesday is devoted to foreign language study, Thursday to sports

- the audit of the management system of the regional branches of EDF-GDF - the French National Electricity and Gaz Agency - and Caisse Organic - a French National Retirement Agency - (managers involved: the Regional Directors).

REFERENCES

Klarsfeld, A., & de Saint-Giniez, V. (1999). Construire l'Apprentissage. Groupe ESSEC: *Ouvertures, N. 1*.

Grimand, A. (1995*). L'émergence de la notion de compétence en gestion des ressources humaines : discours, pratiques, enjeux. Actes du 6ème congrès de l'AGRH*, 241-244.

Aubret, J. (1993). *Savoir et pouvoir, les competences en questions*. Paris: PUF.

Baumard, Ph. (1996). Organisations deconcertées. *La gestion strategique de la connaissance*. Paris: Masson.

Dètienne, M., & Vernant, J.P. (1974). Les ruses de l'intelligence: *La Mètis des Grecs*. Paris: Flammarion.

Le Boterf, G. (1994). *De la competence, un essai sur un attracteur étrange*. Paris: Editions d'Organisation.

Minet, F., Parlier, M. & de Witte, S. (1994). *La competence : mythe, construction ou réalité?*. Paris: L'Harmattan.

Wolfs, J.L. (1998). *Méthodes de travail et stratégies d'apprentissage*. Paris, Bruxelles: De Boeck Université.

Goals and Critical Success Factors in a Problem Based Marketing Course

Nils A. Estenstad & Svein Linge Solberg
Trondheim Business School (TØH), Sør-Trøndelag College, Norway

1.   INTRODUCTION

During the last couple of years there has been an intense debate among Norwegian university teachers and students. The focus of this debate has been the students' high drop out figures, poor examination results and the inefficiency of traditional learning methods. One major point in this debate is that university teachers claim that the students' poor examination results are caused by their low motivation and insufficient as well as inefficient use of the time used on study activities. The students' counter reaction is to put the blame on poor and demotivating pedagogical methods. Lectures in gigantic auditoriums with hundreds of students present represent a learning environment based on a philosophy more similar to recitation in the ancient cathedrals. The new generation of students - often called sound bite generation - demand pedagogical methods that to a greater extent can engage, stimulate, activate and put pressure on the students. One way to meet these requirements is a student-centered, independent resource-based learning, which facilitates flexibility to the timing, pace and place of learning (Ottewill & Jennings 1998). Accordingly, the students are expected to be responsible for organizing their own learning.

This type of action-based learning is regarded as relational in the sense that comprehension is developed through social interactions, and learning is closely attached to the students' involvement in various learning activities. The social aspect of the learning process is important. We can say that true learning is only possible within the context of collective discussion

19

T.A. Johannessen, A. Pedersen and K. Petersen (eds.),
Educational Innovation in Economics and Business VI, 19–34.
© 2002 *Kluwer Academic Publishers. Printed in the Netherlands.*

(argumentation). New learning is only possible when it takes place in the dynamics of social interaction.

We will in our paper take the position of active learning, and convey from more than 20 years of experience with Problem Based Learning (PBL) what we have experienced as fundamentally critical for making a successful learning program. Our basic reference in this paper is our Marketing II course. This means that we have chosen a case approach instead of a general approach. By doing this we hope we can give some useful ideas to the reader as to what kind of practical pedagogical challenges the PBL teacher is facing.

Our Marketing II (MII) course is an elective 6 credit, two-term course in our second year. The students have finished an introductory course in Marketing before they enter this course, and they have no experience in problem-based learning. When the students enter the MII course they have their roots in the tradition of Subject Based Learning (SBL). Students who take up this course have to follow a special course in Market Research. The capacity as regards the number of students at this course is 40. These students are recruited from a total of about 300 students.

MII is a discipline-oriented course focusing on the integration of subjects related to a company's marketing function. The main subjects that are dealt with in the MII course are: Strategic Planning, Consumer Behaviour, Service Management and Market Communication.

2.   THE TØH-PBL MODEL

2.1   Making tacit knowledge explicit

In this paper we attempt to present our experience (tacit knowledge) related to PBL. Tacit knowledge is - in contrast to explicit knowledge - deeply rooted in action, highly personal, hard to formalize and difficult to communicate to others (Nonaka, 1991). Therefore we have developed a model in order to facilitate the communication with the reader. The model is called *"The TØH-PBL model"* and is presented in figure 1.

PBL is a way of conceiving the curriculum, which is centered on real problems rooted in real life practice (Woods, 1994). A PBL course starts with problems rather than with the exposition of disciplinary knowledge. The students are "pulled and pushed" through a process where their acquisition of information, knowledge and skills are driven by the search for solutions of an open problem. This is a stage process where teachers, people from the collaborating company and other actors, support and co-operate with the students. In the TØH-PBL model we will therefore view the problem to be the core element in the learning process (Pettersen, 1992; Brinchman-Hansen, 1994). In the model the problem is surrounded by, and linked to a network of actors and environmental factors. This expresses the social interactive setting. The arrows on the oval line indicate the dynamic aspect of the learning process - the student has to adapt to changes over time.

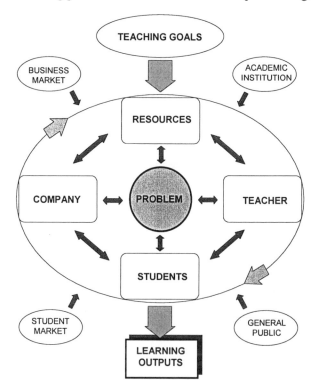

Figure 1: The TØH PBL-model – key components in the learning environment.

2.2   Input to the model - teaching goals

The teaching goals represent the input to the model and to the PBL process. The teaching goals are divided into three types - academic goals, problem-solving goals and personal goals:
- Academic goals
  Academic goals describe what we aim to achieve regarding the transfer of knowledge to the students.

In our course the academic goal is expressed in the following way: *"Extend the students' marketing knowledge and develop their ability to look at marketing problems in an integrated way."*

- Problem solving goals
  Problem solving goals describe what we aim to achieve regarding the development of the students' problem solving ability. In our course this goal is expressed in the following way: *"Develop the students' ability to diagnose, analyze and solve marketing problems."*

- Personal goals
  Personal goals describe what we aim to achieve as far as the personal development of the student is concerned. The ability to relate to actors taking part in the learning process, to live with and handle stress and conflict situations and give written and oral presentations.
  In our course this goal is expressed in the following way: *"Develop the students' ability to relate to other group members, to representatives of the collaborating company, to the teachers and to various informants , to live with and to handle stress and to give written and oral presentations."*

2.3   The four surrounding elements

The four surrounding elements in the model (Business Market, Student market, Academic institution, General public) represent an important basis for securing the future PBL programs and make long term planning possible. Two of these elements represent the recruitment of students and collaborating companies, in the model called the student market and the business market respectively. Internal goodwill and resource support from the academic institution is vital for implementing a successful PBL course. Positive word of mouth from the general public function as gate opener to various external relations needed.

2.4   Learning output

The output of our PBL-process comprises learning benefits for all actors involved - students, teachers and representatives from the collaborating company. The output of our MII- program in relation to the students has to be measured against our teaching goals. In this respect we believe our problem-solving goal to be most important:

The feedback we have received from our students and collaborating companies prove that there are various kinds of benefits experienced from the MII course. Major benefits experienced by students are increased self-confidence, ability to master stress and conflicts, motivation from the feeling of group solidarity and of making progress. The major benefits experienced by the collaborating companies are consciousness and increased motivation (Estenstad, 1995).

3.   CRITICAL SUCCESS FACTORS

Critical success factors (CSF) are generally speaking the key things we have to do right in order to succeed. Transferred to our course, the CSF are the factors that will decide to what extent the three types of teaching goals will be achieved. To illustrate this we will use the format of the TØH-model where the CSF become a second dimension, and establish a relation to the components making the learning environment. Figure 2 shows the model.

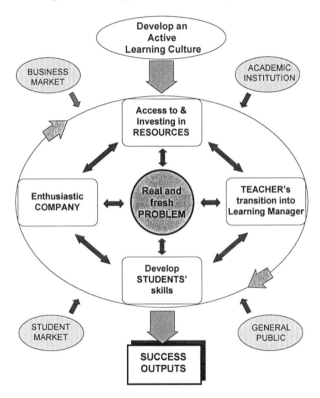

Figure 2: The TØH-PBL model – critical success factors.

The model presents the factors that are critical for the success of our PBL course. In the following sections we try to emphasis what we do in order to overcome these critical success factors:

1. Active learning culture. A PBL course depends on an active learning culture. In section 4 we point out what we do in order to develop such a culture.
2. Teacher as a learning manager. A PBL course must be run by teachers who are willing to and able to adapt to a new teaching role - namely that of the learning manager. This is dealt with in section 5.
3. Problem attributes. Fresh and real problems seem to be an important motivating factor. See section 6.
4. Collaborating company. On a PBL course with our format we need to collaborate with a company that can deliver a marketing problem that is real and fresh. The collaborating company must also be willing to operate as an important resource for the students in their problem-solving process. See section 7.
5. Access to resources. A PBL course needs certain kinds of resources different from what is needed in SBL courses. It is therefore important that the institution itself has a positive attitude towards PBL and shows willingness to place the necessary PBL resources at the students' disposal. See section 8.
6. Students' role and skills. On a PBL course we need students who are enthusiastic about active learning and willing to develop the special attitudes and skills needed in such a course;
    willingness to take the responsibility for their own learning (section 4)
    willingness to work hard in order to develop group skills, problem-solving skills and communication skills. This is dealt with in section 9.
7. Building relations. In order to succeed it is important that the main actors (students, teachers and CC) are willing to invest time and effort in building good relations. See section 10.

4.   DEVELOPING A PBL LEARNING CULTURE

The teaching goals in our PBL-course are rather different from goals we find in SBL. The problem solving goals and the personal goals will be hard to realize in a SBL program. As the goals are different, the learning culture must also be different in these two learning contexts. Values are the core of any culture (Deal & Kennedy, 1982). Therefore the values provide a sense of common direction for all members of a certain culture and guidelines for day-today behavior. We have found the following values to be important in our PBL learning culture:

• Responsibility
  Responsibility is they key value in this kind of learning culture - the students must be willing to take the responsibility for their own learning

and develop an action-oriented culture in the group. Perotti, Gunn, Day, Coombs (1998) put it like this:

"The program design creates a "need" to learn. Students do not see themselves completing assigned tasks, but rather performing the work necessary to deliver the required outcomes, seeking help and retrieving information and skills on a "just-in-time" basis".

- Mastering ability
  In order to take responsibility the students must be in position to master the acquisition and application of knowledge. The students have to discover that they are able to solve the problem they have defined and in the end be able to present a report that will meet the expectations of the CC. In this connection various kinds of skills have to be developed and access to resources is necessary (section 9 and 10).
- Confidence
  Mastering ability is also linked to the students' feeling of confidence. It is important that they have faith in the promises given by the teachers and word-of-mouth from previous course participants. The students must feel confident that they are going to master the new learning situation. They wonder: Will we be able to meet the expectations of fellow group members, teachers and CC, and do we have the necessary skills, facilities, support systems and other resources?
- Enthusiasm - motivation
  The students must have faith in the active learning concept. To initiate the development of a PBL learning culture we have found the key factors to be the stimulation of social interaction, make the students enthusiastic about the PBL idea, and create enthusiasm about the CC and its problem. The CC's contribution by showing enthusiasm will also be important.
- Team feeling - group solidarity
  The students are going to work together very intimately for about 8 months meeting various kinds of challenges and conflicts. A developed strong fellow feeling within the groups will be a valuable asset for having good social interactions. (section 9).
- Creativity
  Creativity is an important element at any stage in a problem solving process, particularly with regard to developing solutions to the defined problems. Students have the advantage over the management of the collaborating company that they are not bound by tradition, and can look at a problem with fresh and young eyes.

5.   THE TEACHER'S TRANSITION INTO A LEARNING MANAGER

The teacher initiates the first step in making the learning program, and will have the central managing position in developing and running the program. By referring to our model in figure 2, we will describe more closely the teacher's role.

A teacher used to SBL programs will per se be a directive teacher who maintains control over the students' behavior in class. (Kirch & Carvalho, 1998). In a PBL-program the teacher has to play a different role – a role, which more or less is similar to that of a good football coach. The transition from the directive teaching role to that of the learning manager is not easy (Nijhuis & van Witteloostuijn, 1998). But it is critical for the success of a PBL program.

The teacher's transition from traditional learning to active learning is normally a difficult step to take. This can be even more challenging when the transition is to be performed in a SBL dominated educational culture.

Kirch and Carvalho (1998) have put forward the following demands on the learning manager which we fully share:

"The learning manager must be competent in the discipline in which he is managing the learning. He or she must also be at least cognisant of the rudimentary aspects of other disciplines. The learning manager must be careful not to promote a myopic view of the problem and its solutions. It is important that we recognise that our particular time and focus with the student are but a part of the total development of the student as a human being and as a business professional. We must be willing, even eager, to address other areas of student development when the topics under consideration lend themselves to such".

The decisions and activities of the learning manager can be divided into three phases, namely the preparation, implementation and evaluation phases:
1.   The preparation phase
   •   selection of the CC;
   •   formalization of the relationship with the company;
   •   definition of the superior problem;
   •   development of a complete program presenting subjects, basic literature, guest lecturers and student tasks/involvement.
2.   The implementation phase
   •   group composition;
   •   create a learning situation in which the students feel safe;
   •   help the students in defining the problems they are going;
   •   to discuss in their projects;

- guide the students so that they obtain the knowledge relevant to;
- their problems;
- guide and put pressure on the students so that they are able to finish;
- their projects within the time limit;
- give a hand in conflict solving;
- ensure a satisfactory quality of the students' projects.
3. Evaluation
    - evaluation of the students' report;
    - evaluation of the written individual exam;
    - evaluation of the course itself;
    - evaluation of the benefits to the various actors.

The students' projects are being evaluated and graded by the teachers and by representatives from the collaborating company. It is critical for the students to know the assessment criteria used by the teachers as these criteria will be a guide for students when they are working on the project (see section 9.2).

The students also have to sit for a written individual exam where the students marketing knowledge is being tested. This exam is being arranged in the beginning of February. This is done to put pressure on the students' work with the core curriculum. The student's final grade in this course is the average of the grade achieved on the report and in the individual exam.

6. DEVELOPING AND WORKING WITH REAL AND FRESH PROBLEMS

In the presentation of their ALPS Model Poole & Thomas (1998) stress that:

"For action learning to be effective, then the learners must be involved directly in **real** problems".

We share their experience and have made this the central element in the TØH model. We would also like to add that problem has to be fresh. "Yesterday's" problem will not catch the same interest and bring about the same enthusiasm. The problems we deal with should be relevant to the Collaborating Company, and the company should find it useful to have the problem explored.

This is how we work to develop problems:
1. Developing a Superior Problem
    Below we present two examples of superior problems:
    - Development of marketing plans for the various business units and concepts within the collaborating company.

- The marketing of the company's logistic system - as a tool for increased service quality and added value
2. Presenting the Superior Problem to the students
   At the very start of the course the superior problem is presented to the students. The collaborating company gives a broad presentation of the company including the background to the superior problem.
3. Developing Operational Problems
   These problems are developed by the students in collaboration with both the teachers and the company and have finally to be approved of by the CC and the teachers.

7.   COLLABORATION WITH AN ENTHUSIASTIC COMPANY

The search for a Collaborating Company (CC) starts several months before the beginning of the autumn term. Several meetings are often needed to make sure that we can collaborate with an enthusiastic company. The company must sign a contract, which binds the company to fulfill its obligations.

We make the following demands on the Collaborating Company:

- The company must be in possession of the resources needed (time, people, and competence) to give the students the necessary inputs for their projects.
- The company must be ready to supply the students with the information they need.
- The company will be at the disposal of the groups and answer questions raised by the groups and give feedback.

8.   ACCESS TO RESOURCES

In order to carry through our MII program various kinds of resources are needed. The students should be confident that they have the right tools available. This will give the students the feeling of mastering and confidence (see section 4). We talk about two types of resources:

1. Physical resources
   Physical resources include the physical infrastructure like group rooms, PC's, audio-visual equipment, a well-equipped document center, telephones, telefax, etc. Software is included as a part of the information technology.

2. Information and system resources

Most important here is a well-equipped library with a service-minded staff. The students must also have access to other kinds of information sources like Internet and databases, and take the advantage of available experts.

The use of resources requires competence on behalf of the user, and necessary training is given.

9. DEVELOPING THE STUDENTS' SKILL

9.1   Group skills

We start the course by preparing the students for the PBL challenge. We present the PBL-philosophy and the TØH –PBL model to the students. In this way we stress the different demands on the students and emphasize the difference between Subject Based and Problem Based Learning. We point out to the students that focus is now on the use of knowledge – and that acquisition of knowledge is a means for developing and solving problems.

Competence profiles and getting to know each other

The students have to work in groups of 4 to 6 members. Very seldom they know each other before they meet in the group. The groups are randomly formed except for one condition - there should at least be one girl in every group. Our experience shows that homogenous groups are more likely to have conflicts. It is important that the group develop an action-oriented culture and that the members do agree upon a common level of ambition.

It is extremely important for the group members to develop a team feeling. In the first week of the course we initiate this in two different ways:

1. Each student is given the task of working out his or her CV. On the basis of the individual CV´s each group has to work out a strength and weakness analysis for the whole group - evaluated in the light of the demands of the PBL-project.

2. We arrange a meeting where the students, teachers and representatives of the collaborating company will come together in a social setting.

Attitude towards co-operation

The students must show a positive attitude towards co-operation. It is important that they are able to relate to the various actors in this learning process. First they must learn how to relate to other group members in order to avoid conflicts in the group. They must also learn how to relate to representatives of the collaborating company, the teachers and other resources representing knowledge and information (section 10).

Stress and frustration

The students have to learn to cope with stress and frustration in relation to problem formulation and time pressure. In particular the students will feel stress when they are developing their operational problem and waiting for the final approval. Frustration will also occur in connection with handling conflicts within the group, something that often involves the teachers.

9.2   Problem-solving skills

The students have to go very actively into the problem-solving process. This means that the students in their reports will give recommendations to the management of the CC about what the company ought to do to solve the problems that have been formulated.

The students are - so to speak - playing the role of business consultants (Kesner & Fowler, 1997). According to responses from representatives of the CC the qualities of the projects are astonishingly high taking the freshness of the students into account.

Below we present the criteria we are using for evaluating the projects. These criteria will also function as guidelines for the students when working with their project.

1.   Formulation of the problem. We believe in the old saying, "a problem well defined is half-solved". A considerable amount of time is spent on this aspect - it takes the students a couple of months to analyze the situation and define their operational problem.

Our experience is that this is time well spent. The students develop a genuine ownership to the problem, which seems to be an important motivating factor. (Perotti, Gunn, Day & Coombs, 1998)

We work very closely with the students and try to play our coaching role as best as we can. We stress that professional problems do not present themselves as well-formed structures, but as "messy indeterminate situations". This leads to active search for relevant theory and information. . The CC's acceptance of their problem formulation is probably their greatest victory in the autumn term.

2.   Model building - structure of the project. It is important to make the students understand the value of theory as a practical tool. We do our best to guide the students, when they are searching for the right kind of theoretical framework on which to develop useful models.

3.   Collection and analyses of data. Data collection plays an important part in the students' work. The students have to collect, record and analyze secondary and primary data in order to describe and analyze the

problem situation, come up with good ideas, recommendations and solutions to the marketing problems of the CC. The students first start searching for data in secondary sources. The information needed cannot always be found in secondary sources. The students, therefore, will be dependent upon primary data, which they have to collect specifically for the project. To design data collection methods and forms, is a very challenging job for the students. Some of our collaborating companies have invested money in primary data collection executed by a research agency. The students then get the experience of working with professionals.

4.   Theory - description and application. The students have to explain well their choice of theory, describe the theory and the way it has been applied as a practical tool for solving their problem. Their personal experience of mastering theory application has a significant impact on their attitude towards theory. In this respect the teachers coaching role is important as well as difficult, as it should balance very carefully between criticism and praise.

5.   Recommendations. The recommendations in the projects are of major interest to the CC. The students have to argue convincingly in favour of the recommendations they present to the CC. They are, of course, not in a position to carry out the decision, but they will suggest how the company should go about implementing and controlling the recommended course of action.

6.   Layout and language. We do stress the importance of a well structured report with good illustrations and figures. The students must bear in mind that their report will be read by different people in the company.

7.   Creativity. Creativity is an extremely important part of the problem solving process. Creativity is not just a matter of inventing new ideas, it is equally important to find out how theory can be utilized. Creativity is linked to the students selection and application of theories, their model building and finding a good structure for the project. Creativity is also important for making good and practical recommendations to the defined problem.

9.3   Communication skills

How do we train and improve the students' ability to communicate? We let the students play the major role in the following ways.

1.   *Theory presentations from textbooks.* The students will on group basis give summary presentations of given chapters and subjects in textbooks. We will in the class discuss various theoretical aspects, discuss the content of essential concepts and the structure the author of

the textbook has used. Our objective is to learn about the theory and its concepts.

2. *Presentation and discussion of articles.* The articles are taken from various sources of periodicals and newspapers. The objective is to let the students find the link between the problem, theoretical framework and solution. The students task is to analyze the problem in the article, evaluate the theory being used, and try to draw some practical marketing implications.

3. *Group discussions.* When the groups meet problems when working with the project they contact the teachers for help and discussions. In this connection we challenge the students to play the active part, by communicating their problem and ideas for solutions. The interactive coaching role is to stimulate every group member to take active part in the group discussions.

4. *Presentation of the operational problem.* One of the most critical tests of their communication skill is when the groups are presenting the operational problem and the structure of their project to the CC. The objective of this meeting is to get acceptance from the management that this operational problem is of interest to the company.

5. *Presentation of the report.* The final test of the students' communication skills is the audio-visual presentation of the report to the representatives of the CC. This presentation is a great event. In some instances there has been up to fifty people from the CC attending the presentations of the students. A grand dinner party paid by the CC ends off this presentation.

10.   BUILDING RELATIONSHIPS

In order to achieve our teaching goals we talk about three types of relations that have to be developed to make our PBL course successful.

10.1   Building an academic network

The teachers have to build a network securing that they get the right kind of impulses for developing and improving the course program. These impulses could either be of a pedagogical or a factual character. Examples of pedagogical impulses are previous students who later have entered PBL programs at other institutions (e.g. Ålborg, Denmark), contact with the PBL entrepreneurs at the Norwegian University of Science and Technology (NTNU) and EDINEB literature. Factual impulses would be more or less the same as when you are preparing other types of teaching programs. But we are very conscious of selecting literature and guest lecturers with a practical approach and background.

10.2   Building a problem solving network

The relationship between teacher and CC is of vital importance and has to be built on trust and confidence. Therefore it is wise to spend some time to get to know each other so that we can develop a good personal chemistry.

The development of the Superior Problem is the most important issue in the discussions between the teachers and various representatives of the Collaborating Company in the initial phase.

The relationship between teacher and students has be organized so that the students are stimulated and motivated to work hard in order to meet the expectations of the Collaborating Company regarding the quality of the final report. This means e.g. that the teachers must adopt an open-door policy, and be helpful whenever the students feel for it (coaching the students).

The collaborating company must be sure that the students are discussing the problems the company find relevant in a realistic and sensible way. This relationship has to be organized so that the students get the necessary information and feedback for questions and proposals that they put forward. As some of this information will be of sensitive character, we formalize this aspect of collaboration by signing a promise of secrecy (both students and teachers).

10.3   Building a personal network

The quality of the final report is to a large extent dependent upon the information the students are able to obtain from other sources than the collaborating company and the teacher. In this respect the students have to show creativity and initiative. The collaborating company's customers, suppliers and competitors can be important sources of information. In this course we are using several guest lecturers - some of them have been previous students of this course. These guest lectures often turn out to be valuable sources of information and part of the students' personal network during the course. We stress the importance of network building and ask the students to use this course as a foundation stone for their future network building. As an example of this we would like to point out that previous students often make contact with their former teachers when they have matters they want to discuss.

REFERENCES

Brinchman-Hansen, Å. (1994). *Prosjekt og PBL*. Universitetsforlaget.

Deal, T.E., & Kennedy, A.A. (1982). *Corporate Cultures - The rites and Rituals of corporate Life*. Addison Wesley.

Estenstad, N. (1995). Benefits from PBL in the Teaching of Marketing, *TØH-serien nr. 12*.

Kirch, D.P., & Carvalho, G. (1998). The Delivery of Accounting in the Problem-Based Learning Environment. In R. Milter, J.E. Stinson, W.H. Gijselaers, (Eds.), *Educational Innovation in Economics and Business III* (pp. 169 -188). Dordrecht, London, Boston: Kluwer Academic Publishers.

Nijhuis, J., & Van Witteloostuijn, A. (1998). Teaching and Organising: The Case of Problem-Based learning. In D.T. Tempelaar, F. Wiedersheim-Paul, & E. Gunnarsson, (Eds.), *Educational Innovation in Economics and Business II* (pp. 171-189). Dordrecht, London, Boston: Kluwer Academic Publishers.

Nonaka, I. (1991). The Knowledge-Creating Company. *Harvard Business Review*, November-December.

Ottewill, R., & Jennings, P.L. (1998). Open Learning versus Lecturing. In R. Milter, J.E. Stinson, & W.H. Gijselaers, (Eds.), *Educational Innovation in Economics and Business III,* (pp. 169 -188). Dordrecht, London, Boston: Kluwer Academic Publishers.

Perotti, V., Gunn, P.C., Day, J.C., & Coombs, G. (1998). Business 20/20; Ohio University's Integrated Business Core. In R. Milter, J.E. Stinson, W.H. Gijselaers, (Eds.), *Educational Innovation in Economics and Business III* (pp. 169 -188). Dordrecht, London, Boston: Kluwer Academic Publishers.

Pettersen, R.C., (1992). *PBL- konsept, modell, metode , Østfold*. Vernepleierhøgskole, Fredrikstad.

Poole, D., & Thomas, I.D. (1998). The Action Learning Partnership (ALPS) Model. In R. Milter, J.E. Stinson, & W.H. Gijselaers, (Eds.), *Educational Innovation in Economics and Business III* (pp. 65 -75). Dordrecht, London, Boston: Kluwer Academic Publishers.

Solberg, S.L. (1995). Use of Problem-Based Learning in the Teaching of Marketing, *TØH-serien nr. 15*.

Søderlund, M. (1998). Problem-Based Learning, Interpersonal Orientations and Learning Approaches. In D.T. Tempelaar, F. Wiedersheim-Paul, & E. Gunnarsson. (Eds.), *Educational Innovation in Economics and Business II* (pp. 155-169). Dordrecht, London, Boston: Kluwer Academic Publishers.

Woods, D. (1994). *Problem-based Learning - How to Gain the Most from PBL*. Waterdown.

The Use of the Action-Research Methodology in the Development of Business Education a Case Study

Martin Kelly
The University of Waikato, Hamilton, New Zealand

1.   INTRODUCTION

This paper discusses the use of the action-research methodology in the classroom to help improve the academic environment. Action-research appears to have grown in popularity with academics generally, and in educational research particularly, over the past few years. In this paper action-research is defined, and a critique and counter-critique are provided. I explain how I have found it useful as an agent for change in my teaching environment. Difficulties, which attach to the use of the action-research methodology, are discussed.

My case study relates to a business studies course, which has been developed to include several modes of learning. I describe how the course development has benefited from a large measure of student input and provide examples of student input relating to the various modes of learning employed.

2.   WHAT IS ACTION-RESEARCH?

The term "action-research" is not uniquely defined, rather it embraces a collection of similar methodologies. The lack of one, universally accepted definition of action-research does allow a broad range of related techniques to meld and develop with usage over space and time. However, the lack of

T.A. Johannessen, A. Pedersen and K. Petersen (eds.),
Educational Innovation in Economics and Business VI, 35–50.
© 2002 *Kluwer Academic Publishers. Printed in the Netherlands.*

such a singular definition becomes problematic when researchers use action-research and then attempt to describe their methodology. Nevertheless it is possible to provide sympathetic readers with some appreciation of what the methodology involves, firstly in a general sense and then more specifically within education. The World Congress on Action Research (1989) attempted to capture the essence of action-research:

If yours is a situation in which
- people reflect and improve (or develop) their own work and their own situations
- by tightly interlinking their reflection and action
- and also making their experience public not only to other participants but also to other persons interested in and concerned about the work and the situation (i.e. theories and practices of the work and the situation)

and if yours is a situation in which there is increasingly
- data-gathering by participants themselves (or with the help of others) in relation to their own questions
- participation (in problem-posing and in answering questions) in decision making
- power-sharing and the relative suspension of hierarchical ways of working towards industrial democracy
- collaboration among members of the group as a "critical community"
- self-reflection, self-evaluation and self management by autonomous and responsible persons and groups
- learning progressively (and publicly) by doing and by making mistakes in a "self-reflective spiral" of planning, acting, observing, reflecting, replanning[1]
- reflection which supports the idea of the "(self-) reflective practitioner"

then yours is a situation in which ACTION RESEARCH is occurring (Altrichter et al., 1989, p. 19).

The need for this exercise in definition at the Congress, and the cumbersome outcome, provide evidence of the difficulty of finding an accepted and all-encompassing definition of action-research. However, McNiff (1988) has specifically targeted education when she describes action- research as:

... an approach to improving education, by encouraging teachers to be aware of their own practice, to be critical of that practice, and to be

---

[1] Lewin in the 1940s first developed what have become four, widely-agreed elements in the action-research cycle: plan changes, act and observe results, reflect on the outcomes, and revise the plan (Elliott, 1982; Kemmis and McTaggart, 1988; Lewin, 1952). They have been used in many working environments including education (for example Stenhouse, 1980).

prepared to change it. It is participatory, in that it involves the teacher in his (sic) own enquiry, and collaborative, in that it involves other people as part of a shared enquiry. It is research WITH, rather than research ON (p. 4).

Zuber-Skerritt (1992) terms action-research within the classroom "action learning" and describes action learning as:

A process by which groups of people... work on real issues or problems, carrying real responsibility in real conditions. The solutions they come up with may require changes to be made in the organization, and they often pose challenges to senior management, but the benefits are great because people actually own their own problems and their own solutions (p. 48).

Action-research is the study of a social situation in order to improve the quality of action within it. It involves self-evaluation and professional development. Gibson (1986) advocates the use of action-research better to understand education, and close the gap between theory and practice:

In the traditional view [of education], 'theory' has been applied to 'practice'... The insights and concepts of, for example, psychology or sociology have been drawn upon to explain, inform or direct practice. Both action research and critical theory challenge this approach as they urge the fundamental indivisibility of theory and practice. Theory is in all practice, is grounded in it (p. 162).

Action-research avoids the opening of the theory/practice gap, because theory and practice are developed together and in unison. Action-researchers maintain that, "there is nothing so practical as a good theory" (Greenwood, et al., 1993, p. 187). Carr and Kemmis (1986) suggest that action-research provides an excellent educational research methodology because:

The purpose of educational research is to develop theories that are grounded in the problems and perspectives of educational practice (rather than the problems and perspectives of some social scientific practice) (p. 122).

The action-research perspective can reveal different images concerning curricula, different suggestions concerning who is best placed to develop curricula, and different ideas concerning the roles of course controllers. Action-research is the assertion of a democratic social and political ideal, the ideal of a creative and involved citizenry in research. Action-research is political because it involves continuous social/organizational change which affects people, and which may be opposed. It involves seeking-out and implementing changes which have the greatest support from the individuals concerned, and are acceptable to all, "Two of the ideas which were crucial (in Lewin's work) were the ideas of group decisions and commitment to improvement" (Kemmis & McTaggart, 1988, p. 6).

There is a large literature on the action-research methodology[2] and there is close agreement as to its main characteristics. Key aspects of the methodology are summarized below, it:

- is concerned to critique what "is" and examines "what is" from an holistic perspective.
- seeks to close the gap between theory and practice.
- does not assume that there is an ideal state awaiting discovery, but that the research process itself allows progress towards an ideal.
- requires extensive communicative processes before action.
- suggests a research cycle involving: an initial overview, followed by a detailed critique of systems in order to gain enlightenment and provide a base from which to plan strategies.
- is an iterative process.

Carr and Kemmis (1986) describe the reasons for applying action-research to education as follows:

1. Educational theory must reject positivist notions of rationality, objectivity and truth.
2. Educational theory must be rooted in the self-understandings of educational practitioners.
3. Education theory must distinguish ideologically distorted interpretations of practices and overcome them.
4. Education theory must expose those aspects of the existing social order which frustrate the pursuit of rational goals.
5. Educational theory must recognize that it has to relate to practice.

Ledford and Mohran (1993) point out that one of the central issues in action-research is the recognition that socially active action-researchers create and define their own realities. Creating realities demands action, the substance of action-research is **action**, and every action-research project must recognize this. Action-research is not simply an interpretivist methodology, the action-researcher are challenged to go beyond an understanding of what "is" to an investigation of what "might become", and to create this. The broader the action-researchers can cast their minds in determining what might become then, potentially, the better can be the results. Society will almost certainly continue to be characterized by rapid change and by diminished traditional anchors such as

---

[2] For example: Elliot, 1982; Kemmis and McTaggart, 1988; Kember and Kelly, 1993; McKernan, 1991; Stenhouse, 1980; Whyte, 1990, to name but a few.

ethical/moral/religious/social codes. Management education must respond to these changes by promoting ideologies that allow the students to emerge as independent learners, challenging and changing society.

Research labeled as action-research may encompass work on two broad levels. At one level of use the operating environment is largely accepted as "given" and the protagonists strive to identify the best way of progressing within that environment to the desired ends. For an example of this type of approach see Greenwood, Whyte and Harkavy (1993) which refers to three such projects and provides some of the assumptions behind such research, for example, "We believe that the social sciences exist to assist society in solving problems" (p. 176). They suggest that the action-research methodology has something to offer in such a context:

> Action-research encourages integrative, interdisciplinary social science based on both local knowledge and social science expertise. The multidisciplinary approach has proved quite elusive in standard research approaches... Action-research is also important because self-management is a moral and political value that we seek to promote (p. 177).

These claims are worthy of respect. However, an alternative approach to the action-research methodology leaves researchers loathe to assist society in 'solving social problems' *identified in society*. Rather the researchers 'should' advocate action-research be used to determine what the social problems are. Greenwood et al. recognize that the 'correct' definition of a problem is often not achieved by traditional methods, and therefore action-researchers should avoid addressing predefined problems:

> We are critical of the academic research community's general infatuation with abstract, static models, expert control of research, and their lack of commitment to testing ideas through genuine application... The applied research communities [too]... often simplify problems to match them to the modest solutions they have at hand. Such an approach is as closed to participation as orthodox research and does not promote ongoing learning (p. 189).

The distinction is described well by Chisholm and Elden (1993). They suggest that traditional action-researchers attempt to improve organizational performance and generate social science theory; that is to change organizations and social science. However, a newer group of action-researchers, "Attempt to raise levels of consciousness, explore new approaches to basic social problems, and empower the oppressed" (p. 285).

Today individuals are assailed from every angle by divergent and contradictory value claims. Business education has been dominated by the perspective of training students to know facts and techniques - often a narrow and limiting perspective. We should be empowering students by fostering independent learning. It might be argued that in many universities the students are "the oppressed", since the education they receive (in some sort of passive knowledge transfer) does not actually prepare them for the realities of living. Action-researchers promote holistic thinking in education, opening up educational practices and research to rational, psychological and spiritual values.

3.   A CRITIQUE AND COUNTER-CRITIQUE OF ACTION-RESEARCH

Main-stream organizational research generally allows one set of people (the researchers) to study another set of people (the subjects). There are several reasons why such research is unlikely to provide practical outcomes useful to those being researched (Bartholomew, 1972). The action-research methodology makes educational research an integral part of educational practice, and thereby improves the chances of the outcomes being relevant to the practice of education. The research (if it can be isolated and labeled as such) concerns *the education* of both the action-researchers and the clients, which become identical groups.

The action-research methodology is more 'realistic' than many other research methodologies because it is based at the local level where the people involved are fully aware of, and able to talk about, "real"[3] problems. It involves talking with the people who are living their normal lives in the environment being researched. It necessitates bringing these people and their ideas into the research project, not just at the observation end, but also into the design and framework setting stages of the research project.

The action-research methodology does not attempt to build grand theories. Its aim is to build transient local theories to help individuals better to understand, control and profit from their environment. The measures of 'understanding', 'control' and 'profit' are to be made by the individuals in the classroom rather than by researchers in distant offices. Although the action-research methodology accepts the need for evidence and reliability in substantiating discovery, it allows for diversity in acceptable methods.

Action-research is not appreciated by some, it: "is resisted by entrenched interests... It challenges the 'expert' authority of academic educational researchers... It challenges bureaucratic authority in its notion of participatory control" (Carr & Kemmis, p. 210). Many orthodox social

---

[3] "Real" in the sense that the problems have meaning in the decision making models of the people involved, concerning how they organise their lives.

science researchers are not pleased with the advent of action-research; they attempt to discredit it. With action-research the researcher must be "willing to relinquish the unilateral control that the professional researcher has traditionally maintained over the research process" (Whyte, 1990, p. 241). Some orthodox researchers respond to the challenge of action-research to their hegemony by stating that they do "science" while action-researchers merely "tell stories" (Greenwood et al., 1993). However, the narrative dimensions of supposedly "objective" social scientific accounts have been successfully 'exposed' for what they are, for example: Bourdieu, 1984; Clifford and Marcus, 1986; Habermas, 1984; Mitroff and Mason, 1981.

Action-research is sometimes criticized for 'obvious' bias because it involves the researcher in analyzing his or her own practices. Such criticism implies that there is a 'neutral, value free' point from which 'proper' research can be conducted; any such point is illusory, "There is no objective knowledge of reality... reality can only be known through our constructions which are subject to constant revision; we do not have direct access to an interpretation-free reality" (Zuber-Skerritt, 1992, p. 56).

Narratives emanating from action-research environments provide vicarious learning experiences for their readers. However, it must be recognized that researchers bring their own biases to models which they create in attempting to understand and describe their environments. These biases will influence the researcher's 'skeletal'[4] generalizations concerning the reality within an environment (Laughlin, 1995). Nevertheless the skeletal generalizations can provide useful insights to others with similar interests.

Action-research treats the 'actors' as both the bearers and the 'victims' of ideologies. It recognizes the actors' ability to change the world. The collaborative nature of action-research can offer an approach to overcoming those aspects of the existing social order, which frustrate rational change. Action-research is, "The expression of individual self-reflection which contributes to community self-reflection both by extending and by challenging the formation of common practices, theories and institutional structures" (Carr & Kemmis, p. 205).

---

[4] 'Skeletal' is used metaphorically to signal the incompleteness of any general theory. The skeletal framework can be fleshed out within chosen empirical research locations. 'Whole beings' thus created must be considered to have no more than local meaning. The skeletal framework will itself remain more stable, enduring and transferable.

4.   BRINGING ACTION-RESEARCH INTO THE CLASSROOM

Action-researchers recognize that all concerned in the classroom situation, especially the students, should be encouraged to help challenge and shape the social system in which they live, be it the educational setting and/or the environment in which they are/will be employed. Thus rather than being value neutral they select problems to solve that contribute to practice, and are concerned with democratic, humanist values. McKernan (1991) notes that action-research is expressly political because it seeks continuous change in the environment being studied:

> Critical action research is seen as a politically empowering process for action-researchers; the struggle is for more rational, just and democratic forms of education... As a theoretical activity it invites... practitioners to consider... the totality of relationships within the social system and structure of the society in which they live and work (p. 27).

As educators we are responsible for initiating iterative changes and noting their effect in improving the environment. At the same time the environment which we create changes continuously, as we promote changes through our research. Changes in the environment need to be constantly recognized, but the need to report changes to a distant 'client' is obviated. I have adopted action-research in the development of the course, *Accounting, Organizations and Society* (AOS). I have conducted five iterations; each one adapted in response to student and teacher interactions. The adoptions had to occur within a framework set by the University systems (for example the formal grading systems) but the educational practices were refined and changed in a participative and interactive program. The course is described further in the following section.

It is because of action-research's power in challenging assumptions that it is potentially so useful in reshaping current practices in tertiary education, and thereby providing the opportunity for greater productivity in learning. Action-research requires the active participation of those who have to carry out the work which they identify and anticipate. The group must also agree as to how progress will be monitored. In the AOS course example, students were required to participate in deciding what was to be learned, how the learning was to take place and how it was to be measured. There are some obvious problems with the introduction of such an approach into a structured educational environment, but none which are insurmountable, for example:

- It requires courage to arrive at the first meeting of a class and commence by asking fee-paying students what direction they would like the class to take rather than providing them with clear instructions concerning exactly what they will be required to learn in order to obtain a good pass grade.

- Once choice in class is opened up to students it may be difficult to achieve consensus. The 'controller' may find him/herself having to accommodate the supervision of several different paths to knowledge without having any subgroup come to believe that their chosen path is iniquitously difficult. This may cause the controller additional work and stress.

Action-research attempts to allow the action-researchers to create alternative views to those portrayed in the media and accepted generally:

> Recent pressures on teaching staff from students and government have caused a crisis in higher education... students have demanded that institutions adapt their curricula, teaching and assessment methods to the changing needs of society... funding bodies have demanded greater accountability and effectiveness in terms of costs, resources and the quality of teaching and research in higher education (Zuber-Skerritt, 1992, p. 4).

Such pressures must be recognized but, wherever possible, they should not be allowed to become constraints. Academics must maintain flexibility in responding to societal pressures. Adoption of the action-research methodology encourages the establishment of self-critical communities of people. It does not assist people to implement pre-designed fixed systems; it involves people remaining open to surprises and responsive to opportunities. It involves the examination of new practices to compare them with previous practices. Whatever current practice is adopted it must be subjected to ongoing critical assessment and to change when appropriate.

5. THE MODES OF LEARNING EMPLOYED IN THE CLASS

I developed six modes of learning for use in the course based on suggestions in Rogers (1983):
1. General Expositions
2. Self Assessment Tests
3. Dialectical Enquiries
4. Discussions with Visitors
5. Small-group Project
6. Open Book Invigilated Course Test.

These modes were created in order to improve the learning environment in the classroom, and bring me closer to the students. They are intended to deliver deep (Ramsden, 1992) learning opportunities to the students. Brief descriptions of each follow:

5.1   General expositions

Each week two pairs of students volunteer to present journal articles, chosen by myself, to the rest of the class. All students are required to present at some time. The presentations are used to allocate 15% of the students' total course marks. The chosen articles contain a lot of challenging ideas. The course explores the manner in which Accounting is used in society and I want the students to be alerted to the concerns of commentators. The readings encourage students to question the uses of Accounting. Students are encouraged to realize that many controversies involve clashes of several valid perspectives; that seldom is one party totally 'correct' in on-going controversies. The presentations are followed by class discussions led by the presenters.

5.2   Self assessment tests (SATs)

In order for the general exposition sessions to be successful it is essential that all involved have done the required readings. The SATs contain questions on the readings and require the students to respond. They are used to allocate 15% of the total marks. The students grade their own efforts but I randomly audit a few tests each week and discuss the allocated grade with the student if necessary. I am aware from taking classes previously that when I ask for readings to be done, many students arrive at class without having done them. An incentive is required to encourage students to undertake the readings. The SATs were introduced for this purpose. SATs aid the general exposition sessions.

5.3   Dialectical enquiries

Students divide into groups of six to discuss a problem in society which they have identified in the areas of the recent class expositions. It is necessary for the students to identify a problem that has different students believing that different 'solutions' provide the best way forward. The initial different approaches to the problem area are termed the "thesis" and the "antithesis". The students argue about the problem for around two hours and agree on the best way to proceed (if possible). The students are given an introduction to Jungian Psychology to help them appreciate the behavior of their colleagues during the argument. The agreed best way to proceed is termed the "synthesis". Students produce a written report of their group arguments and their synthesis. These reports are used to allocate 20% of the total course marks.

5.4   Discussions with visitors

The *Discussions with Visitors* seminars bring the students into contact with members of the business world. Students are provided with the opportunity to interact with citizens who are active in the business community, and question them on their beliefs and motivations. They can learn about career development, and societal pressures encountered in the commercial world. The visiting speakers introduce issues which currently are helping to shape New Zealand business and society. The seminars are designed to encourage two way communication. Introductory speeches from the visitors are used to provide brief details of their own career development, and a general introduction to their business activities. The visitors provide short handouts prior to attending class. They know that the students have read the information in the handouts and it does not have to be presented during the visit. The visitors are asked to speak for only 15 minutes. The class members then question them, for about 90 minutes. Thus the sessions are not visitors' lectures, but discussions with visitors. Students are required to produce reports of the visits and the reports are used to allocate 15% of the course marks.

5.5   Small group project

Many new management graduates may not be aware of how accounting figures are used in society to define, and help solve, problems. The Small Group Project necessitates the students forming themselves into groups and identifying empirical research topics. Students must learn to function within their group, in order that a good written report is produced. This is excellent preparation for their coming careers. The task is used to allocate 20% of the course marks.

5.6   Open book invigilated test

This test is similar to the traditional "final examination". However, the test is "open book" and worth only 15% of the total marks for the course. Students are told that they will be expected to finish within two hours because they will find that time adequate; they are allowed three hours. This helps relieve the traditional time-pressure associated with examinations.

6.   STUDENTS RESPONSES IN THE ACTION-RESEARCH ENVIRONMENT

This class is very different from most other classes at my university. Students are put under pressure to cope with the new style of learning which is provided:

> The only aspect of this course I found annoying was that the workload was very heavy compared to other courses I have taken. The work was also different, not so much essays but short projects or write-ups. I found I was devoting all my spare time trying to complete course work for the following week. I sacrificed working on my other courses for this one.

Students must develop much of the detail to be included on their learning agenda. They must also realize that they have a responsibility in shaping their own learning environments. They may be sensible to argue for changes, and thereby educate the teacher. Although grade percentages are given above for each mode of learning, I tell the students that these are negotiable and the class members determine the final splits democratically. The splits do change from iteration to iteration. Students are encouraged to give feedback and suggestions for improvements continuously. Three major criticisms of the course have been:

- The number of readings required - over the five iterations these have been cut from 72 to 12.
- The time and effort required for SATs - these have now been abandoned and students are required to produce précis instead.
- The overall workload has been too high - it has been reduced but is still higher than for other 'equivalent' courses.

Examples of feedback from the students, which has helped me to develop the course, follow:

6.1   General expositions

We did not tend to participate actively in the discussions that followed the expositions. I believe that a possible reason for this, is because our opinions and ideas were not encouraged during our earlier years of study. We have got used to the idea of the lecturer speaking and us listening and find it hard to adjust to the new role required.

6.2   SATs

The amount of readings that we had to read was an annoying part of this course. The obvious solution would be to have fewer readings. Fewer articles would mean that if students did not understand an article, with lots of complex issues in it, then they could spend time trying to understand the complexity.

I often found myself running out of time to read designated articles. Thankfully, I have managed to catch up on these readings as I feel they are invaluable in "teaching" the issues.

6.3   Dialectical enquiries

I found it unnerving that lecturers tried to teach us the idea that there is one rule for everything. I did not agree with this concept, especially as some of my seventh form high school study had already indicated that there was often more than one rule for anything.

I have learnt to listen to other students' opinions and feelings... I have become more tolerant of opposing points of view and realized that my view may not always be right, and by listening and sharing I am becoming a better and richer person.

6.4   Discussions with visitors

I have really appreciated having guest speakers come into our class... While at university I feel that we are isolated from the "real world"... Contact with business people helps to break that isolation... [it] has inspired me to become "somebody".

6.5   Small group projects

I have really appreciated the small group project. Apart from enjoying working with others and the challenges involved in-group work I appreciate the lack of real structure in the group project. I liked the way we could choose our own topic, design our own project according to what we wanted or felt necessary and then just be left alone to get on with it. This is the first course in which I have experienced no structural requirements in a group project. I know I have (and I am sure my colleagues have) enjoyed the independence and autonomy involved in the production of these reports.

6.6   **Open book invigilated test**

This test, well what a surprise. The strengths are obvious. This course was all about learning how to learn and developing your own thoughts on the issues raised. It was not about learning the authors' opinions on each topic, it was about promoting yourself to think and expand your ideas about accounting... This test has given me the opportunity to reflect on the tools I have developed to be able to communicate, understand others' views, encourage team work, develop other people's ideas and learn from everyday experiences.

Despite some criticisms many students have grown to appreciate the class environment that has developed:

- The course ... made me realise what it is like in the "real world" and has given me an idea of what my role in society will be... I have learnt about myself, and to be myself.
- This course ... has taught me to question everything. Discussion is imperative. I have learnt that change is good, and the way things have always been done, status quo, is not always right just because the majority of people accept it.
- I thoroughly enjoyed the loose structure of this course and the empowering feeling that this course provided me with. Having a learning environment where students and lecturers are both partaking of a learning process is a change for the better.
- I really appreciated the structure of this course compared to other accounting classes. It encouraged learning through becoming proactive, and overall it has restored my faith that learning can be enjoyable[5].

7.   METHODS OF OBSERVATION AND ENQUIRY IN THE ACTION-RESEARCH ENVIRONMENT

The use of action-research in universities will primarily relate to the classroom. The action-research approach to research does not predetermine exactly what is to be observed and measured, rather it commences with an objective to achieve, and seeks the help of those involved in attempting to achieve that objective. The way to proceed will be agreed, but will remain subject to revision, if the action-researchers want change. Developments may suggest that the primary objective be changed in favor of a better objective as the study proceeds.

---

[5] Further details concerning the course will be supplied to interested parties on request.

The variables to be measured in educational research will generally involve human motivations and behavior. The specific variables to be measured may only become apparent once the research is commenced, and the responses to opening plans become apparent. The action will lead 'where it will' as the research proceeds, and the methods adopted will be in response to the situations that evolve. There cannot be an opening method 'blueprint' in action-research, as those familiar with the scientific methodology may require. The specific data to be collected will be determined in response to the problems that are identified as the research progresses.

For example, the students appeared more critical of the courses in anonymous written feedback notes, than they were in providing feedback directly to myself. However, the written feedback was often short on detail and did not adequately explain the students' problems. In response I arranged for students to provide anonymous feedback on the course to external interviewers (post-graduate anthropology students), after their final course grades had been allocated. Thereby I received better quality feedback that was not provided under fear of grade reprisal, or in fear of offending me directly. I had not initially proposed to obtain feedback by this method but I adopted the practices when I realized the need to do so.

I am concerned with monitoring changes in the classroom environment in order to 'improve' the learning environment, diagnose problems, plan actions, implement actions and observe the results. The data collected are used also for evaluation of my own performances. Methods of data collection, which I have employed, include tape recordings and videos made in the classroom. These provide records of developments and assist reflection. Feedback from students has been obtained formally through questionnaires and through set written exercises. Informal feedback has been obtained in conversations, note exchanges, and E-mail exchanges, usually instigated by the students. When students have visited my office to talk about the courses, the conversations have sometimes been recorded (with the students' permission). The official documentation gathered by the university on all courses is brought into the reflective process (eg. students' grades and course evaluations). My personal observations are often re-enforced by student comments and written submissions. This triangulation creates confidence in the reported results.

8. CONCLUSION

This paper has championed the use of the action-research methodology in educational research. I hope that a growing adoption of action-research in education will help to change the educational status quo in our universities. I attempt to help my students to develop the abilities to promote changes in their environments. Establishing an action-research neighborhood, in which students have some control over their classroom environment, provides opportunities for students to cultivate confidence in themselves. Action-research encourages individuals to challenge "what is". It is with the hope of encouraging such challenges that I prepared this paper.

REFERENCES

Altrichter, H., Kemmis, S., McTaggart, R., & Zuber-Skerritt, O. (1989). Defining, confining or refining action research? In O. Zuber-Skerritt, (Eds.), *Proceedings of the first world congress on action research*, Brisbane.

Bartholomew, J. (1972). The teacher as researcher. *Hard Cheese No. 1*, Goldsmiths College, University of London.

Bourdieu, P. (1984). *Distinction: A social critique of the judgment of taste*, translated by R. Nice. Cambridge: Harvard University Press.

Carr, W., & Kemmis, S. (1986). *Becoming critical: Knowing through action research*. Victoria: Deakin University.

Chisholm, R.F., & Elden, M. (1993). Features on emerging action research. *Human Relations, 46* (2), 275-298.

Clifford, J., & G. Marcus, (Eds.), (1986). *Writing culture: The poetics and politics of ethnography*. Berkeley: University of California Press.

Elliott, J. (1982). Action-research: *A framework for self-evaluation in schools*. Working Paper No. 1. Teacher-pupil interaction and the quality of learning. London: Schools Council.

Gibson, R. (1986). *Critical Theory and education*. London: Hodder and Stoughton.

Greenwood, D.J., Whyte, W.F., & Harkavy, I. (1993). Participatory action research as a process and as a goal. *Human Relations, 46* (2), 175-192.

Habermas, J. (1984). *Theory of communicative action: (Volume I)*. Cambridge: Polity Press. First published as Theorie des Kommunikativen Handelns (1981).

Kember, D., & Kelly, M. (1993). *Improving teaching through action research*. Campbelltown: Higher Education Research and Development Society of Australasia.

Kemmis, S., & McTaggart, R. (1988). *The action research planner, 3rd edition*. Geelong: Deakin University Press.

Laughlin, R. (1995). Empirical research in accounting: Alternative approaches and a case for middle-range thinking. *Accounting, Auditing and Accountability Journal, 8* (1), 63-87.

Ledford, G.E., & Mohran, S.A. (1993). Looking backward and forward at action research. *Human Relations, 46*(11), 1349-1365.

Lewin, K. (1952). Group decisions and social change. In G.E. Swanson, T.M. Newcomb, & F.E. Hartley, (Eds.), *Readings in social psychology*. New York: Holt.

McKernan, J. (1991). *Curriculum action research*. London: Kogan Page.

McNiff, J. (1988). *Action research - Principles and Practice*. Basingstoke: Macmillan.

Mitroff, I.I., & Mason, R.O. (1981). *Creating a dialectic social science*. Dordrecht: Reidel.

Stenhouse, L. (1980). *Curriculum research and development*. Heinemann: London.

Whyte, W.F. (1990). *Participatory action research*. Sage: London.

Zuber-Skerritt, O. (1992). *Professional development in higher education*. Kogan Page: London.

Managing Teams of Teams: Lessons Learned

Gail Corbitt[1] & Ben Martz[2]

[1]*California State University, Chico, USA &* [2]*University of Colorado at Colorado Springs, USA*

1. INTRODUCTION

Recruiters continuously report that one of the attributes that they like about California State University (CSU), Chico graduates is that they know how to work in teams and they are good team players. In addition, every year our Industry Council (an Advisory Board to the MIS program) identifies team skills as one of the most important recruiting characteristics. They consistently vote for continued emphasis of these skills in our program. For the MIS discipline, the ability to work in teams is a given prerequisite for the competitive workplace; one that bases more and more work performance evaluation on group and team skills and less on individual accomplishment.

In 1994, we reviewed our curriculum's use of project teams and this critical characteristic. We found that in nearly every case, we had groups of students in 3-5 person teams where each team was responsible for the same deliverable. For example, students worked in project teams to complete programming assignments, systems analysis projects or database design projects. In some cases, the projects were not true "group" projects. That is to say that the tasks could reasonably be completed by individuals and merged together toward the end of the semester for a final deliverable.

What is more common in the information system industry for which we are preparing our students, however, is a large team where sub-teams are responsible for one aspect of a complex interdependent project. Collectively the large project team is responsible for one deliverable and the smaller individual teams, functional teams, may only see one aspect of the whole

T.A. Johannessen, A. Pedersen and K. Petersen (eds.),
Educational Innovation in Economics and Business VI, 51–62.
© 2002 *Kluwer Academic Publishers. Printed in the Netherlands.*

project. For example, there are functional teams responsible for quality assurance processes, testing programs and systems, designing code, writing code, etc. In spring 1995, the new goal of the Systems Design course at CSU Chico, became to simulate this larger project team environment and thereby provide our students with the experience of working on a large systems project development team. In addition, we wanted to try to create an atmosphere of true collaboration as defined by Michael Shrage:

> "Collaboration is the process of shared creation: two or more individuals with complementary skills interacting to create a shared understanding that none had previously possessed or could have come to on their own. Collaboration creates a shared meaning about a process, a product, or and event. In this sense, there is nothing routine about it. Something is there that wasn't there before." (*No More Teams!*, 1995, p.33)

Managing this environment of teams of teams is not easy, however, but after 4 years we have learned how to create an atmosphere that at least approaches collaborative learning. The purpose of this paper is to explain the theoretical and practical background to our approach, describe the large team environment and present some lessons learned from our experience. While the emphasis is designed for systems development projects, we believe the basic concepts can be applied to any discipline where large project teams may be present, such as Engineering, Product Development, Marketing, etc.

2.   BACKGROUND ON HIGH PERFORMING TEAMS

Looking to support our idea took us to popular literature that characterized successful team projects and as a result important team characteristics. While it is not our intent here to exhaustively look at the literature surrounding teams and team building, we have chosen a limited number of authors who have popularized common attributes of high performance teams. For example, Schrage's definition above defines a collaborative situation as one in which the 2 or more participants realize that they cannot do the job alone. Furthermore, as the team members work together they build a "social matrix" of relationships, friendships, and mutual respect. (Schrage, 1995) Our goal was to draw on this definition in order to help create an atmosphere that is most conducive to creating high performing teams. This way, we can maximize the student's opportunity to succeed and still offer the students a collaborative large project team experience.

Team performance resides at the heart of the learning organization using what Senge (1990) calls the "discipline of dialogue." This discipline includes studying and understanding the "patterns of interaction in teams" with the ultimate goal to create team learning. Similarly, popular literature has recently advocated collaborative team environments so that companies can achieve extraordinary results. In some ways, the "principles" advocated by Peters and Waterman (1982) in *In Search of Excellence*, the "fishnet organization" of Johansen and Swigart's (1994) in *Upsizing the Individual in the Downsized Organization*, the "task-oriented transient organization" (TOTO) from Warfield's (1989) *Societal Systems* and the "reengineering teams" called for in Hammer and Champy's (1993) *Reengineering the Corporation*, all have some degree of high performing team concepts within their foundations. Extraordinary results are seldom the result of an individual effort; teams are at the core of achieving, if not greatness, at least success. Two books looked explicitly at teams and their contribution to corporate success; *The Wisdom of Teams* by Jon Katzenbach and Douglas Smith (1994) and *Teamwork and Team Players* by Glenn Parker (1996).

In order to explain the team environment we tried to create, it is helpful to review the classification of teams as presented by Katzenbach and Smith. These authors present 5 levels of team development: 1) Pseudo-teams; 2) Working Groups; 3) Potential Teams; 4) Real Teams; and 5) High Performing Teams (Table 1). Pseudo-teams and Working Groups are typical in many academic settings where the group performance does not go beyond the sum of its parts; these groups do not achieve synergy. In these groups, the work is divided and assigned to individual team members, each does his/her part and the result is the final product that is a collection of the parts. In short, there is no significant increase in value due to collaboration (because collaboration has not truly occurred). The only noticeable advantage to having a team may be some timesavings in producing the output. When evaluating a team for efficiency, a Pseudo-team is one step below the Working Group in that the final product may not be well-coordinated and individual style and performance actually detracts from the final product. The performance of the Working Group is equal to the sum of its parts, while the Pseudo-team performance is actually less than the sum of its parts (1994, p. 91) (As academics we certainly have group projects that fall into both of these categories.)

The last 3 team types actually produce better performance products than the sum of their member's individual effort and each type moves closer to a true collaborative effort. For example, a Potential Team truly wants to be better than the sum of its parts. Individual team members care about the common output, they expect it to be better than they can do on their own, and work towards or coordinate a common working approach. Team members agree ahead of time how they will achieve results and work steadily at doing this as a group – not just as individuals. As the commitment by the group members to the common goal increases, the group begins to hold individuals mutually accountable. As this happens the Potential Team becomes a Real Team.

Table 1: Team Types and Their Characteristics.

	Characteristics			
	Cooperation	Coordination	Commitment	Collaboration
Pseudo	No	No	No	No
Working	Yes	No	No	No
Potential	Yes	Yes	No	No
Real	Yes	Yes	Yes	No
High performance	Yes	Yes	Yes	Yes

The individuals on a Real Team care about the final output and each person works hard toward the common goal. Each person feels a personal responsibility toward, not only their part of the project, but to the team as a whole. Each person does not want to be the "weak link" and participants work to become contributing members of the team. High Performing Teams have all the attributes of Real Teams but they care about their team members as well. They collaborate by covering for each other's weaknesses and build on each other's strengths so if a person from the outside attacks an individual on the team, the whole team feels attacked. High Performing Teams are rare but they significantly outperform other types of teams (Katzenbach and Smith, 1994). The attributes of High Performing Teams include the following characteristics:

- Small number of people (4-6 on each team)
- Complementary skills
- Commitment to a common purpose
- Integrated performance with an overall goal/purpose
- Commitment to a common approach (agreement on how to work together)
- Mutual Accountability.

Given this framework, there are a number of research questions that one can ask. Can the environment be manipulated across these dimensions in order to maximize the opportunity for high performing teams to occur? Can this "manipulation" be done in an academic environment? How can these concepts of teams be applied to large team environments in order to maximize the likelihood of a high performing team? While these questions remain interesting, the main curriculum question we asked in 1995 was:

How can the academic environment be manipulated to maximize the opportunity for High Performing Teams in a large project setting?

3. CREATING A TEAM OF TEAMS

We created a course syllabus (Appendix A) in order to simulate the large project team environment and enable as many attributes of High Performing Teams as possible. The classroom scenario includes the following characteristics:

- All students in the class work on one project that receives a single grade;
- The project is "live" with real timelines, users and deliverables;
- Students apply for positions on one of six teams (Quality Assurance (process centered QA), Server Development, Client Development; Documentation; Implementation; and, Testing (product centered QA));
- The Project Manager is also a student in the class;
- Team Leaders are appointed for each team and the Team Leaders along with the Project Manager representing the Project Management Team are responsible for the project as a whole;
- All team assignments are selected by the instructor(s);
- Each team, including the Project Management team, has separately defined deliverables;
- Each deliverable is dependent on deliverables from other teams (no team can work entirely independent of interactions with other teams);
- Instruction needed to complete the project is done via mentoring of teams (outside of class) or by Just In Time training by the instructor(s) or other students in the class;
- Performance evaluations of each student are conducted at the 8th week and at the end of the term;
- Team deliverables are reviewed and approved by other student groups in the class using standard business practices like structured walkthroughs and quality circles;
- There is accountability at three levels: individual, team and project;
- Twenty percent of each students grade is the final project grade and another 20% of each student's grade is the team deliverable grade; and
- Each student can assign "performance" points to up to 3 other students in the class for 10% of the class points.

In summary, there are six functional teams and one project management team of 4-6 members each working on the class project. Since students do not self select into teams and have to apply for positions within the class, the instructor can assure to some degree the complementary skill component of high performance teams. The instructor reviews the application in conjunction with other faculty members who know the students from other classes. In this way, each team is carefully constructed and many times students are not given their first choice. As one student said once, "I see you have distributed the 'loafers' so we each get one." In reality, the structure of this class, more than any other, gives the 'loafers' a chance to shine and we have seen many students who do not perform well in other classes really get involved with this class. It seems peer pressure works as an advantage here. They no longer are letting themselves down, but the whole team and in some cases, the whole class – so pressure to keep up and to perform is created by fellow classmates.

Making the project grade a single grade for the whole class ensures more commitment to a common purpose; the "A" students drive the rest of the class to their standard. Individual performance is integrated with the overall goal by making the individual team deliverables highly integrated with each other. No team can work alone – each team relies heavily on input from other teams and each team provides output to other teams. This interdependence provides a real opportunity to learn and grow as both team members and software developers. The students catch on very quickly that they can't work alone and they are dependent on others. Through regular status meetings, a major use of class time, they see how their actions (or in-actions) help or hinder the project as a whole. They see how an error on their part has far reaching consequences and they learn about cooperation in a way that is rare in an academic setting.

The class achieves commitment to a common approach by participating in the Quality Assurance plan developed by the QA team. This QA process plan outlines: 1) how changes are made to the plans as we go along 2) what the deliverables are 3) how quality of the deliverables is measured 4) what the review process is for moving the project forward (in other words, when is a deliverable finished), and 5) how the class time is used. The whole class has an opportunity to review and approve this document, and once approved, it becomes the common approach (the social contract) to completing the work. Mutual accountability is also supported when the class collectively defines and accepts how to achieve the generally described deliverables. In addition, applying the grade from the overall project as a major portion of the individual's semester grade increases accountability. In addition, team-building activities at the beginning of the class, peer points that each student can "give out" to others, and 2 performance evaluations conducted by Team Leaders and the Project Manager help support the accountability. These activities also account for 20% of the overall student grade and rely on input from peers. A portion of the class syllabus outlining the point structure and the team responsibilities is presented as Appendix A.

4. CHALLENGES AND LESSONS LEARNED

There were several fundamental challenges that had to be overcome. For example, we did not have grading criteria that matched the time commitment of the students. We had a midterm and a final exam worth 40% of the grade and yet the actual time spent on the project was 90% of the work. Students resented (some with good reason) the disproportionate grading criteria. The grading criteria represented in Appendix A have evolved over the years and more closely match the time spent by the students among the class activities. One continuing problem is the quiz points associated with team presentations. The stated purpose of the team presentations is to give the rest of the students in the class as chance to see what each of the other teams in the class is responsible for. The presentation should describe how the group presenting contributes to the final project in the context of the whole systems development process. The intent of the quizzes is to assure attention to the presentation both by the presenters and the audience. Students complain about this, but agree that there is no other more appropriate alternative.

Other challenges that have been addressed over the years include instructor differences when the class is team-taught, use of class time (we have found that the class needs to meet 3 times a week, minimum), and having the students participate more in the evaluation process. We have team-taught this class most of the time it has been offered. Sometimes we sent mixed messages to the students when the 2 instructors had different answers. We also found the students were quick to go to "mom" when "dad" said something they did not like, or visa versa. We learned to coordinate better among ourselves, which added to the faculty workload. The major disadvantage to teaching this course is that the time outside class to mentor the teams is high. One semester that the time was carefully tracked showed that we spent 5 hours outside of class for every hour we spent in class – over 2 sections of this class it was about 25 hours a week per faculty member that was devoted to this course. (The rewards are also great, however, as the students learn a lot and are quick to share their insights and experiences. In addition, the course is extremely engaging from the faculty's perspective.)

Assigning individual student grades remains a continuing challenge. The academic system at CSU, Chico requires individual grades and yet the class consists of 80% or more of group work. We (the faculty and students) have tried a number of options including having the HR class create a performance evaluation based on group activities. We have settled on a simplified performance evaluation that Team Leaders complete for each team member, and the Project Manager completes for each Team Leader, and the Instructor(s) complete for the Project Manager. This is done twice during the semester and is supplemented by peer points that each student can give out. In the peer point process, each student is "given" 50 points twice a term that can be distributed across a maximum of 3 people in the class. The students do not have to give the points to anyone, but they do not get to add them to their own score. Most students take this seriously and hand out points to deserving students.

Still the instructor(s) often find it difficult to assign individual grades, especially to Team Leaders and Project Managers who go unrecognized or resented by their peers. Most of the time the grading system of peer points and performance evaluations take care of the inequity but from time to time the instructor has had to "adjust" point grades so that a fair letter grade can be assigned. The class also has personnel policies so that a student who does not perform can be fired if the procedure is followed. A fired student must find another job in the class or negotiate with the Project Manager and the Instructor(s). There has been only one firing in the 5 semesters that the course has been offered in this format and the student ended up taking the class over.

One continuing problem is that the workload of teams is not equal. Typically, the team doing the coding for the client part of the system is at least twice as much work as the other teams. The classes consistently feel that the workload for the teams other than the client team is more or less equal. In response, we expanded the size of this team (Client team) and splitting the deliverables into the detailed design and the actual code. We hope this addresses the workload issue. Most students believe that the course consumes as much time as the students give it, so they need to learn how to budget time for the project. Most also say that they see the value in working on this project and it is more interesting than sitting in on lectures and taking tests, etc. As a result they end up spending more time on the course than they planned just because it engages them.

Another problem from the student perspective is that the course is not structured enough for them. The concepts of Just-In-Time learning, and asking for help when they don't know something are intimidating to many students. They still expect to be "spoon fed" material and told exactly what to study. We believe that the unstructured nature of the course is part of its value. The students learn to learn and learn how to find answers to questions when they have them. They have to decide what needs to be done and how to do in the least amount of time.

While every class encounters different problems, all of the students go away with a more realistic idea of what it is like to work on a systems development project. Some (only a few) learn that they really do not want to major in MIS. The most important thing that each and every student leaves this experience with, however, is that collaborative teamwork takes on a whole new meaning. They see the frustration in not knowing everything.

This means that they are not better at identifying information they do need. They understand better both the absolute need to share information as well as the type of information that needs to be shared in order to coordinate a large project. Finally, the class experience provides some insight into the management required of large project.

APPENDIX A: GRADING AND TEAM RESPONSIBILITIES PORTION OF SYLLABUS

Grading:
Plus and minus grades are given. Grades are based on both individual and team work.

- Class Final Project   200
- Team Final Project   200
- Quizzes   140
- Group report & presentation 100
- Performance evaluations   100
- Peer Points   100
- Class/QIF participation   100

The quizzes are short answer essay and multiple choice. They are given the day after each class group presentation and no make up quizzes are given.

Each student is given two performance evaluations during the semester; one at about the 7th week and one at the end of the term. The Team Leader and the Project Manager review each team member and turn in a written evaluation, including a point allocation, into the Instructor. The instructor reserves the right to change the points assigned upon consultation with the student, Team Leader and Project Manager. During the review, overall performance is discussed along with any areas that may need improvement. Team goals are set for each team at the time teams are assigned and during the first performance evaluation. Students are evaluated with respect to these team goals, in addition to the following goals that are expected from every student:

1. The student is a valued team member contributing high quality work assignments on time.
2. The student is willing to participate in team meetings, and
3. The student is willing to learn new skills, and contributes to the team's work as required.

The peer evaluation points are done twice a semester. Each student is given 50 points (each evaluation) that they can give away to other students in the class. You can divide the 50 points, you can not distribute points to more than 3 people at a time. The points do not have to be given away. During the semester if you work with someone on your team or on another team that goes beyond what you'd normally expect, you can give that student points. A form will be available to use to record the points that you give away.

In addition, each student will be given 10, "210 Bucks" to be used for a similar purpose. If another student in the class surprises you with extra help and/or knowledge that you didn't expect you can give the student a "210 Buck." At the end of the semester we auction off prizes that you can buy with your 210 Bucks. Any Bucks that have not been given out to others are collected and cannot be used during the auction. (Note that there are no class points associated with this activity. This is just for fun.)

The whole class is developing one system. The class final project grade (worth 200 points) is added to your individual grade for this class. You are required to work in teams responsible for one aspect of the project and you are part of the total project team that is ultimately responsible for the completion of the project. In other words, if the project fails, the whole class bears responsibility in its failure and the class is only as strong as its weakest team. The teams along with their corresponding duties and deliverables are available below.

You are to prepare a job application for a job on one of the project teams. If you desire to be a team leader you need to indicate this as well. Systems Management is ultimately the responsibility of the faculty instructor. The Project Management, however, is the responsibility of one student in the class (who is chosen to be Project Manager). The faculty instructor mentors the teams as needed. In the event of a conflict, the following is the desired pattern for resolution:

- Person to person within the team
- Team Leader
- Project Manager
- Systems Manager (Faculty Instructor)
- Whole Class.

Just like in business, people can be fired from their jobs. If a team member continually shows no interest in the project, does not participate and/or does not follow through on team assignments, the Team Leader needs to warn the student in writing of the problem (send copies to Project Manager and Systems Manger in charge). If after the written warning the negative behavior continues, a second letter is sent to the student putting the student on notice for possible firing. If still no corrective behavior occurs, a third letter firing the student is sent. If you receive a letter indicating you are fired, you need to find a team that is willing to hire you or negotiate with the faculty instructor for a new assignment and the project grade points. A fired student automatically loses 100 of the total points assigned to the course and is in jeopardy of failing the class.

PRIMARY TEAM	DUTIES	PRIMARY DELIVERABLES
Server Development	Create Data Model Code the server system Create Program documentation Create System Flowchart Design and implementation of security Fix errors found in testing	Working system Detailed Data Model with Repository Program documentation
Documentation	Construct documentation plan or specifications Write user guides Integrate system's documentation Help fix errors found in testing	User Documentation System Documentation On-line help (if any) Documentation "Plan"
Testing	Create overall project test plan Produce test data for each phase Test system prior to end-user install Present final system	Test plan Testing data and results
Client Development	Produce detailed design client system Prototype screens, reports, etc. Fix errors found in testing	Design details Working system Program documentation
Implementation	Develop implementation plan for data conversion and training Install all components for the user	Implementation Plan Installed User System with Initial data
Evaluation	Develop quality assurance plan to monitor the project process Conduct process control audit Conduct final system audit	Quality plan Final system audit

Project Management	Composed of the Project Manager and Team Leaders from the above teams :
	    Coordinate the project
	    Provide inter-team communication
	    Conduct status reports
		Final Project Deliverables

REFERENCES

Hammer, M., & Champy, J. (1993). *Reengineering the Corporation.* Harper Business Publications, 109-114.

Johansen, R., & Swigart, R. (1994). *Upsizing the Individual in the Downsized Organization.* Addison Wesley, pp. 8-10.

Katzenbach, J., & Smith, D. (1994). *The Wisdom of Teams.* New York: Harper Business Books.

Schrage, M. (1995). *No More Teams!* Mastering the Dynamics of Creative Collaboration. Currency Doubleday Publications.

Senge, P.M. (1990). *The Fifth Discipline: The Art and Practice of The Learning Organization.* Doubleday Publications.

Parker, G.M. (1996). *Team Players and Teamwork.* New York: Jossey-Bass.

Peters, T.J., & Waterman, Jr., R.H. (1982). *In Search of Excellence.* Harper & Row, p. 127.

Warfield, J.N. (1989). *Societal Systems.* Intersystems Publications, p. 73.

Issues in Team Teaching: Point and Counterpoint

Michael K. McCuddy, Wendy L. Pirie, David L. Schroeder, &
Sandra E. Strasser
College of Business Administration, Valparaiso University, Valparaiso, Indiana, USA

1. INTRODUCTION

Team teaching can be both a satisfying and frustrating experience. Kulynych (1999, p, 144), for instance, describes the team-teaching experience as "both exhilarating and exasperating". Among the satisfying—even exhilarating—aspects of team teaching are the opportunities to learn from one another and the support faculty members can receive from colleagues. Among the frustrations associated with team teaching are faculty members' insecurity and their fear of power imbalances (Speer & Ryan, 1998), lack of institutional support (Speer & Ryan, 1998), and lack of attention to detail (Arnold & Jackson, 1996; Bakken *et al.*, 1999; Lehmann & Gillman, 1998; Speer & Ryan, 1998).

The authors of this paper have experienced both the exhilarations and the frustrations of team teaching. Many of the issues and concepts in this paper arise from three semesters of the four of us teaching together in a team format. Four stand-alone, three credit functional courses (Financial Management, Management and Organizational Behavior, Marketing Management, and Management Information Systems—all at the junior level) were combined to create a twelve credit hour, integrated functional core course. In the first semester, the course met four days a week for just less than three hours each day. In the second and third semesters, the course met each morning of the week for approximately two and one-quarter hours each day. This team-taught integrated format raises the first issue—what is team teaching?

T.A. Johannessen, A. Pedersen and K. Petersen (eds.),
Educational Innovation in Economics and Business VI, 63–74.
© 2002 *Kluwer Academic Publishers. Printed in the Netherlands.*

2.   THE ISSUE OF TEAM TEACHING: A SHARED VISION VERSUS A KALEIDOSCOPE

A shared vision of team teaching needed to be established. Using "sports" similes; team teaching could be like a gymnastics team, a relay race team, a wrestling tag team, or a soccer team. On a gymnastics team, the members perform separately and independently, relying on each other to perform well and thereby contribute to the overall team effort. While they may be performing at the same time, they are not performing in the same venue. On a relay team, all members are present but only one member is performing until the time of pass-off to the next member. On a wrestling tag team, each member is present but not all members are performing. The non-performing members have the option of tagging in at any time. On a soccer team, all members on the field are actively performing simultaneously.

Examples of expectations for each of these existed among the four faculty involved in the course, among the faculty not involved in the course, among the students in the course, among the students not involved in the course, from the administration, and from external stakeholders.

Initially, an approach that might be likened to the soccer team approach was used. The design was four faculty members in the classroom all the time, interacting with one another and with students. One faculty member was generally in charge at any one time—or had the ball. Linkages with the other disciplines—or handoffs—arose from activities like sharing specific concepts and examples from each of the four disciplines, or from reviewing articles in *The Wall Street Journal* (this occurred at the beginning of each class session and is referred to as *The Wall Street Journal* discussion). Everyone was on the field at the same time, working toward a common goal.

Some faculty not involved in teaching the integrated functional core anticipated that perhaps two of us might be in the classroom at the same time, but never all four. They anticipated an approach like that of a relay team. One of us would be performing with a second faculty member waiting for the hand-off. They did not see any need for all team members to be present simultaneously.

Other faculty not involved in the core anticipated that only one of us would be in the classroom at any given time. They anticipated an approach like that of a gymnastics team. One of the team members would be performing at a given time, with others having set times to perform. They did not see a need for more than one member to be present.

Some of the students involved anticipated an approach where one faculty member would be "up front"—with perhaps another waiting to go. Like a relay team, one faculty member would be "running" (the course) until he or she passed the baton to the next. Eventually everyone would run, but no one would be running at the same time, even though someone would always be waiting to have the baton passed from another faculty member.

Some of the students not involved in the functional core anticipated a trade-off approach, where two faculty members would be covering a related topic in the class at the same time. This is like a wrestling tag team, where one would be "wrestling" with an issue, with the other team member waiting at the ropes to tag in and take a turn in the struggle.

External stakeholders—such as administrators, parents of students, and potential employers—liked the soccer team approach and the "added value" of four faculty members in the classroom at the same time. Administrators were excited about the approach of combining four courses, and anticipated a soccer team approach with four players playing all the time. However, it was as though a player played a whole game but was compensated for only one-quarter of the game. Parents of students perceived a better educational value for their offspring and enhanced employment opportunities for them. Potential employers appreciated the added value of a more realistic simulation of the integrated business environment.

The four different conceptions of team teaching are summarized in Table 1. The extremes were from each faculty member alone in the class for three contact hours per week to four faculty members in the classroom for all twelve contact hours per week. In the former situation, the only "team" was the class that remained a constant group. In the latter situation, the class and the faculty comprised a "team".

Table 1: Conceptions of team teaching.

	Gymnastics Team	Relay Team	Wrestling Tag Team	Soccer Team
Faculty in class simultaneously	One	One or two	Two or more	All
Class contact time per faculty member per week	3 hours	6 hours	At least 6 hours	12 hours

All four approaches were used at some point in the three semesters. For example, the soccer team approach, with all four on the field at the same time, occurred during *The Wall Street Journal* discussions, where all four faculty members offered input on article topics; or during critiques of group projects, where all shared their assessment. The wrestling tag team approach occurred on several occasions when the same topic was addressed from the perspective of two different disciplines, such as the concept of decision making from both an information systems standpoint and an organizational behavior standpoint. The relay team approach occurred on days where one faculty member would be "up front" during part of the class time, followed by another, and then another. The gymnastics approach, although rare, happened when one faculty member took the entire two-hour plus class time for a day.

3.   THE ISSUE OF TEACHING STYLE: "SAGE ON THE STAGE" VERSUS "GUIDE ON THE SIDE"

In addition to dealing with the issue of what team teaching is, we had to deal with the issue of teaching styles. Teaching styles are characterized as topic-based, outcome-based, or problem-based. These classify teaching styles by the degree of involvement of faculty members and students in defining the problem for discussion and in developing the solution(s) to the problem. This is summarized in Table 2.

Table 2: Characteristics of teaching styles.

	Faculty	Student
Topic-Based (e.g., Lecture)	Defines problem and develops solution(s)	Is a passive receptor of knowledge
Outcome-Based (e.g., Seminar)	Becomes active in developing solution(s)	Selects problem but is passive in developing solution(s)
Problem-Based (*e.g.*, Case Study or Project)	Defines problem but is passive in developing solution(s)	Becomes active in developing solution(s)

Depending on the circumstances, faculty members choose the appropriate teaching style. Most faculty members have used all three at some point. In a team-taught course this choice is no longer at the discretion of an individual faculty member but rather the result of a team decision. Some faculty members may prefer a lecture-based approach (sage on the stage) while others prefer a project or case approach (guide on the side). Unless consensus can be reached, conflicts can occur.

In our case, the interdisciplinary aspect of the course exacerbated some of the difficulties we experienced in establishing a shared vision of team teaching and in adopting an appropriate teaching style for each occasion. While connections between the disciplines being coordinated existed, there were also differences in the disciplines. Some disciplines were more conducive to one teaching style versus another. Methods of evaluating student progress varied from discipline to discipline. The objectives of the courses in each discipline varied in their orientation towards behavioral objectives versus cognitive objectives. All of this made the transition from course to course more difficult in some ways and more exciting in others.

Rather than merely handing off to one another, we were constantly involved in comparing, contrasting, relating, and revealing the aspects of multiple disciplines. This was exciting and challenging but also difficult and time consuming. It also created some frustration for the students who spent a great deal of time and energy trying to put things into neat blocks. A typical comment was: "I cannot tell where finance ends and marketing begins." The students wanted the disciplines more discretely defined so they would know "what to study". This tension between integration of disciplines and a separate disciplinary focus is difficult to resolve for students and faculty. This tension involved many additional issues that are addressed in the remainder of the paper.

4. THE ISSUE OF CONTROL: SHARED RESPONSIBILITY VERSUS LOSS OF CONTROL

While it is exciting to share the responsibility of the classroom with other faculty and to an extent with students, it is threatening to give up control of the classroom to other faculty and to an extent to students. Team teaching must address the varying needs for control of each team member and the necessity to control each team member.

Who is in control? With the gymnastics team, each individual is in control of his or her own performance and trusts that other team members will perform as well. With the relay team, control passes to the person running with the baton. With the tag team approach, control is more fluid with the person in the ring having obvious control but the individuals on the sidelines retaining some control, given their ability to enter the fray at their discretion. With the soccer team, each individual on the field has control simultaneously over some aspect of the play. This issue of control relates directly back to an understanding of the definition of team teaching.

A further issue deals with the responsibility of the faculty members and students for defining the content of a team-taught class. To the extent the instructor acts as the "guide on the side" and that a problem-based or outcomes-based style is used, the students must assume responsibility for the class. This entails a further loss of perceived control for the faculty. The acceptance of responsibility for the class is challenging for the students. This transference of control is problematic for students and faculty alike.

On the one hand, giving up control is threatening; on the other hand, having a team to support you and to step in when the need arises is exhilarating. In a stand-alone class with a single instructor, the instructor has control along with the responsibility that entails. In a team-taught class, the control is more fluid. The degree of comfort in giving up control depends upon the personality of each instructor. We observed that individuals who had a higher need for control imposed control in other ways to compensate for their perceived loss of control. This can take the form of rules, schedules, etc. While it is exciting to be part of a team and to share the control and responsibility, it is also threatening.

5. THE ISSUE OF STANDARDS AND MEASUREMENT: OBJECTIVE VERSUS SUBJECTIVE EVALUATION

Teaching style differences affect the standards for and measurement of student output and performance. A topic-based style usually leads to a greater reliance on objective evaluation mechanisms such as multiple choice or true/false exams. The faculty member defines both the problem and the solution, and students react in a relatively passive fashion. Faculty members, rather than students, are responsible for the learning process. Faculty members are responsible for defining the desired outcomes of the learning process, whereas students are responsible for demonstrating the acquisition of knowledge. A problem-based teaching style or an outcome-based teaching style is more amenable to subjective methods of evaluation. Rather than a precise answer, there are imprecise—perhaps even multiple—answers. Faculty members assume somewhat less responsibility, and students assume much greater personal responsibility for both the learning process and learning outcomes.

Differences in teaching styles lead to differences in evaluation mechanisms. The four faculty members utilized quite different approaches for evaluating student performance in course specific material. One faculty member relied heavily on quizzes and exams with objective questions. Another faculty member utilized short essays and some objective questions. A third faculty member relied on problems and extended essays. The fourth faculty member relied very heavily on extended essays. Based on these differences, students formed differing expectations for the evaluation process as each professor applied it.

The evaluation process was challenging from another perspective as well. Forty percent of the course grade in each of the four disciplines was based on common requirements that were to be evaluated by all four faculty members. The vast majority of these common requirements were subjective rather than objective in their evaluation orientation. Resolving differing faculty viewpoints on student performance regarding requirements such as a book report or a consulting project typically necessitate some negotiation and compromise.

This issue also involves the comparisons that students naturally make among their professors regarding who is an "easy grader" and who is not. With such comparisons in a team-taught course, there may be real pressures or perceived pressures to adjust one's grading standards upwards or downwards. Another comparison that students make is with the grades awarded in the comparable stand-alone courses. There was a perception by some students that the grades in the integrated functional core were lower than grades in the corresponding stand-alone courses. Other students believed the grades in the functional core were higher, and it was an easier way of taking the courses. This is a function of the fact that poorer students tended to benefit from and better students tended to be harmed by the common grade component.

Faculty members are not immune to making comparisons either. Faculty perceptions regarding differences in performance standards and expectations can affect their judgments about and working relationships with their peers.

6. THE ISSUE OF OUTCOMES: INTEGRATED OBJECTIVES VERSUS DISCIPLINARY OBJECTIVES

While the objectives of integration enhance those of the specific disciplines and make the experience fulfilling, there is a fear that the objectives of integration gain too much precedence and detract from the objectives of the individual disciplines. The balance between integration objectives and individual disciplinary objectives has to be established up front or problems will arise.

Each discipline has specified affective, cognitive, and behavioral objectives. How should a student feel, what should a student know, and what should a student do (or be able to do)? There are also objectives inherent in the integration. Some disciplines focus more on cognitive objectives while others are oriented more toward affective and behavioral objectives. The objectives of integration tend to be more affective and behavioral. To the extent that the disciplinary objectives align with the integration objectives, less difficulty occurs for faculty members. This was a crucial issue for faculty who were not teaching in the integrated core. They were very concerned that disciplinary objectives were being sacrificed for the sake of integration objectives.

Faculty and student satisfaction with the experience depends on their belief in the importance of integration objectives. To the extent that disciplinary objectives are not met, there is cognitive dissonance. This dissonance is even more prevalent on the part of faculty members when they are teaching the same course concurrently in a stand-alone manner.

7. THE ISSUE OF RIGOR: LOWEST COMMON DENOMINATOR VERSUS A NEW PLATEAU

Team teaching in an integrated course also raises the issue of rigor. How rigorous can a course be, with regard to content, methods, and performance expectations, when four faculty members have an impact on the course? What, if anything, is compromised? With multiple disciplines and multiple personalities involved, is there a tendency to sink to the lowest common denominator; to rise to the challenges of the occasion with collective improvements; to engage in trade-offs so that no one is neither too irritated nor too happy; or to persist in doing what one normally does and ignoring the reaction of others? The issue of rigor raises specific content-related questions as well, including the following: How much discipline-specific material must be delivered in order to be fair to the introductory course for the discipline? Can this be done at the same time as the introduction of the interdisciplinary nature of business? How might rigor be affected by different teaching styles, different visions, and different disciplines with different standards and measurement tools?

Some faculty members believe that rigor is sacrificed in a team-taught course where integration is emphasized. Each discipline represented in the integrated course has it specific content, methods, and traditions. Each faculty member naturally feels the pull of his/her content, methods, and traditions. The pull of one discipline may be incongruent with the pull of another discipline. For example, one discipline (or a faculty member's approach to the discipline) may be more oriented toward learning vocabulary as opposed to learning and applying concepts or understanding and using theoretical frameworks. Disciplines differ with regard to qualitative and quantitative orientations. Disciplines and the professors teaching in them differ in their use of lectures, discussions, case analyses, problems, and exercises, to name but a few activities.

Rigor also is sacrificed because fewer class contact hours are devoted to the content of each discipline in order to accommodate integrative activities. At times, faculty members feel rushed to cover the same amount of material that they would cover in the corresponding stand-alone courses. A faculty member's allotted discipline time may not proceed according to plan because other faculty members who are present in the classroom interject questions and comments intended to reflect the integrative nature of the course. Thus, the students receive less discipline-specific exposure, and may be less prepared in the fundamentals of business than are students taking the stand-alone courses.

An alternative perspective is that rigor is not sacrificed in a team taught integrative course. Faculty members are not viewed as the fountain of all knowledge. Students assume a more active role in and responsibility for their own learning. While it is true that fewer class contact hours are devoted to discipline-specific material, this does not mean that students do not learn the content. However, students are expected to be more responsible for their own learning, and to take appropriate initiative to inquire about those ideas and topics about which they experience confusion.

One of the benefits of team teaching in an integrated course is the provision of multiple perspectives on given topics or issues. Multiple perspectives are encouraged and shared by faculty doing the right thing. The right thing is to be flexible and adaptable in the management of discipline-specific time, and in responding to and utilizing input from the other faculty members. Contributions can be supportive and reinforcing—both of the specific content of the discipline and the linkage of the discipline's content to the integrative nature of business.

Some faculty members argue that undergraduate students must know the fundamentals of business before they can begin to understand and appreciate the integrated nature of business. Doing both together undermines each. Fundamentals and integration must be developed sequentially. Based on this perspective, students cannot understand integration of the fundamentals unless they first understand the fundamentals themselves.

Other faculty members argue that the fundamentals of business and integration need not be taught in a sequential fashion—there is nothing magical, or even realistic, about this approach. Life in the business world is not doing the functions of business, and then integrating them. Rather, life in the business world is the integration of business functions. From this viewpoint, students can better understand the purpose of the various business fundamentals by simultaneously knowing how they fit into "the big picture".

8.   THE ISSUE OF RESOURCE UTILIZATION: EDUCATIONAL BENEFITS VERSUS RESOURCE COSTS

A team-taught course is no more costly in terms of resources than a stand-alone course. Alternatively, offering team-taught courses is costly in terms of faculty resources. The former statement is only true from the perspective of administration when there is no course relief offered to faculty. In that case the entire burden is borne by faculty, and administration attaches no cost to the team-taught courses. In fact, there is a cost to team teaching regardless of which team-teaching approach is adopted.

With the gymnastics team approach, the class contact time is not significantly greater than for a stand-alone course but there is a significant increase in coordination and planning time. With the relay team approach, the class contact time increases slightly and there is a significant increase in coordination and planning time. With the tag team approach, there is another incremental increase in class contact, coordination, and planning time. Finally, with the soccer team approach there is an exponential increase in class contact, coordination, and planning time. If administration recognizes this increased time commitment by providing teaching load relief, extra teaching assistance, or a stipend, there is a clear cost. Unfortunately, administration frequently views team teaching as having no extra cost because they expect the "cost" to be borne by the faculty.

Potentially, offering a team-taught course imposes an extra burden on faculty not participating in the team-taught course. This occurs if class sizes increase in other sections due to lower enrollment in the team-taught courses than in corresponding stand-alone courses. Further, if teaching loads are reduced for faculty in the team-taught course, the burden of this relief may be passed onto other faculty. Once again the cost of the team-taught course is borne by faculty—just different members of the faculty. It is difficult to get administration to commit resources to bear the true cost of team-taught courses.

9.   CONCLUDING OBSERVATIONS: WITH A BANG OR WITH A WHIMPER?

Team teaching of the integrated functional core at Valparaiso University was a noble experiment but it has ended. The demise could be attributed to a lack of a shared vision between and among the various stakeholders: faculty, students, administration, and external stakeholders. Team teaching creates multiple and diverse demands and expectations from the different stakeholder groups for participating faculty and students. These demands and expectations can produce numerous conflicts in how the faculty members' roles and the students' roles are played out. Being aware of the potential for numerous role conflicts is an important initial step toward effective team teaching. Being committed to proactively resolving these role conflicts is an essential subsequent step. Part of this proactive resolution is to ensure that both faculty members and students truly understand that in "the real world" there are multiple ways of doing things, and that one must be adaptable to those multiple ways if one wishes to be effective.

Effective team teaching in an integrated course requires an appropriate balance of the faculty roles of being the "sage on the stage" versus the "guide on the side". The "sage on the stage" role is more appropriately adapted to the transmission of information about the language, concepts, and theories of business fundamentals. The "guide on the side" role is more amenable to the application of language, concepts, and theories.

Students who are well prepared to function effectively in contemporary businesses must have a solid grounding in both business fundamentals and the integrative nature of those fundamentals. Even those faculty who traditionally have operated quite happily within their tunnel-vision of discipline loyalty often come to realize—just as businesses already have— that solid grounding in both business fundamentals and the integrative nature of business is essential. Discipline-specific content cannot and should not be sacrificed for integration. Integration cannot and should not be cast aside to provide for greater coverage of discipline-specific content.

The bottom line is that effective team teaching of an integrated course takes on many faces. Tensions can arise from these many faces. If not well managed, the tensions can be destructive. If well managed, the tensions can be a catalyst for improvement. Managing these tensions well means several different things. It means being open to alternative viewpoints. It means not being so rigid in one's thinking and ways that the team-taught course has to be "my way or the highway". It means being interested in, rather than bored by, the other disciplines—particularly after the first semester. It means genuinely listening to and responding to others' concerns, while striving for a standard of excellence.

Was team teaching challenging, exciting, and rewarding? Or was it disappointing, confusing, and frustrating? The answer is yes!

REFERENCES

Arnold, J., & Jackson, I. (1996). The keys to successful co-teaching. Thought & Action: *The NEA Higher Education Journal*, 91-98.

Bakken, L., Clark, F.L., & Thompson, J. (1998). Collaborative teaching: many joys, some surprises, and a few worms. *College Teaching, Vol. 46* No. 4, 154-157.

Kulynych, J.J. (1998). Crossing disciplines: postmodernism and democratic teaching. *College Teaching, Vol. 46* No. 4, 144-149.

Lehmann, J., & Gillman, R. (1998). Insights from a semester of collaborative teaching. *Primus*, 97-102.

Speer, T., & Ryan, B. (1998). Collaborative teaching in the de-centered classroom. *Teaching English in the two-year college (TETYC)*, pp. 39-49.

Project Seminars: One way of Developing Reflected Practical Competence

Brigitte Gütl & Heike Welte
Business Education and Evaluation Research, University of Innsbruck, Innsbruck, Austria

1.   INTRODUCTION

In this article we want to discuss the basic ideas underlying our program of "project seminars", its structure as well as the consequences which will be the results of this form of teaching and learning within the study of business education or business administration. We want to show that we have reached already many of the aims underlying the conception (specially in the field of qualification) but that there are still a lot of experiences or a complex of problems respectively which are the starting point for a further development of the design of these courses. The aim of our concept of education is the development of reflective practical competence: The main question is: How should scientific and experience orientated education be organized, if we want people to get used to complex situations.

2.   THE MODEL OF TECHNICAL RATIONALITY

The starting point in our description is a criticism of the traditional education at universities and the view of vocational activity as a complex professional performance. The main point of our concern regarding this education program is the concept of the "reflective practitioner" by Donald Schön (1983). His main question is: How do we get high quality performance in working situations which are complex and uncertain. Usually universities give the following answer: People use their theoretical

T.A. Johannessen, A. Pedersen and K. Petersen (eds.),
Educational Innovation in Economics and Business VI, 75–91.

knowledge to solve the problems of their professional work. This approach is called "a model of technical rationality" (Schön, 1983, p. 39).

This technical rationality as a way of conceptualizing political and administrative intervention in educational systems follows three basic assumptions (Altrichter, Posch & Somekh, 1983, p. 201):

- There are general solutions to practical problems.
- These solutions can be developed outside practical situations (in research or administrative centers).
- The solutions can be translated into teachers' actions by means of publications, training, administrative orders etc.

So professional individuals need and learn general theoretical knowledge in their education and this knowledge is produced through research. The concept of the traditional education at universities is characterized by the following (Schön, 1987, p. 309):

- Professional know-how is privileged information which has been formed through scientific methods. This leads to the assumption that this knowledge is seen as constant and beyond doubt.
- Scientific knowledge is specialized, isolated and divided into subjects (Bromme, 1992, p. 34, p. 149). People act as if everything is arranged hierarchical, differentiated, objective and without any past.
- Teaching is the transmission of this form of structured information through teachers and teaching-books. They have a monopoly as sources of knowledge.
- Practical know-how is of less importance than theoretical knowledge.
- The acquisition of social qualifications can only be acquired outside the universities.

The consequences of such a conception can be seen in the main strategies of learning as passive consumption of information and determinated from outside. Discussion what to learn and self-responsibility are rare. The validity of this theoretical knowledge is not set in question. In this way learning is a process without relevance to experiences and social activities.

This concept of using theoretical knowledge to solve problems shows a picture of enterprises, which is characterized by clear aims and a stable institutional context (Salzgeber, 1996, p. 57). Perhaps these are found in simple jobs with lots of routines. But that is not the situation in which graduates will be confronted with in their vocational life. There will be rather complex, uncertain and ambiguous situations. So in these situations - as we see it - reflection is required professionally as a main addition.

3. THE MODEL OF REFLECTIVE RATIONALITY

Before we explain the model of reflective rationality we want to show what is meant by a complex situation (Dörner, 1994, p. 58):

- There are many influencing factors which are connected to each other and affect each other. Complex practical problems demand specific solutions.
- The net result of this is that one needs to take into consideration all of these elements in one's decision with all the following effects.
- These situations have their own dynamic, which means the system is always changing and it's hard to calculate the results or build on a specific situation.
- These solutions can be developed only inside the context in which the problem arises and in which the practitioner is a crucial and determining element.
- The solutions cannot be successfully applied to other contexts but they can be made accessible to other practitioners as hypotheses to be tested.
- There are rarely solutions which are defined as right or wrong. Many actions contain elements which are partly new.

Performing in these highly qualified vocations can be described by the following characteristics (Altrichter, Posch & Somekh, 1993, p. 202f):

- In complex situations people cannot use their knowledge to solve a problem because the problem is not obvious. Only through the process of defining the problem it becomes clear. And this process of defining the problem assumes that using theoretical knowledge takes effect. From the perspective of technical rationality, professional practice is a process of problem solving. Problems of choice or decision are solved through the selection, from available means, of the one best suited solution to established ends. But with this emphasis on problem solving, problem setting is ignored, the process by which the decision to be made is defined, the ends to be achieved, the means which may be chosen. In real-world practice, problems do not present themselves to the practitioners as given. They must be constructed form the materials of problematic situations which are puzzling, troubling and uncertain. In order to convert a problematic situation to a problem, a practitioner must do a certain kind of work. He must make sense of an uncertain situation that initially makes no sense. When we set the problem, we select what we will treat as the 'things' of the situation, we set the boundaries of our attention to it, and we impose upon it a coherence which allows us to say what is wrong and in what directions the situation needs to be changed. Problem setting is a process in which, interactively, we name the things to which we will attend to. Even when a problem has been constructed, it may escape the categories of applied science because it presents itself as unique or unstable.

- This first definition of the problem is not yet fixed. Successfully performing people observe their actions and at the same time the correctness of their definition of the problem regarding the situation. Through reflecting on their actions they develop their definition of the problem continuously.

- Finally, problems are not always special cases of a general well known theory. Successful people have the competence to develop knowledge out of the working situation through their experiences. Professionals do not only have theoretical knowledge which they have acquired through a long period of education, they also have this knowledge gained from experiences and reflection. The sum of both of them put people in the situation of solving problems of their vocation competently, and with know-how in connection with the situation.

The demands of these situation concern qualifications such as the ability to work independently, creatively, with social competence, sense of responsibility, and so on. This means we must partly disqualify 'traditional' knowledge such as theories, instruments or methods. But the manner in which this knowledge is used, how it is acquired, how we can develop social and self competence has to be reconsidered - knowledge alone does not lead to the security of a professional performing in complex situations.

The 'reflective practitioner' sorts out the balance between defined knowledge and professional reflection on the one hand and between individual autonomy and the network of interactions with others on the other hand. It is a question of recognizing uncertainty, accepting them and developing solutions. The case studies showing highly qualified vocational work by Donald Schön show that successful and competent performance will emerge through "research in the context of practice" (Schön, 1983, p. 68). Competent acting demands for the integration and situational use of three competences (Schön, 1983, p. 48ff; Altrichter, Posch & Somekh 1993):

action type 1: tacit knowing-in-action:
When professional practice flows smoothly and appears simple to an onlooker, performance is based on 'tacit-knowing-in-action'. This type of professional action has the following characteristics:

- thinking and acting are not separate (skilful, practical activities take place without being planned and prepared intellectually in advance);
- the professional is frequently unaware of the sources of his or her practical knowledge or how it was learnt;
- the professional will usually not be able to give a straightforward verbal description of this practical knowledge.

Nevertheless, these actions could not have resulted without knowledge. Their skillfulness, their situational appropriateness and their flexibility indicate a knowledge base which is 'tacit' for the time being: we know more than we can tell.

The most important example of tacit knowing-in-action are 'routines'. Routines are actions which have been built up through frequent repetition, which are carried out comparatively quickly, and which are executed largely unconsciously. Routines do not indicate "lack of knowledge" but rather a specific quality of knowledge organization, a concentration of task related knowledge.

action type 2: reflection-in-action

Whenever new and complex situations have to be dealt with or disturbances and problems disrupt the smooth flow of routinized action, another type of action is additionally necessary: reflection-on-action. Such reflection occurs within action, it is not at all rare and need not be verbalized to be useful in problem-solving. When someone reflects-in-action, he becomes a researcher in the practice context. He thinks about what he is doing, even while doing it. He is not dependent on the categories of established theory and technique, but constructs a new theory of the unique case. Reflection-in-action resembles, as Schön (1983, p. 68) says, a 'reflective conversation with the situation'. It is the competency for self-reflexive transformation of one's own thinking, the competency to import knowledge from one context to another, using analogues, to evaluate this knowledge, and to develop it on the basis of evaluation.

The practitioner allows himself to experience surprise, puzzlement or confusion in a situation which he finds uncertain or unique. He reflects on the phenomena before him, and on the prior understandings which have been implicit in his behavior. He carries out an experiment which serves to generate both a new understanding of the phenomena and a change in the situation.

ation type 3: reflection-on-action

Reflection-on-action occurs when it is necessary to formulate knowledge explicitly and verbally, to distance ourselves from action for some time and to reflect on it. In reflection-on-action, reflection distances itself from the flow of activities, interrupts it, and concentrates upon data that represent the action in an objectified form. It improves our ability to analyze and reorganize knowledge: consciously reflecting on action slows it down and disturbs our smoothly running routines, but it also facilitates careful analysis and allows us to plan changes. By distancing ourselves from the flow of activities, we have a better chance of dealing with the problems that entangle us, redefining them and reorganizing our response. It makes knowledge communicable: the knowledge underlying professional action can be made visible and communicated to others, such as colleagues, clients and interest groups. This ability is a constituent part of professional competency.

In our conception of education there are the following underlying assumptions of organizing some part of the education to get the described competence of reflection:

The heart of our education is a "learning by doing" or a reflective practical training of the students:

Reflection-in-action cannot be removed from practical performance and should be developed ideally in concrete organizations. In this way students get used to their later vocational practice. Therefore a concept of education should create situations in which students are able to perform practically and differently, to deal with this performance, the personal role in performing and the different experiences. The orientation to practice means giving students wider experiences about the relationship of people in enterprises so they can cope with the demands of the vocational life and their later vocational role. A central aim is to get to know the complexity and inconsistency of practice, the variety of demands, aims and relations. They should also be in the position to reflect about their function and situation in enterprises. The practical experiences of the students and the elaboration of them are the focus of interest and not the learning of presented elements of knowledge and facts (Laske/Welte 1993, p. 12). In this teaching and learning process students and lecturers work on the questions, problems and requests of the participants. Knowledge and competence is developed through this way. There is not a prefabricated program to absolve.

Students should recognize the learning situations as being important in itself:

This means that students can make an actual or future connection to their practical and/or vocational life. Students should perform actively, responsibly and independently. They should be able to develop their own ideas, questions and demands during their learning - they should create the set frame in a self-responsible way which is useful for them. Because learning through reflection is only possible when one takes responsibility for one's own performance. For instance, they should decide which information they need to solve a problem, they should demand this information and they should perform with this information.

Learning means searching, means trying one's own knowledge through performing. The discussions and dealing with behavior and theoretical knowledge takes place if they are introduced by the students as a problem, whether the students need them to perform. ... Added to that knowledge gains an other dimension, it is necessary for the concrete performance, connections can be made and it becomes something to talk about and to work on (Salzgeber, 1996, p. 282ff).

Learning situations should contain the student's own possibilities of performing and creating:

That means the problem is not already given, but should be defined, changed or examined by the student. To give free room to work on problems is also a process of letting students go, of questioning their own ideas, of making mistakes and also of being allowed to make mistakes, and to be able to learn out of the mistakes. However, lecturers are confronted usually with the situations that students are used to analyzing more or less clear and already given problems and to develop the solution which is already included in the problem. And this 'security' is demanded by the students of their lecturers. Openness and uncertainty in learning situations means for teachers to be confronted with this demand, it means learners being confronted with unrealizable expectations and requests and to work on them.

The role of the teacher is the one of a coach:

Action and reflection should be possible and promoted through conversation and the arrangement of the learning environment. This is the main task of the teacher - he is getting a coach. The arrangement should contain the right balance between freedom and instruction, between not expecting too much and a net of counseling and discussion. The learning person needs the right degree of help, because help is the condition for independence (Lobenwein, 1996, p. 186).

Learning situations should contain guidelines dealing with the experiences one makes:

An important element of this learning situation is the reflection on action and the counseling by the university. This means, that around the reflective practicum there are many other courses, some of them before the practicum others afterwards. These courses are carried out for the practical performance, by giving students certain knowledge, methods and social skills.

Very important are courses after the practicum which develop the competencies one needs to reflect on action. That means discussing and working on these experiences, to connect them with existing knowledge, to confront and accept expectations, to reflect on one's own behavior are the central elements of this concept of education. This importance is also shown in the fact that students have not much corresponding routines to develop competence out of their performance and experiences. Without systematical and guided discussions it is left to the chance how one uses his experiences.

4.   EXAMPLE OF OUR EDUCATIONAL-MODEL 'BETRIEBSPÄDAGOGIK'

In the following we will illustrate the previously described understanding of education by the example of 'Betriebspädagogik' in the field of human resource management and business education.

4.1   Brief description of 'Betriebspädagogik'

By taking this optional subject our students have the possibility of gaining an additional qualification to their main-studies. Participation is voluntary. The main aim is:

"Students of Betriebspädagogik should be qualified to fulfill their future vocational tasks autonomously and through responsible actions. They should be able to take scientific knowledge into consideration concerning educational, professional, personal development processes as well as economic processes and their function in society." (Salzgeber, 1996, p. 29)

The students negotiate on the basis of an organizational subject the concrete formulation of the problem, collect and analyze data, develop suggestions for improvement, present and discuss their solutions with representatives from the organization. Students learning and working on a project accompanied by seminars where we analyze, reflect, make statements founded on theory, systematize and shape the student's experience made during the projects is the root of the concept. The aim of this educational concept is the orientation of one's own performance, which is closely related to the research into one's own education.

Therefore the 'extension of the capacity to act' as one aim of the learning process means creating the possibility to learn on the level of content, social, methodical and personal competence. If this is based on experience and on following practice, there has to be action and reflection, nearness and distance in the learning process. Kolb's 'clock-model of learning' figured on Kolb (1984, p. 42) illustrate this view of education:

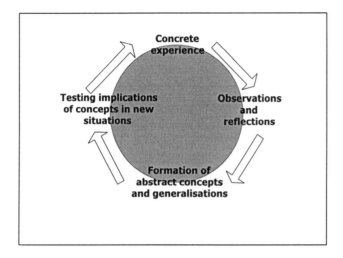

Figure 1: 'Clock-model of learning'.

4.2 The education-network of 'Betriebspädagogik'

To reach the described aims, there is a close connection between theory and practice in the accompanying seminars and in attending the students. Lecturers, supervisors from the organizations and consultant are involved in this education concept. The learning process in a practical context is accompanied by subject orientation and methodological inputs (for example: project-management, methods of empirical research, ...) on the one hand. On the other hand counseling-dialogs between student-groups and their supervisors lead the learning process. The center of this is professional, methodical and social reflection. The following picture shows the network and aims of seminars accompanying the students:

Accompanying seminar:

This part is given by a consultant. He is competent in practice and management of organizational-projects. He supports students with his high consulting-experience in their project consulting work. His competence in dealing with organizational learning-processes is a vital chance for learning and an important help for our students.

Project- and learning-reflection:

In this part of their studies students are supported by a lecturer with high competence in theory and methodology. Besides the discussion of the subject and the student's project intentions, the focus is put on one's own learning process. This is done with the intention to motivate and

support the 'practical theory-foundation'. The idea is that students
develop their own theories of learning processes through practical work.
Lectures on Betriebspädagogik:

Projects are shown in a wider social context than the organizational
view. This meta-respect is the topic of the lectures. An education-
researcher discusses relevant questions with the participants concerning
social political policies in relation to learning, profession and work.
Supervisor in the organization:

The student groups can fall back upon a person in charge of the project-
partner firm. On the one hand he supports the students in their work (e.g.:
collecting information in the company, making contacts with interview-
partners, ...) but on the other hand he pays attention to suitable and
problem oriented process.

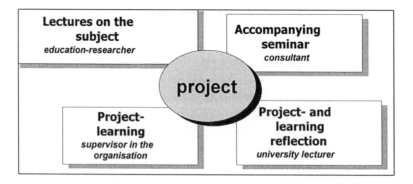

Figure 2: The education-network.

For all that work and processing emphasis we tend to a co-operative and
well-coordinated sharing responsibility of this educational network. The
intensive collaboration in the team and with the partner company proves the
necessity of a co-operative and guided processing of social activities and
conflicts.

4.3   Course procedure

The basic procedure of this type of seminar is based on the following
description (Salzgeber, 1996, p. 33f):

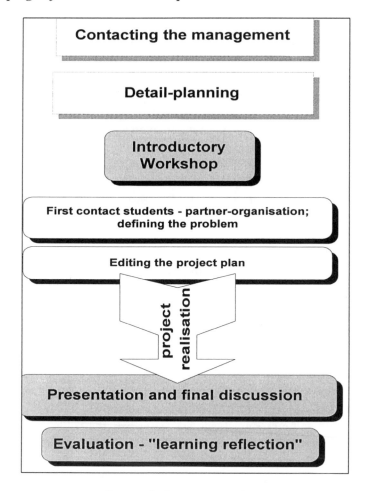

Figure 3: Course procedure.

Contacting the management of the organization in question:
The aims of a preparatory talk with the representatives of the organization are to get a general agreement with management concerning the project-work and developing possible main areas for the exploration. Besides clarifying the contents and the educational aims it is also very important to make clear the relationship between costs and benefits.

Detail-planning of the course:
Co-ordination of the lecturers, participants, putting together the teams in quality and quantity, ... are just a selection of things to be done in this phase.

Introductory workshop:
The introductory workshop informs about the aims, contents and methods as well as the procedure during the course. Students get a short insight into the organizations, commentaries on the project-topics and a more or less

intensive preparation for the first steps in project work as a whole and on their own projects in detail (such as training for the first meeting with management of company, basic knowledge in making contracts, ...). A most important part of the procedure is the building of student project teams.

The first contact between students and the partner-organization - defining the problem:

The next step is creating a contract between the students and the representatives of the organizations. This means to get to know the problem they have to work on it. Students must develop responsibility for their work in the company, the university and - last but not least - for the team. From experience we can say that this is a very intensive and time-consuming part of the whole project.

Editing the project plan:

The aim of this plan is to get a good base of knowledge and methodical preparation for the problem. Students have to substantiate their task, based on suitable theory and have to adapt this knowledge to the special situation of the company in question. The confrontation of theoretical knowledge with practical experience - which is really the confrontation of incomplete theory with incomplete practice - contains substantial learning possibilities.

Project realization:

During the following weeks students work on the performance of their projects in the partner companies, accompanied and supported by the lectors, supervisor and the consultant. Some important possibilities of making experience and gaining competence are teamwork, the collecting, analyzing and interpretation of data, as well as the general question of usability of empirical results, subjects of "Betriebspädagogik" such as instruments to help initiate learning processes in organizations, evaluation and so on.

Presentation and final discussion:

At the end of their project work students have to present their results and knowledge they gained during the project in the firm. They get feedback on the use of their practical work. Furthermore they have the possibility to train how to present and discuss in front of an important audience. The practitioner gets – hopefully - inspiring information and material for pursuing discussions.

Evaluation - 'Learning Reflection':

In this final step of the course the students get feedback on their project work from the lecturer. They also have the possibility to give feedback concerning their experiences during the course, with the lecturers regarding the quality of support. However, in the last few years the main aim of this part became the reflection of the student's own learning process. During the whole year the most important thing for students is their practical work with all its demands. Now the focus is put back on the virtual aim of the concept: the education of the student himself as a professional who is working with special in-company educational processes. Students should learn from their experiences they made in their own learning process in a way that helps them gain basic knowledge in the subject of learning procedures in general - "a practical theory". Here are some examples of questions we work on in this phase:

- What did I learn about my own learning?
- What makes the difference between this course and other typical university courses? Which relevancy does this have for my ideas of learning and education?
- Which educational aims became important to me during this work?
- What helped me in my work and what was obstructive? What was about the general conditions?
- What roles did the lecturers have? Are they teachers? Trainers? Coaches? Mentors? What role do I prefer and why? In which context?
- What roles did the learners have? What was my role?

5.   EXPERIENCES WITH THIS EDUCATIONAL MODEL

It is not possible to create learning situations perfectly (but improve them), especially if learning should be more than the reception and reproduction of knowledge. So the conception described here is only one purpose to reach certain aims. The problems, which are connected to the courses, can be seen as the starting point for a further development of the design. In this part we want to discuss some of our main experiences as lecturers we collected in the last few years (they have been discussed in detail in Auer, Salzgeber & Weiskopf 1998; Salzgeber 1996). These experiences have been the reason for a current further development of the curriculum. They show us the possibilities of this model on the one hand as well as the limits on the other hand. In this context it is important for us to get a realistic view of the educational potentialities of 'Betriebspädagogik'. We limited our expositions to two dimensions of our progress report:

5.1   Project- and problem-based seminars as a challenge for students

Critical questions are mostly filtered out, the view and the definition of the problem by the supervisor in the company forms the starting position and determines the students 'thinking'.

Students find themselves located between university and practice, the system of education and the system of work in a great complexity of unclear roles and functions. On the one hand they have to execute a job, which should satisfy the management as much as possible. The evaluation, if the results they worked out are good one's or not, is done by practice. This leads to an orientation at the demands of the client and only in a second dimension at the actual problem. On the other hand many things they have to do in practice are not the things they have to learn in our system of education. Examples of different requirements would be the searching for alternative definitions of the problem and critical distance to statements made from only one management-hierarchy.

The perceived gap between 'theory' and 'practice' doesn't change for our students. For some, the gap is even growing bigger.

Working on a practical problem often has negative influences on the theoretical quality of (written) project-reports. The critical dealing with theories is seen as pressure for many students. Literacy gives no concrete help - it gives no direct advantage. Above all theory supports dealing with and arguing about the problem. The question for practical-oriented teaching is - not only at our faculty - widespread. What we find problematic in this matter is that mostly this question is understood synonymously with the refusal of theory and often also the request for a 'reflection-stop'. Students tend to generalize examples taken out of the practice experience and interpret them as an 'economic truth' although described and interpreted only from one company supervisor. The theoretical meta-view is outside the field of perception. As a consequence of this it becomes a threat to one's own definition of the situation, which then has to be justified. This is not satisfactory - not even in a one-sided instrumental view.

Students move in a trouble spot between high motivation and excessive demands.

In our experience - and what we learned from student's feedback - motivation and engagement of the participants is much higher in project-seminars than in the usual ones. Working on practical problems in a company has positive effects in most cases. On the other hand the high demands of those projects have the consequence that students come near to the limits of their physical and mental ability. The complexity of the situation of learning (technical questions, project-management, dealing with management, ...) produce individual insecurity as· well as tensions and conflicts in the teams. Moreover, they are confronted with dual and often contradictory demands of the university and the company. The pressure of solving the problems and performing in the project comes to the fore. The demands of the educational system are often found to be a nuisance and pedantic to the teams in such things as theoretical substantiation, written project-reports, which are made in a scientifically correct way of using references and so on. They have a similar point of view to the requested reflection on the project's progress, which is perceived as wasted time and unnecessary.

Experience in teamwork

Making experience in the work with other students is often the most important impression students get from this course. On the one hand the intensive work on content, experiencing and reflecting on this process and with the others is invaluable for all involved persons. On the other hand there is a high interdependence between the students which is not seldom the reason for emotional conflicts. If the structure of the teams change - for example if somebody leaves during the time of the education for long - this has big consequences for the rest of the team.

Organizational questions superimpose technical questions.

In the center of a student's work are often the administrative questions like the design of letters or shaping a brochure. Problems of getting an appointment with a busy client, how to argue about the expenses in a contract, ... all that has a high priority. The important questions regarding content are thrust into the background. The very complex situation with which they are confronted, is more than they can handle and could be a possible explanation for that mentioned above. In this case those questions become important which are easily dealt with, those which make them feel secure - although these are not the central questions!

Projects raise the consumer-oriented approach of students to their education.

In this context education really has to be useful - useful for the concrete project-situation. Everything that doesn't help in the project cannot be utilized and is ignored by the students.

Failure in practical situations (especially in the context of work) has other consequences than a failure in a university's examination situation.

In a student's life it is often normal to fail an examination. Sometimes it is good form to do it twice in our western-European-culture. But there is another approach to failure in a vocational situation. The effects and threats have another dimension than in conventional examination situations. Hard personal crises, conflicts in the teams, flight in other - easier - topics, orientation on 'project success' on which price ever ... are the consequences.

5.2   Project- and problem-based seminars as a challenge for lecturers and the institution 'university'

The practical (inter-discipline) project contradicts the discipline of imparting knowledge.

The work on a concrete practical problem often creates questions beyond the narrow scientific discipline. In contrast to that studies are structured in subjects highly oriented to a special knowledge. Key-qualifications are developed - if at all - unsystematically. Especially the realization of projects requires interdisciplinary and extra functional competence from the students. That may have the consequence that technical aspects are thrust into the background - in relationship to project-management for example. Also the professional expectations of the person who is looking after students' work is too high. The lecturers are professionals in their own subjects.

There is a high discrepancy between small project groups with the need of high support and the quantitative needs of a mass-university.

The aims and content of education often have to be subordinated to pragmatic needs of project-acquisition.

The aims and the content of "Betriebspädagogik" - they are hand in hand – is based on vocational qualification processes. Now it is very difficult to find 4 or 5 projects every year in our region which demands this work. Sometimes content is defined anew. So it is possible, that students work on an image-analyses of the educational concept of a partner company rather than evaluating the vocational concept.

The presented experiences give an overview of the chances and especially the limits of this educational model. If we formulate them sometimes very critical we don't do this with the intention, to impeach them fundamentally. But making us aware of this limits makes us feel more secure in handling the process and gives us the possibilities of it's further development. Above all it helps us sometimes to understand situations, which are on a first view not comprehensible.

REFERENCES

Altrichter, H., Posch, P., & Somekh, B. (1993). *Teachers Investigate their Work.* London, New York: Routledge.

Auer, M., & Welte, H. (1997). Projektseminare als praxisorientierte Ausbildungsform. In M. Auer, & S. Laske, (Eds.), *Personalwirtschaftliche Ausbildung an Universitäten - Grundfragen, Konzepte und Erfahrungen* (pp. 326-340). München, Mering: Hampp.

Bromme, R. (1992). *Der Lehrer als Experte.* Zur Psychologie des professionellen Wissens. Bern, Göttingen, Toronto: Huber.

Dörner, D. (1994). *Die Logik des Mißlingens.* Strategisches Denken in komplexen Situationen. Reinbek bei Hamburg: Rowohlt.

Kolb, D.A. (1984). *Experimental Learning.* Experience as the Source of Learning and Development. Englewood Cliffs: Prentice Hall.

Laske, S., & Welte, H. (1993). Unternehmensanalyse-Seminar als Spurensuche - Ein Ansatz für ein lebendiges Lernen. *Zeitschrift für Hochschuldidaktik 1*, 9-22.

Lobenwein, W. (1997). *Reflexion der Praxis.* Die Entwicklung reflektierter praktischer Kompetenz in der (wirtschaftspädagogischen) LehrerInnenbildung. Innsbruck.

Salzgeber, G. (1996). *Reflexion (in) der Praxissituation im Projektstudium Betriebspädagogik.* Innsbruck.

Schön, D.A. (1983). *The Reflective Practitioner.* New York: Basic Books.

Schön, D.A. (1987). *Educating The Reflective Practitioner.* San Francisco, Oxford: Jossey-Bass.

Mindfulness Theory, Technology and the Transfer of New Learning

Lyn Murray
School of Computing and Information Technology, University of Western Sydney, Australia

1.   INTRODUCTION

Students who are being educated today in order to practice a profession tomorrow must interact with vast, complex and exponentially increasing bodies of knowledge. How are they to organize and respond to these bodies of knowledge, and how are they to apply the knowledge that they are presently acquiring to situations which have not yet evolved? It seems clear that they will need to be taught ways of thinking, rather than factual content which is likely to be obsolete by the time they come to implement it. Learning about process in education rather than product will need to become the focus of the new age., and yet frequently knowledge about the educational process has been perceived to 'belong' to the teacher, whose professional expertise activates this process on behalf of the student. Students participate in the learning process while actually having no knowledge or understanding of how it operates, but this will have to change in order to provide students with more control over their own learning.

As a way of approaching teaching for and about process, I utilize the constructs of mindfulness and transfer. The ability to effectively transfer existing knowledge and experience to new and very different contexts will be a critical skill of workers who wish to adapt to career and environmental change. The explicit teaching of mindfulness theory according to a mechanism which I present in this chapter effectively facilitates transfer of learning because it operates to empower students to be cognitively flexible

93

T.A. Johannessen, A. Pedersen and K. Petersen (eds.),
Educational Innovation in Economics and Business VI, 93–105.
© 2002 *Kluwer Academic Publishers. Printed in the Netherlands.*

and responsive to emergent circumstances, without imposing previously constructed commitments to meaning on those emergent circumstances.

2.   MINDFULNESS: WHAT IS IT?

Mindfulness is a construct developed by Ellen Langer of Harvard University. It is characterized by active distinction making and differentiation (Langer, 1997). A mindful individual engages in the process of creating new categories and differentiating information more finely, and remains "open to the processes through which meaning arises within and among people. This openness to the perspectives of others and to information viewed as novel allows us to construct meaning" (Langer, 1994, pp. 50-51).

Mindlessness, on the other hand, is characterized by a rigid use of information during which the individual is unaware of its potentially novel aspects (Langer & Piper, 1987). Information is managed as though it has a single meaning and is available for use in only that way, and this results in a lack of attention to details which might in fact invalidate such assumptions if they were considered carefully. After limited experience with one solution to a problem, simpler or more effective solutions are not considered even when they are available and appropriate. In a similar vein Reardon and Rogers (1988) argue that there is a tendency for categories, once formed and found to be efficacious, to persist in use even when the earlier situation of utility has changed.

Research would seem to support the idea that in many situations adults tend to interact mindlessly with the environment unless they are provoked into mindfulness, for example by a circumstance such as an unfamiliar situation for which existing conceptions are no longer adequate (Langer & Imber, 1980). In fact "the research on mindlessness suggests that much of the time people are not hearing what is being said to them or reading what has been written to them, as long as the structure of the communication is familiar. Moreover, they are unaware that this is occurring" (Langer & Imber, 1980, p. 361).

The degree of awareness with which an individual operates varies directly with the degree of repeated experience of a particular activity, so that the more frequently an individual has engaged in the activity the more likely it is that scripts will be relied upon to complete the activity (Langer, 1978). Citing Abelson (1976), Langer (1978, p. 41) refers to "scripts" as "large units of varied behavior (which) can be chunked together to form fewer coherent cognitive units that are capable of being over learned". These scripts, or "abstracted essences of social events" (1978, p. 41) eventually come to be processed instead of the actual event which is being participated in. The following of a script may be equated with interpersonal mindlessness.

Of course scripts are useful because they reduce the cognitive work which is required to engage in interaction, so that the individual is able to engage in less mental activity and effort for those interactions that it would appear are invariably repeated. If the individual had to execute a complex cognitive search of every possible strategy or response every time he or she wished to engage in communicative interaction, the demands on his or her cognitive processing ability would be debilitating (Spitzberg & Cupach, 1984, p. 83), and to this extent the following of a script is a pragmatic and adaptive activity. Further work in this field has moved in the direction of the concept of informational encapsulation, which suggests that encapsulated processes are impenetrable by other cognitive processes. This means that they are unresponsive to context, and that they are automatically activated by particular stimulus events. A significant characteristic of encapsulated processing is that it engages a minimal resource load, and it is in this characteristic that its major advantage can be found (Royer, Cisero & Carlo, 1993).

The difficulty, however, seems to lie in the fact that certain recurring activities or behaviors are likely to impress themselves on the individual and to result in the individual's automatic recognition of particular structures inherent in interactions. With repeated exposure to an emerging structure in the interaction, the individual begins to pay less and less attention to the semantics of the interaction and more attention to the structure. As the interaction and its underlying structure are repeated without challenge or negative consequences, the individual is reinforced in the belief that the structure is in fact a reliable and predictable indication of how the interaction will be best conducted. According to this perspective, the more people engage in particular activities, the more they rely on scripts to realize these activities, and this leads Langer (1978) to argue that much of the interaction that takes place in the everyday world would seem to rely on the scripts and their recognition of the underlying structures of ordinary activities rather than on the active processing of information.

It would seem that the emergence of a regular script structure in an interaction acts as a signal that attention does not need to be paid to semantics, because if the structure is congruent with previous encounters of the activity, then it is assumed that the semantics will be congruent with previous encounters, and consequently a minimal amount of the information which is available will actually be processed. The problem here is that while structures may appear initially to be regular and 'normal' they may actually diverge quite markedly in ways which the individual is unable to perceive.

Although seemingly similar scripts may in fact contain quite distinctive sets of semantics, the individual is unaware of these distinctions and assumes the ability to act on the basis of a minimal amount of scripted information. This may be the case even when the original scripts did not necessarily provide the individual with the most efficacious tools with which to deal with the situation, and when the most minimal of mindful approaches will indicate a better method.

An important component of mindfulness theory is the notion of premature cognitive commitment, which is a commitment that is unconsciously made to the meaning of information and its anticipated implications. Once a premature cognitive commitment is made the relationship between the information and the experience which it represents can remain fixed. In fact the information "in essence, only exists in the single, rigid form in which it was initially encoded. Alternative understandings of the information are not available" (Langer, 1989, p. 149). Premature cognitive commitment is characteristic of mindlessness.

Mindfulness, by contrast, is a cognitively active state in which an individual consciously engages with the immediate elements of his or her environment, and challenges premature cognitive commitments in regard to the meaning to be constructed from and in that environment. Mindfulness is characterized by cognitive differentiation rather than by categorization. Mindfulness theory essentially challenges a commitment to previously constructed meanings, and to the circumscribed nature of the meanings so constructed. Teaching from a mindfulness perspective may have the potential to facilitate transfer of newly acquired knowledge and strategies to other contexts, because by taking a mindful approach such contexts are not conceptualized, constructed or interpreted in rigid and constricted ways. The inclusion of a mindfulness perspective in education may empower students to identify the instability of experience as it differs across a range of events and over a period of time, and to accept and accommodate the resulting uncertainty.

However, the construct of mindfulness is not accurately represented by the concept of the reflecting solitary mind studying complex alternatives and selecting among them. This representation may lead to a false belief in objectivity, and ignore the obvious point that any 'fact' is an assertion by an individual in a context, based on a background of prior understanding. Problems or difficulties or predicaments are ultimately questions of meaning, and questions of meaning can rarely be resolved, but rather need to be attended to, interpreted, and interacted with (Van Manen, 1991; Marcotte & Niosi, 2000).

Mindfulness is not taught or modeled in our society in general or in our education systems in particular because of a traditional emphasis on the acquisition of "facts" and on the search for the "right" answer to a variety of problems, and this leads to the formation of premature cognitive commitments that subsequently remain unquestioned. As Langer & Brown (1992, p. 15) suggest, "Learners are often taught to view facts as immutable, unconditional truths", but actually the "facts" will often change when the context changes. Rogers (1997, p. 687) notes that under present pedagogical approaches "students devote their efforts to mastering a set of facts, often without the sense that those facts connect in a significant way to some process, some experience." (For further discussion see also Kruglanski, 1989; Nicholls, Nelson & Gleaves, 1995; Breuer & Streufert, 1996; Mezirow, 1996; Yeatman, 1996; Hofer & Pintrich, 1997; Candy, 1998).

It is rare that an individual will continue to seek solutions to a problem once he or she has come upon one that will serve the purpose. After a time the first solution that he or she has found will come to seem to be the best and only solution and no further questioning of propositions or assumptions will occur. However, if the perspective is adopted that consequences have meaning within a context, and contexts keep changing, then the positive or negative aspects of the event/problem keep changing, and it probably would be appropriate at some point to seek alternative methods and solutions (Langer & Brown, 1992). The awareness that the "evidence" which is frequently cited to support the discussion of a particular topic is actually conditional and open to interpretation allows students to countenance differing interpretations of the same topics, ideas or issues and helps to prevent a mindless commitment to the meaning and significance of previously unquestioned evidence or information.

For example, a mindful perspective on communication and technology would involve an orientation towards the new possibilities which are constantly being created by the use of technology as well as an awareness of the possibilities which are constantly being eliminated by it. A mindful perspective on technological processes, such as technologically mediated communication, would involve an awareness of the novel and unique aspects of that technology and would not simply be an attempt to impose familiar existing processes onto new communication technologies. At the same time a mindful perspective on communication and technology would involve an awareness of the dangers inherent in technological determinism, or "the blindness created by design" (Winograd & Flores, 1987, p. 166), whereby the opening of new possibilities closes off other possibilities and the nature of the technology itself seems to automatically determine and frequently restrict the range of possible responses to it (Olesen & Myers, 1999; Golden & Powell, 2000).

When people adapt to new technologies and restructure their behaviors based on what the technologies currently allow them to do, they tend to take technologies for granted and do not question their social effects (Dutton, 1999). In fact, the "social possibilities offered by information technologies are in large part products of "deep" design, characteristics and properties not readily, or not at all, open to modification by users." (Fountain, 2000, p. 47). Technology incorporates certain assumptions about the identity and nature of users, their capacity to actually use the technology, their requirements and their expectations. These assumptions become built into the new technology during the process of design, development, marketing and implementation. "During this process views and assumptions become fixed and set within the emerging technology. The technology comes to embody an assembly of ideas about social arrangements. Technology, we might say, is this network of congealed social relations." (Woolgar, 1998, p. 444).

Following from this argument, and because adult learning is incremental and grounded in previous experiences (Brookfield, 1986), even a new topic is approached with preconceived ideas. The explicit teaching of principles of mindfulness addresses this issue because it provides students with a mechanism which enables them to contest premature cognitive commitments to meaning. Students who can apply the principles of mindfulness will necessarily be more competent because they are interacting on the basis of the information which is present in the immediate context, and not on the basis of previously established and presently uncontested commitments to meaning.

3.   HOW DOES MINDFULNESS RELATE TO THE TRANSFER OF LEARNING?

The construct of transfer of learning is critical to a consideration of thinking and of learning in general. In fact, the boundaries between transfer and learning are so indistinct that knowledge transfer is commonly used as a measure to assess learning. If students can only solve a problem about which they have been instructed within a specific context but cannot solve the same problem in a related context, then they are not considered to have attained subject mastery (Pea, 1988; Greeno; 1997).

Of course the issue of transfer and the question of whether or not cognitive skills and strategies are domain specific or domain independent have been debated at very great length. Comprehensive reviews of research relevant to the debate (Lave, 1988; Perkins & Salomon, 1989; Pea, 1988) suggest that the answer still appears to be equivocal. Further discussions by Anderson, Reder & Simon (1996), Butler (1996), Greeno (1997), and Anderson, Reder & Simon (1997) support this view.

Fogarty, Perkins & Barell (1992, p. xv-xvii) identify three historical perspectives on transfer in teaching and learning, which they summarize in the following distinctive way:

- The Bo Peep Theory of Transfer: Transfer Takes Care of Itself
  (Leave them alone and they'll come home)
- The Black Sheep Theory of Transfer: Transfer Doesn't Happen
  (Transfer stubbornly refuses to do what it is supposed to do)
- The Good Shepherd Theory of Transfer: Transfer Will Happen With Mediation
  (Teachers can 'shepherd' knowledge and skills from one context to another)

In a somewhat more formal manner Perkins & Salomon (1989) express a similar view. Early advocacy of domain independent cognitive skills assumed that general heuristics would readily make contact with an individual's knowledge base and that transfer was a process which operated automatically. When this failed to occur in experimental situations a view developed that cognitive skills were in fact context bound. However, recent emphasis on domain-based knowledge may well undervalue the importance of general heuristics, so that common accounts of failure of transfer may be explained in terms of lack of conditions needed for transfer, rather than in terms of domain specificity (Perkins & Salomon, 1989). This position would lead to the interconnection of general cognitive and domain specific material in instruction (Perkins & Salomon, 1989), and has obvious applications to strategies for teaching about mindfulness in its emphasis on the salient nature of context.

Pea (1988) has developed what he calls an interpretivist perspective on transfer, and argues first of all that transfer is selective because 'appropriate' transfer is socio-culturally defined for particular purposes, tasks, and thinking situations. When transfer involves more than the straightforward access and application of knowledge, then complex personal issues based on cultural practices and value systems are invoked.

He also argues that the perception of common elements or factors between one context and another is in fact primarily socio-cultural rather than objective, and that contexts "… are 'read' as texts, with multiple possible interpretations, according to the thinker's culturally influenced categorization system of problem types … . There are thus likely to be significant developmental, individual, and cultural differences in the situation perception on which knowledge transfer depends." (Pea, 1988, p. 204). Most knowledge is in fact an interpretation of experience based on schemas that both enable and constrain the individual processes of constructing meaning (Resnick, 1991).

Many difficulties encountered by learners are not simply the result of lack of basic knowledge or of unavailability of relevant problem-solving strategies alone, but the result of "executive" problems in not managing their mental resources effectively. It would seem that learners need to acquire not only problem-solving strategies but also self-management skills which would enable them to direct their own thinking and learning episodes.

Consequently, students need to acquire executive thinking skills such as goal setting, strategic planning, checking for accurate plan execution, goal-progress monitoring, plan evaluation, and plan revision. Yet commonly these fundamental executive processes remain under the control of the teacher in a teaching/learning interaction, and any teaching approach that emphasizes the acquisition of complex thinking processes should be developmentally responsive to the need for such teacher intervention to fade as the processes become increasingly autonomous in the students (Pea, 1988). This would involve teaching/learning interactions in which thinking processes are made explicit, or modeled, because this seems to provide important fostering conditions for learning to think well and transfer knowledge to new problem contexts within a broad domain such as reading, writing or mathematics.

Ceci and Roazzi (1994, p. 83), working from a somewhat different perspective, nevertheless come to a similar conclusion when they suggest "It may be that the use of proximal examples and explicit instructions are a necessary first step to inculcating transfer, at least in most people", while Anderson, Reder & Simon (1996, p. 6) argue for the need to include "ability to transfer as a specific goal in instruction, a skill that is given little attention in most current instruction."

However, while acknowledging a range of perspectives on learning and transfer, it should be remembered that in attempts to take them all into account, "we could be forever lost in appreciating the complexity of the situation and never get on to doing something about it." (Anderson, Reder & Simon, 1997, p. 20).

4.   HOW DO THE CONSTRUCTS OF MINDFULNESS AND TRANSFER CONVERGE?

I believe that the explicit teaching of mindfulness theory according to a mechanism which I now present will "get on to doing something about" effectively teaching for transfer of learning (Murray, 1997), because it involves the facilitation of metacognitive processes which provide students with insight into their own learning activities. This insight empowers students to more effectively manage their own learning as well as to apply that learning more successfully in authentic situations (Elen & Lowyck, 1999; Georghiades, 2000).

In effect this mechanism operates to empower students to be cognitively flexible and responsive to emergent circumstances without imposing on those emergent circumstances the students' previously constructed commitments to meaning. That is, this mechanism may equip students to transfer previous learnings to emergent circumstances in a way which is functional and adaptive rather than rigid or prescriptive.

This mechanism consists of the concept of a communication environment. This is based on the premise that people do not interact without regard to their surroundings, but rather within a communication environment, which consists of those factors which are immediate and dynamic in an interaction.

This communication environment can be classified into three components which are:
• Topic
• Situation
• Participants.

I do not suggest that these three components comprise the total intrapersonal and interpersonal elements of the communication environment. Factors such as past experience, past learnings, perceptions, relationships, attributions, status and so on may well be expected to influence interactants, so the significance of such factors is clearly not to be underestimated. In fact, a consideration of such issues is fundamental to the understanding of interactive processes. However, these factors are not immediate or dynamic, but rather they are brought to the interaction by the participants, and are essentially fixed for the course of the interaction.

Focusing attention on elements which are dynamic and grounded in the present by attending to the topic, situation and participants will promote a mindful approach to their interactions. I have described this process of attending to the topic, situation and participants as *enhancing immediacy*. My own research indicates that teaching students to enhance immediacy together with explicit statements about theories of mindfulness and transfer enables students to be mindful in authentic interactions.

The method which I used in my research involved the explicit presentation of principles of mindfulness, followed by the introduction of the concept of the communication environment. I then asked students to work in small groups to identify particular interactions from their own authentic workplace experiences wherein the topic, the situation and the participants were reasonably discrete. The students did not find this difficult. I then asked them to reconsider their perceptions of the interactions if one of the elements of topic, situation and participants was varied and the other two remained stable. For example, the topic being considered might be recent changes in the workplace, the situation might be the workplace, and the participants might be a peer group of workers. An alteration to the situation such that the discussion took place in a bar after work, or an alteration to the participants such that the discussion was being conducted with a superior rather that a peer, would obviously result in significantly different interactive strategies if the interaction were being conducted mindfully.

Students were then asked to consider how such variations in the communication environment affected their perspectives on the interaction. They were consistently able to identify additional significant factors and perspectives which had not occurred to them previously in their reflections on the interaction. In consequence, they were also able to identify a range of strategies which would operate to greater or lesser effect to bring the interaction to a satisfactory resolution depending on the circumstances. I consider that they thereby demonstrated increased cognitive flexibility as a result of using this device. I found that by mindfully considering facts not as stable commodities but as potential sources of ambiguity students were able to gain a more insightful perspective on everyday interactions and became more open to perceiving the many perspectives from which any activity may be viewed.

5. CONCLUSION

Education based on a mindfulness approach will generate social interactions in which thinking processes are made explicit, and this will provide important fostering conditions for learning to think well and transfer knowledge to new problem contexts within a broad domain. In a mindful state, learning and change occur constantly because the very nature of mindful interaction with the environment means that both the environment and the individual are different.

In a time of change, where the immutability of factual information is no longer the only appropriate perspective from which to conceptualize and construct meaning and interaction, the construct of mindfulness has much to offer. Teaching that values and fosters a recognition of variability and multiple frames of reference may be a way of providing students with the cognitive and behavioral flexibility to respond to interactions in a genuine and appropriate fashion, and to view issues from a range of perspectives which are neither linear nor exclusive in their orientation (Murray, 1996). This will allow students to transfer their existing knowledge to emergent contexts in a flexible and creative fashion.

Education which emphasizes a mindful approach allows changing interactions to be evaluated and responded to in contemporaneous and relevant terms, and essentially allows for the "creation of new categories" to describe the new situation, rather than assuming that the existing situation is similar to previous situations. The adoption of such an approach means that crucial skills would include the ability to mindfully evaluate the situation and then mindfully adapt strategies to suit it. The mindfulness approach presented here thus provides a device for becoming aware of more than one perspective and for shifting perspective as this might be appropriate, and this will necessarily extend the interactive competence of those who use it.

REFERENCES

Anderson, J.R., Reder, L.M., & Simon, H.A. (1996). Situated Learning and Education. *Educational Researcher, 25*(4), 5-11.

Anderson, J.R., Reder, L.M., & Simon, H.A. (1997). Situative Versus Cognitive Perspectives: Form Versus Substance. *Educational Researcher, 26*(1), 18-21.

Breuer, K., & Streufert, S. (1996). Authoring of Complex Learning Environments: Design Considerations for Dynamic Simulations. *Journal of Structural Learning, 12* (4), 315-321.

Brookfield, S.D. (1986). *Understanding and Facilitating Adult Learning.* Milton Keynes: Open University Press.

Butler, J. (1996). Professional development: Practice as text, reflection as process, and self as focus. *Australian Journal of Education, 40* (3), 265-284.

Candy, P.C. (1998). Knowledge navigators and lifelong learners: producing graduates for the information society. In C. Rust, (Eds.), *Improving Students as Learners.* Oxford: The Oxford Centre for Staff and Learning Development.

Ceci, S.J., & Roazzi, A. (1994). The effects of context on cognition. In R.J. Sternberg, & R.K. Wagner, (Eds.), *Mind in context: interactionist perspectives on human intelligence.* Cambridge: Cambridge University Press.

Dutton, W.H. (1999). The Web of Technology and People: Challenges for Economic and Social Research. *Prometheus, 17* (1), 5-20.

Elen, J., & Lowyck, J. (1999). Metacognitive instructional knowledge: cognitive mediation and instructional design. *Journal of Structural Learning and Intelligent Systems, 13* (3-4), 145-169.

Fogarty, R., Perkins, D., & Barell, J. (1992). *How To Teach for Transfer.* Cheltenham: Hawker Brownlow Education.

Fountain, J. (2000). Constructing the information society: women, information technology, and design, *Technology in Society, 22*, 45-62.

Georghiades, P. (2000). Beyond conceptual change learning in science education: focusing on transfer, durability and metacognition, *Educational Research, 42*(2), 119-139.

Golden, W., & Powell, P. (2000). Towards a definition of flexibility: in search of the Holy Grail? *Omega, 28*, 373-384.

Greeno, J.G. (1997). On Claims that Answer the Wrong Questions. *Educational Researcher, 26*(1), 5-17.

Hofer, B.K., & Pintrich, P.R. (1997). The Development of Epistemological Theories: Beliefs about Knowledge and Knowing and Their Relation to Learning. *Review of Educational Research, 67*(1), 88-140.

Kruglanski, A.W. (1989). The Psychology of Being Right: The Problem of Accuracy in Social Perception and Cognition. *Psychological Bulletin, 106*(3), 395-409.

Langer, E.J. (1997). *The Power of Mindful Learning*. Reading: Addison-Wesley Publishing Company.

Langer, E.J. (1994). The Illusion of Calculated Decisions. In R.C. Schank, & E.J. Langer, (Eds.), *Beliefs, Reasoning and Decision Making*. Hillsdale: Lawrence Erlbaum Associates.

Langer, E.J. (1989). *Mindfulness*. Massachusetts: Addison-Wesley.

Langer, E.J. (1978). Rethinking the Role of Thought in Social Interaction. In J.H. Harvey, W. Ickes, & R. Kidd, (Eds.), *New Directions in Attribution Theory and Research Volume 2*. Hillsdale: Erlbaum.

Langer, E.J., & Brown, J.P. (1992). Mindful Learning: A World Without Losers. *New Directions for Adult and Continuing Education, 53*, 11-20.

Langer, E.J., & Piper, A.I. (1987). The Prevention of Mindlessness. *Journal of Personality and Social Psychology, 53* (2), 280-287.

Langer, E.J., & Imber, L. (1980). Role of Mindlessness in the Perception of Deviance. *Journal of Personality and Social Psychology, 39* (2), 360-367.

Lave, J. (1988). *Cognition in Practice*. Cambridge: Cambridge University Press.

Mezirow, J. (1996). Contemporary paradigms of learning. *Adult Education Quarterly, 46*(3), 158-17.

Murray, L. (1997). *Mindfulness Theory and the Transfer of Interpersonal Communication Skills*. Paper presented to the 5th International Improving Students as Learners Symposium, University of Strathclyde, Glasgow, Scotland.

Murray, L. (1996). Communication and uncertainty: The role of mindfulness in communication skills training. *Australian Journal of Communication, 23* (1), 104-117.

Marcotte, C., & Niosi, J. (2000). Technology Transfer to China: The Issues of Knowledge and Learning. *Journal of Technology Transfer, 25*, 43-57.

Nicholls, J.G., Nelson, J.R., & Gleaves, K. (1995). Learning Facts Versus Learning that Most Questions Have Many Answers: Student Evaluations of Contrasting Curricula. *Journal of Educational Psychology, 87* (2), 253-260.

Olesen, K., & Myers, M.D. (1999). Trying to improve communication and collaboration with information technology. *Information Technology and People, 12*(4), 317-332.

Pea, R.D. (1988). Putting Knowledge to Use. In R.S. Nickerson, & P.P. Zodhiates, (Eds.), *Technology in Education: Looking Toward 2020*. Hillsdale: Lawrence Erlbaum.

Perkins, D.N., & Salomon, G. (1989). Are Cognitive Skills Context-Bound? *Educational Researcher, 18*(1), 16-25.

Reardon, K.K., & Rogers, E.M. (1988). Interpersonal Versus Mass Media Communication: A False Dichotomy. *Human Communication Research, 15*(2), 284-303.

Resnick, L.B. (1991). Shared Cognition. In L.B. Resnick, J.M. Levine, & S.D. Teasley, (Eds.), *Socially Shared Cognition*. Washington: American Psychological Association.

Rogers, B. (1997). Informing the shape of the curriculum: new views of knowledge and its representation in schooling. *Journal of Curriculum Studies, 29* (6), 683-710.

Royer, J.M., Cisero, C.A., & Carlo, M.S. (1993). Techniques and Procedures for Assessing Cognitive Skills. *Review of Educational Research, 63*(2), 201-243.

Spitzberg, B.H., & Cupach, W.R. (1984). *Interpersonal Communication Competence*. Beverley Hills: Sage.

Van Manen, M. (1991). Reflectivity and the pedagogical moment: the normativity of pedagogical thinking and acting. *Journal of Curriculum Studies, 23* (6), 507-536.

Winograd, T., & Flores, F. (1987). *Understanding Computers and Cognition*. Norwood: Ablex Publishing Corporation.

Woolgar, S. (1998). A New Theory of Innovation. *Prometheus, 16*(4), 441-452.

Yeatman, A. (1996). The roles of scientific and non-scientific types of knowledge in the improvement of practice. *Australian Journal of Education, 40* (3), 284-301.

PART II

TECHNOLOGY SUPPORTED EDUCATION

Collaborative Learning and New Learning Technologies: Coordination of Pedagogy

Catherine Carey & Felicia Lassk
Western Kentucky University & Northeastern University, Bowling Green KY, USA

1.   INTRODUCTION

Two trends, among many, in pedagogy are rising in relevance in today's higher education. One advocates the use of collaborative learning; the other advocates the use of new learning technologies. These pedagogies are often found diverging in opposite directions. Collaborative learning focuses on learning with one another and from one another in small groups. New learning technologies often focus on the individual learning at home or in a lab, alone, quietly with a computer. Both methods can fall under the realm of "active learning" where students are actively involved with the subject rather than simply listening to a lecture on the topic. We would like to use this discussion paper to illustrate how both types of active learning can be combined to further enhance the educational experience for students.

Our purpose here is not to discuss various group or web assignments, how to conduct an on-line course, or the virtues of distance learning. Instead, the focus is on how to incorporate collaborative work and technology into the actual classroom atmosphere to enhance teaching, learning, and effective communication between professor and student and between the students themselves. There are many ways to do this that are adaptable to accommodate both the large and small class size and that meet the needs of the many diverse learning styles associated with the business student. We provide a summary of the current literature on both collaborative work and instructional technology, and we provide a wide variety of references of actual techniques so that readers can easily find out more information about

109

T.A. Johannessen, A. Pedersen and K. Petersen (eds.),
Educational Innovation in Economics and Business VI, 109–125.
© 2002 *Kluwer Academic Publishers. Printed in the Netherlands.*

ideas they like. We confess at the beginning, however, that fully incorporating both types of pedagogy may involve a large initial time commitment, but the rewards are high in both teacher and student satisfaction.

2. COLLABORATIVE LEARNING AND NEW LEARNING TECHNOLOGIES: A REVIEW OF TECHNIQUES

Vygotsky (1978) illustrated the importance of "play" (experimentation) and "social interaction" in the learning process. Collaborative learning techniques and new learning technologies allow for both of these components in a way like never before. Group activities allow students to get to know each other, tackle difficult questions, and actively think and learn from one another. When this is complemented by utilizing the Internet, including a course web page, the World Wide Web, and e-mail, along with other types of simulation software as learning tools, this can be a way of making learning "fun." Through the use of technology, students are introduced to a new world of information that stimulates their curiosity.

Both the increased use of collaborative learning and new technologies are leading to a new role for the professor in the classroom. Many colleagues fear the loss of importance in the classroom with either pedagogy (Arbaugh, 2000 & Murphy, 2000). Our experience is that this is certainly not the case. The combination of collaborative learning and new learning technologies actually increases the role of the instructor. Careful development of group and on-line assignments along with the proper mentoring guidance are important to maintaining student attention and enhancing learning when using these teaching styles. Reckless abandonment of students with difficult assignments in an effort to teach them to think entirely for themselves or as a group can be counterproductive when students do not know where to start or have not had the proper background preparation.

Collaborative learning involves problem solving in small groups. "Collaborative activities enhance learning by allowing individuals to exercise, verify, solidify, and improve their mental models through discussions and information sharing during the problem-solving process (i.e., while working on the assigned academic task)" (Alavi, 1994, pp. 161-162). Studies have shown that collaborative learning improves a student's critical thinking skills through an increase in direct student involvement with the subject, thus promoting academic achievement (Johnson et al., 1981). This simply means that collaborative learning provides "hands on" experience and, as a nice side effect, it encourages class participation, debate, and attendance.

New learning technologies surface in many forms. It can be as simple as allowing students to communicate through e-mail to as high tech as distance learning through courses on the Internet and interactive telecourses (ITV). The use of technology to enhance teaching and learning in business is not new. Grimes and Ray (1992) summarize the literature and discuss the impact of microcomputer simulations and tutorials in economics classrooms prior to 1992. They conclude that student performance is improved through this form of integration of technology in the classroom. Since the time of that writing, new learning technologies have become increasingly more interactive through the growing use of the Internet. The percentage of U. S. college classrooms using e-mail in 1998 reached an astonishing 44.4% while one-third of all classes use Internet resources as part of the syllabus and one-fourth use WWW pages for class materials and resources (Green, 1998). Agarwal and Day (1998) test the impact of the Internet's communication and conferencing capabilities and information access, retrieval, and use on student performance in economics classes. They found a positive impact of using the Internet on economic education. This finding is repeated in other business disciplines as well (Smart, Kelley, & Conant, 1999).

Increasingly, however, we have found references through casual comments at technology conferences, through written media (e.g., Huber, 1991, Manicas, 1998), and even through new courses at our university about shutting down the "outmoded classroom" at the university level. As firm believers in the importance of social interaction as an integral part of learning, we are personally frightened at the thought. This has lead to our concerted effort to illustrate how technology can enhance teaching rather than replace it. Our focus is somewhere in between these extremes where technology enhances teaching and prevents loss of the "social interaction" that is often important to learning. In the sections that follow, we review the advantages and disadvantages of each pedagogy, and then we present ways to combine the two pedagogies to enhance teaching and learning.

3. SOME ADVANTAGES AND DISADVANTAGES TO USING COLLABORATIVE LEARNING TECHNIQUES

Collaborative learning provides many advantages to students by contributing to their active participation in the learning process. While a lecture format often provides discussion between the professor and student, all students do not participate. With collaborative learning students participate with the professor and with each other. Activities are designed so that all students participate to some degree. Participation allows students to familiarize themselves with and use the language of the discipline. Collaborative learning allows students to feel more comfortable in team situations that are becoming increasingly more valuable in the real business environment. Finally, research has shown that a higher level of learning occurs with collaborative learning (Thomchick, 1997).

A disadvantage of these learning techniques is the increased time necessary both inside and outside of the classroom to prepare, facilitate and brief these activities over the straight lecture format. Professors might also fear the problem of sacrificing quantity for quality that may be associated with in-class group activities. Sometimes the activity will fail in the classroom. Tasks may not be well developed and thus may not be very effective. A project that works well with one group may not work as well in a different type of class. The failure may be reflected in the professor's teaching evaluations. Students may also resist participating in class activities. Some students find their comfort level higher when working alone. And finally, while some students prefer to work on their own, others may try to free ride on the efforts of other group members[1].

4.   SOME ADVANTAGES AND DISADVANTAGES OF INTEGRATING TECHNOLOGY IN THE CLASSROOM

Instructional technology provides advantages to learning that we are only beginning to fully understand. Its importance is being reviewed from administrative levels, as well as, at the faculty and student levels. At least one-third of respondents in a national U.S. survey of college campuses identified "assisting faculty integrate technology into instruction" as the single most important instructional technology issue confronting their institution, while 26.5% find "providing adequate user support" most important (Green, 1998). However, these same institutions send a mixed message to faculty when only one-eighth of these institutions recognize and reward the use of technology in the classroom as part of the tenure and

---

[1] Bartlett (1995) has developed an interesting technique using a random drawing process to control the problem of free-riding in group assignments. Schibrowsky (1995) addresses the incidence of cheating in many experiential/collaborative learning activities, provides suggestions for controlling cheating, and has many references to articles on how to deal with cheating.

promotion process. Even so, it is estimated that 51.6% of all faculty and 45.1% of undergraduate students use the Internet routinely in their daily lives.

Faculty that use instructional technology, such as the Internet, presentation software, and distance education to enhance learning have found many very worthwhile advantages. Technology allows them to communicate more often and, perhaps, more effectively with individual students. It provides the students with more resources available through the Internet, off-campus library access, national databases, etc. Professors may invite outside experts to speak to the class via teleconference, or they may use pre-recorded presentations via digital video or streaming video over the Internet. Students may be able to interact more easily with each other outside the classroom via e-mail, discussion boards, or chat groups. They may also interact with students of other campuses or with top experts in their fields. Technology provides access to courses that some students who, because of their location, would otherwise not be able to take advantage of a course via distance learning. Since students may also take courses that are not available at their home campus, technology allows a wider selection of courses. And finally, new learning technologies provide students and faculty an opportunity to gain experience with technologies and new media that are currently being widely used in the business world.

There are disadvantages to new learning technologies, however. There are the infamous technological failures such as "system down" or "server down", web forms that do not work, e-mails sent, but not received, failure to properly save or back up assignments, "getting booted" from the Internet provider, "camera droop" or lost remote sites in ITV classrooms. Despite these problems, faculty and students prevail in their use of technology. However, for many faculty and older, non-traditional students, there may be steep learning curve for the incorporation of new technology. Seasoned faculty may view the time spent learning and incorporating technology incurred by their relatively newer colleagues as an undesirable expense, particularly given the lack of reward structure provided for technology use. This, in itself, may also lead to a competitive disadvantage for the university or program, particularly when other universities are attracting good students and faculty are providing impressive technologically equipped facilities. And finally there is the expense. Many universities are simply not financially able to provide the latest technology to their faculty and students for wide use throughout the curriculum. However, as we will show, combining technology and collaborative learning need not always take the most expensive routes.

5.   COMBINING COLLABORATIVE LEARNING AND NEW LEARNING TECHNOLOGIES IN THE CLASSROOM

So you would like to use more collaborative learning techniques, but you have also been charged with the task of incorporating more technology in the classroom? The following table of strategies illustrates some potential ways to incorporate technology while maintaining a collaborative environment in the classroom for teaching and learning enhancement. Interpret Table 1 with caution. What we believe is low/high technology or no/high collaboration may be classified by others differently depending on their use of either method. We classify low technology methods as those which use (a) little or no electronics or (b) electronic equipment requiring a relatively low skill level (e.g., t.v./v.c.r., overhead projector). Medium technology methods require some basic computer equipment/skills. High technology methods require some programming/training skills and specialized software/hardware. Methods with *little or no* collaboration require virtually no interaction between students, and in some cases, little interaction with the professor. Methods with some collaboration involve promoting some feedback between professor and student, and limited communication between students with the professor presiding (e.g., discussion). The high collaboration classification means that some portion of the student's grade results from work with each other.

Using Table 1, we have tried to place higher technology applications that incorporate higher degrees of collaboration in the lower right portion. The lines dividing the cells in Table 1 are somewhat "fuzzy" in reality. The degree of collaboration varies from classroom to classroom, instructor to instructor. An important note: combining pedagogies does not mean that the collaborative exercise must be technology oriented. Sometimes we use some low technology/collaborative exercises combined with high technology/individual oriented tools for the dual effect.

5.1   Moving from "chalk and talk" to "comparing and sharing"

The move from "chalk and talk" to "comparing and sharing" can often be met with some resistance. The inertia comes from fears mentioned earlier such as requiring too much time to prepare, loss of control in the classroom, sacrificing quantity of information delivered in the classroom, and declining performance/student evaluations. But the move to more collaborative activities in the classroom need not occur over night. Try some of the following suggestions as we go from Square 1 to Square 3 in Table 1.

"Great orators should lecture," according to Becker and Watts (1995, p. 699), but the rest of us may need some help. Becker and Watts (1996) find that the median amount of time spent lecturing in economics undergraduate courses is an amazing 83%. This includes the time the chalkboard was used for presentation of graphs and text. For those of use who still wish to lecture or would like to improve upon the time we spend lecturing, some lecture techniques can be found in Saunders and Welsch (1990) and Gottko and Osterman (1987). Tips for improving discussion can be found in Hanson and Salemi (1990). Adding a touch of collaborative learning to a lecture-oriented course can be as simple as a five minute "think-pair-share" or a short in-class group assignment.

What do the students want? Surprisingly in a study by Karns (1993) students ranked discussion and speakers quite highly. Karns provides survey results of students comparing many of the activities listed in Squares 1 through 3. Students ranked the items according to preference and effectiveness. The students in the survey found guest speakers, discussion, films/video, and simulations to be most preferred, and they found discussion, guest speakers, client projects, and case analyses to be most effective. The students ranked term papers and text/readings least preferable, while ranking text/readings and multiple choice tests as least effective. Karns concluded that activities that provide realism and stimulation, yet require reasonable effort, are preferred by students and are perceived as effective.

Involving students in realism and simulation can be accomplished through adding case studies (Carlson & Schodt, 1995). Some business professors, particularly in economics, are less likely to use case studies due to the fear of giving up *theoretical rigor*. Moore (1998) overcomes this problem by combining traditional lecture with an outside collaborative learning lab where students working in groups of three or four take a series of short written quizzes.

A somewhat less realistic, yet novel approach, is to use the *novel approach*. With this activity, students read a novel that is specifically written to include concepts that relate to a particular course. Some examples of these are *The Choice: A Fable of Free Trade and Protectionism*, Jevons (1993), *Murder at the Margin*, Russell (1994), and *The Force*, Dorsey (1994). We have found this approach to be an interesting way to draw students into discussion.

For an even more collaborative approach, Thomchick (1997) provides a review of various collaborative learning techniques including problem-centered instruction (teamwork), writing groups, peer teaching, discussion groups and learning communities. The author compares the work of a traditional classroom atmosphere with a classroom dominated by collaborative learning. Other surveys of collaborative approaches can be found in Johnson and Johnson (1991) and Rea, Hoger, and Rooney (1999). Wright, Bitner, and Zeithaml (1994) discuss the importance of teamwork and the associated skills development in the business world. They provide examples of various active learning activities involving teamwork. In addition, *Great Ideas for Teaching Marketing* (Hair, Lamb & McDaniel, 1998) provides a variety of active learning exercises.

Other structured approaches to collaborative learning include simulations and experiments. These can range from non-computer oriented simulations and role-plays to high technology oriented simulations involving students from various parts of the world. The *Marketplace* simulation can provide competition between student teams in one class or worldwide competitors via the Internet (Cadotte & Matis, 1996). Role playing ideas can be found in Lowry (1999), Rodger (1996), Moncrief and Shipp (1994), Bartlett and Amsler (1979), and Alden (1999). Role plays may be conducted inside or outside the classroom. We have conducted role plays in both settings with either a student, a faculty member, or a business professional as a student's role play partner depending on the assignment. Laughlin and Hite (1993), Wellington and Faria (1996), and Becker and Watts (1995) provide an overview of non-technical role-play/simulations and experiments and their effectiveness.

5.2   Moving from "chalk and talk" to "point and click"

The move from "chalk and talk" to "point and click" simply means involving technology in some way into the classroom presentation. Here we are referring to moving down the left side of Table 1 through Squares 1, 4, and 7. The first step might be to replace the overhead projector with some sort of presentation software such as Power Point or Freelance Graphics. Many textbook companies now offer Power Point presentations with their textbooks. These presentations can be edited so that they are tailored to an individual course or instructor. Faculty that fear getting too involved with technology due to time constraints often fail to realize that once one gets acquainted with presentation software, presentations may actually take less time to prepare than a set of overheads.

Table 1: **Strategies for Teaching and Learning Enhancement with Technology and Collaborative Learning.**

	Little or No Collaboration	Some Collaboration	High Collaboration
Low Technology	Lecture w/Overhead "Chalk and Talk" Independent Study (Text only) Video Presentations/Lectures Written/Typed Homework/Journals Reading Assignment	Lecture w/Discussion Novel Approach w/Discussion Case Studies Video Presentations w/Discussion Student Presentations– Individual In-class Assignments "Think-Pair-Share"	Collaborative Group Work (In and Out of Class) Student Presentations- group Collaborative Learning Labs Classroom Experiments Role-Playing Simulations
Medium Technology	Presentation Software (Power Point, Lotus, etc.) Word Processed Homework Computer Tutorials Simulation Software	Discussion w/Presentation Software (Power Point, Lotus, etc.) Discussion w/Simulation Software Student Power Point Presentations Individual	Student Power Point Presentations- group Collaborative Group Work w/Simulation Software Games
High Technology "Low-End" (Square 9)	Web Page Utilization Information Retrieval and Use (for homework, research papers, journals) On-line Courses On-line Assignments/Testing Interactive Software Webforms/E-mail assignments	Discussion w/Network Links Interactive T.V. Courses Discussion Boards, EMail Discussion w/Interactive Software and Web Pages On-line Courses w/discussion board	▪ Chat groups ▪ Simulations via Internet ▪ The "Inverted Classroom" ▪ Classroom Web Page Development Streaming Video and Real Audio w/discussion board
"High-End" (Square 9)			Desktop Videoconferencing (Collaborative Telelearnin Real time component via Internet Information-technology-enabled-partnership Groupware

Getting the students involved with technology may be accomplished by simply requiring or recommending that they purchase simulation software with their texts or use software available via the university's computer lab. Simulation and tutorial software provide practice that gets the student actively involved with their subject. Some software simulates real world situations, while others provide examples and sample tests with answers and explanations. Boyd (1993) reviews microcomputer software in response to Walbert's (1989) suggested improvements for economics software designers. Other reviews of non-collaborative simulation and interactive software can be found in Katz (1999), Bulter and Herbig (1992) and Clopton and Perreault (1992).

To spice up presentations even more with technology, Ronchetto *et al.* (1992) present a wide array of multimedia applications (combination or integration of electronic, video, audio, and/or computer technologies). They first illustrate how multimedia fits and enhances learning according to the Kolb learning model. They report on the interactive nature of laserdiscs and how these disks can direct and monitor student progress, provide a standardized communication format, and allow feedback and practice. The interactive nature of these and the software presented in this section is between student and computer rather than with other students.

With an Internet connection, students and faculty can access interactive software or interactive web sites on WWW. Textbook companies again will provide these materials often free of charge. The students can access tutorials, sample multiple-choice questions, real world examples, etc. Some textbooks are now on-line (e.g., *EconWeb* and *International Trade Theory & Policy Analysis*). On one of our websites, http://www.wku.edu/~carey, students can find many interactive links concerning topics discussed in class, such as a purchasing power parity calculator, currency calculator, national budget simulation, or national debt clock. These web sites are often brought into the lecture presentation to promote discussion and interest in the topic.

Daniel (1999), Smart, Kelley, and Conant (1999), Sosin (1997), Agarwal and Day (1998) discuss the impact of the Internet on education. Agarwal and Day suggest two broad categories into which Internet methods can be classified: (1) computer communication and conferencing and (2) information access, retrieval and use. The former relates to our Squares 8 and 9, to be discussed later, while the latter relates to Square 2. Atwong and Hugstad (1997), Monaham and Dharm (1995), Kaynama and Keesling (2000) and Siegel (2000) discuss basic integration of Internet technology into the classroom. Professors can provide a web page for students with course information. Students and faculty can access references and databases on the Internet. Some professors have success with the use of web forms. Our experience is that students enjoy web forms (answering questions directly onto the web page for submission to the instructor over the Internet), but occasionally assignments are lost in cyberspace.

A high-tech delivery system can even significantly reduce the amount of face-to-face contact between student and faculty member. Faculty can put lectures on-line on their course web page via typed, taped, or video taped presentations. Students will often communicate with the faculty member via e-mail, discussion boards, or chat rooms, discussed in the next section. An example of such a course can be found in Johnson and Bretz (2000). They discuss a web-based, self-paced, competency-based introductory computer literacy course. Students work at their own pace. They take online exams in computer labs on scheduled dates. Their exams are graded instantly and the scores are sent directly to the instructor. The instructors rarely see the student in this situation, but the students have reviewed the course structure positively.

5.3 Linking the professor and student with technology

Linking the professor with the student through technology is most commonly accomplished via the Internet or Intranet, as in Square 8, while microcomputer simulations that lead to some class discussion would be classified in Square 5. Also, simply combining the multimedia presentation approach with the appropriate amount of discussion in the classroom or on an electronic bulletin board would accomplish this same goal. Gregor and Cuskelly (1994), Berge (1994), Manning (1996), and Zack (1995) present many ideas regarding the use of e-mail and bulletin/discussion boards. An example of the use of multimedia can be found in Lage, Platt, and Treglia (2000) who use video tapes, Power Point with sound, WWW course page, and handouts to present materials traditionally presented in class *outside* of class, while doing homework in groups during class time.

A more high-tech way linking professor and student through technology is via ITV. Students at remote locations can sit in on lectures via a satellite hook-up, and can even participate in class discussion. Webster and Hackley (1997) evaluate teaching effectiveness in technology-mediated distance learning using ITV. They report the advantages and disadvantages they encountered during two semesters and offer advice to administrators and first time ITV faculty. They encountered significant problems with "medium richness" (e.g., lack of eye contact, teaching methods such as pointing a finger on a document, and instructor focus on the technology at the expense of students). Reducing these problems might enhance the learning experience for students in this environment.

Another rather sophisticated form of high-tech delivery can be found in Keeva (1997) which discusses the use of the real time component of a class taught completely on the Internet. The class involved students at four law schools interacting by a live video link with the professor. E-mail and discussion boards are used to "call-on" students throughout the week, and the WWW is used to distribute a full digital set of readings.

5.4   Connect students in cyberspace

Finally we are ready to combine higher forms of technology and significant amounts of collaborative learning. On Table 1 we might find ourselves in Squares 6 and 9. But recall our most important point mentioned earlier: the professor does not have to be located in Squares 6 and 9 to be combining high technology and high collaboration. Combining techniques from, for example, Squares 3 and 7 can reach the same goal. However, let us look at techniques that innately combine the two desirable goals. These techniques can be found in Square 9. Square 9 is divided into two groups of strategies. We will classify these as lower-end *high* technology and higher-end *high* technology. We feel this classification is necessary due to a wide range of technology access on college campuses today. While e-mail and discussion boards may represent high technology to many faculty, clearly it ranks fairly low on the scale for faculty involved in collaborative video conferencing.

Siegel (1996) explains simple ways to incorporate networking technology (Intranet and Internet) into classroom assignments. She reports some advantages and disadvantages that she has encountered, and suggests introductory assignments to get students started communicating collaboratively via e-mail, including the *E-mail Icebreaker, Scavenger Hunt*, and *Net Search*. None of these techniques requires sophisticated technology other than access to e-mail and the Internet. Other techniques she recommends include setting up class bulletin boards, inviting Internet guest speakers to interact with class, forming intercollegiate student marketing teams, developing consulting projects, and other various group research projects.

Simulations involving teamwork often involve the use of some type of technology. This technology can fall into any one of our three categories. If the simulation is simply a microcomputer software program, it might fall in the "medium" Square 6 category. If it is found on the Internet, it might fall into the "low-end" of the high technology category in Square 9. Likewise, if it is found on the Internet and it allows students from different locations to collaborate synchronously, it might fall in the "high-end" of the high-technology category. Alpert (1993) reviews a large scale, medium technology simulation known as *The Marketplace* that involves student teams of three to six. He identifies the pros and cons of implementing large-scale games and provides excellent references to other simulations. In addition, ABSEL is an organization that supports simulations, games, experiential learning, and provides two refereed publications devoted to the topic. A listing of simulation packages used in college classrooms can be found at the following web address: www.towson.edu/~absel/Simpack/package.html.

Other types of collaborative efforts can also fall into our designated categories. McNeilly and Ranny (1998) offer an array of ideas that allow the integration of business writing assignments and collaborative activities via the Internet. Alavi, Wheeler, and Valacich (1995) compare three groups of collaborative learners: traditional face-to-face groups, local groups (a same campus telelearning group), and non-proximate distant groups (students on two separate campuses). Their study is grounded in cognitive learning theory, and finds that the three environments were equally effective in terms of student knowledge acquisition. Other examples of collaborative learning on the lower-tech end include those suggested in Natesan and Smith (1998). They discuss ideas such as setting up a classroom homepage, discussion groups, a class bulletin board, Internet guests and a classroom on-line newspaper. However, on the very high-tech end, Alavi, Yoo, and Vogel (1997) talk about the *information-technology-enabled-partnership* where faculty and students from two separate state universities combined using technology. The course required an elaborate set-up, including electronic classrooms equipped with one or more networked computer workstations for each instructor and student and "videowalls". Students and faculty interacted through audio and video mediums, as well as, through e-mail. Collaborative activities between students were facilitated through the use of asynchronous groupware.

A less elaborate discussion of groupware (network-based software designed to facilitate group activities such as discussions, debates, joint papers, or team projects) can be found in Greenlaw (1999). Groupware combines web pages, electronic bulletin boards, and discussion lists. Users can read and edit synchronously or asynchronously. For more information on groupware, Greenlaw cites other studies. Even lower-tech, but similar in result, Canzer (1997) and Siegel (1996) present on-line, asynchronous delivery of an introductory marketing course using a series of discussion boards for both individual and collaborative activities.

6.   CONCLUSION

We have found the combination of collaborative learning techniques and new learning technologies to be an effective, pleasurable experience for both ourselves and our students. As Becker and Watts (1995, p. 699) so adeptly put it, students are "all to willing to vote with their feet in the long run." We believe that technology should enhance teaching - not replace it, but this takes some dedication, willingness to experiment, and plenty of time to make it work.

Many professors are unaware of simple ideas that incorporate collaborative learning and new learning technologies. Other pioneering professors are already trying out ideas and they are discovering what works and what does not. Dardig (1997) writes about the development of the *ODC Technology Ideabook*: *A Sourcebook for Faculty/Staff-Tested Ideas on Using Computers to Promote Student Learning and Make Life Easier* for Old Dominican College. In this database, ODC faculty share their ideas about what they have learned utilizing technology with other faculty members at ODC. Faculty at our university are involved in a similar project. We encourage you to join us in this education adventure by integrating technology with collaboration in the classroom and sharing it with your colleagues.

REFERENCES

ABSEL (1999). The Association for Business Simulation and Experiential Learning. Available from World Wide Web:(http://www.towson.edu/~absel/aboustabsel.html)

Agarwal, R., & Day, A.E. (1998). The Impact of the Internet on Economic Education. *Journal of Economic Education, 29* (2), 99-110.

Alavi, M. (1994). Computer-Mediated Collaborative Learning: an Empirical Evaluation. *MIS Quarterly, 18.*(2), 159-174.

Alavi, M., Wheeler, B.C., & Valacich, J.S. (1995). Using IT to Reengineer Business Education: An Exploratory Investigation of Collaborative Telelearning. *MIS Quarterly, 19*(3), 93-311.

Alavi, M., Yoo, Y., & Vogel, .D.R. (1997). Using Information Technology to Add Value to Management Education. *Academy of Management Journal, 40* (6), 1310-1333.

Alden, D. (1999). Experience With Scripted Role Play in Environmental Economics. *Journal of Economic Education 30,* 127-132.

Alpert, F. (1993). Large-Scale Simulation in Marketing Education. *Journal of Marketing Education, 15,* 30-35.

Arbaugh, J.B. (2000). How Classroom Environment and Student Engagement Affect Learning in Internet-Based MBA Courses. *Business Communication Quarterly 63*(4), 9-26.

Atwong, C.T., & Hugstad, P.S. (1997). Internet Technology and the Future of Marketing Education. *Journal of Marketing Education 19,* 44-55.

Bartlett, R. (Spring)Teaching Economics as a Laboratory Science. *Journal of Economic Education 26,* (Spring), 131-39.

Bartlett, R., & Amsler, C. (1979). Simulations and Economics. In E. Thorson (Eds.), *Simulations in Higher Education.* Hicksville, N.Y.: Exposition.

Becker, W.E., & Watts, M. (October, 1995). Teaching Tools: Teaching Methods in Undergraduate Economics. *Economic Inquiry 33*, 692-700.

Becker, W.E., & Watts, M. (1996). Chalk and Talk: A National Survey on Teaching Undergraduate Economics. *American Economic Review, 86*, 448-53.

Berge, Z.L. (1994). Electronic Discussion Groups. *Communication Education, 43*, 184-193.

Boyd, D.W. (1993). The New Microcomputer Development Technology: Implications for the Economics Instructor and Software Author. *Journal of Economic Education, 24*, (Spring), 113-125.

Bulter, D.D., & Herbig, P. (1992). Export to Win: a Useful International Marketing Simulation. *Journal of Marketing Education, 14*, 58-62.

Cadotte, E., & Matis, P. (1996). *The Management Strategy in the Marketplace: A New Business Simulation.* [On-line] Available from World Wide Web:(http://www.marketplace-simulation.com)

Canzer, B. (1997). Marketing Education on the Internet: a Word Wide Web Based Introductory Marketing Course Design for the Virtual-U Project in Distance Education at Simon Fraser University. *Journal of Marketing Education, 19*, 56-65.

Carey, C. (No Date). Cathy Careys Homepage. [Online]. Available from World Wide Web: (http://www.wku.edu/~carey)

Carlson, J., & Schodt, D. (1995). Beyond the Lecture: Case Teaching and the Learning of Economic Theory. *Journal of Economic Education, 26* (1) 17-28.

Clopton, S.W., & Perreault, Jr. W. (1992). A Computer-Aided Approach for Teaching and Learning Physical Distribution Service Concepts. *Journal of Marketing Education, 14*, 47-57.

Daniel, J. (1999). Computer-Aided Instruction on the World Wide Web: The Third Generation. *Journal of Economic Education, 30*, (Spring), 163-174.

Dardig, J.C. (1997). Enriching the Teaching/Learning Process with Computers: Spreading the Word on a College Campus. *THE Journal*, 52-54.

Dorsey, D. (1994). *The Force.* New York: Ballantine Books.

EconWeb. (No Date). *Online Texts for College Level Economics.* [Online]. Available from World Wide Web: (http://www.econweb.com)

Gottko, J., & Osterman, D. (1987). The Feedback Lecture: An Illustration. *Journal of Marketing Education, 9*, 39-43.

Green, K.C. (1998). *Colleges Struggle with IT Planning.* The Campus Computing Project. [Online]. Available from World Wide Web:(http://www.campuscomputing.net)

Green, K.C. (1997). *More Technology in the Syllabus, More Campuses Impose IT Requirements and Student Fees.* The Campus Computing Project. [Online]. Available from World Wide Web: (http://www.campuscomputing.net)

Greenlaw, S.A. (1999). Using Groupware to Enhance Teaching and Learning in Undergraduate Education. *Journal of Economic Education, 30* (1), 33-42.

Gregor, S., & Cuskelly, E.F. (1994). Computer Mediated Communication in Distance Education. *Journal of Computer Assisted Learning, 10*, (September), 168-81.

Grimes, P., & Ray, M.A. (1992). *The Impact of Microcomputer Simulations and Tutorials in the Principles Classroom: A Review of the Empirical Evidence.* A Roundfigure Discussion Paper, Allied Social Science Association Meetings.

Hair, J. Jr., Lamb, C., & McDaniel, C. (1998). *Great Ideas for Teaching Marketing.* Cincinnati, Ohio: South-Western Publishing. Available from World Wide Web: (http://ww.swcollege.com/marketing/gitm/gitm.html)

Hanson, W.L., & Salemi, M.K. (1990). Improving Classroom Discussion in Economics Courses. In P. Saunders, & W.B. Walstad, (Eds.), *The Principles of Economics Course: A Handbook for Instructors* (pp. 96-110). New York: McGraw-Hill, Inc.

Huber, P. (June 10, 1991). Desktop Schools. *Forbes, 147*, p. 114.

Jevons, M. (1993). *Murder at the Margin: A Henry Spearman Mystery.* Princeton University Press.

Johnson, D.W., &. Johnson, R.T. (1991). *Learning Together and Alone: Cooperative, Competitive, and Individualistic Learning.* 3rd Ed. Engelwood Cliffs, N. J.: Prentice Hall.

Johnson, D. W., Maruyama, G., Johnson, R., Nelson, D., & Skon, L. (1981). Effects of Cooperative, Competitive, and Individualistic Goal Structures on Achievement: A Meta-Analysis. *Psychological Bulletin, 89* (1), 47-62.

Johnson, L.E., & Bretz, R.W. (2000). An Innovative Pedagogy for Teaching and Evaluating Computer Literacy. *Information Technology and Management, 1,* 283-292.

Karns, G.L. (1993). Marketing Student Perceptions of Learning Activities: Structure, Preferences, and Effectiveness. *Journal of Marketing Education, 15,* 3-10.

Katz, A. (1999). A Computer-Aided Exercise for Checking Novices Understanding of Market Equilibrium Changes. *Journal of Economic Education, 30,* (Spring), 148-162.

Kaynama, S., & Keesling, G. (2000). Development of a Web-Based Internet Marketing Course. *Journal of Marketing Education, 22* (2), 84-89.

Keeva, S. (1997). Stars of the Classroom. *ABA Journal, 83,* 18-20.

Lage, M.J., Platt, G. Jr., & Treglia, M. (2000). Inverting the Classroom: A Gateway to Creating and Inclusive Learning Environment. *Journal of Economic Education, 31,* (Winter), 30-43.

Lauglin, J.L., & Hite, R.E. (1993). Game and Simulation Effective in Marketing Education: An Experimental Investigation. *Journal of Marketing Education, 15,* 39-46.

Lowry, P.E. (1999). Model GATT: A Role-Playing Simulation Course. *Journal of Economic Education, 30,* (Spring), 119-126.

McNeilly, K.M., & Ranney, F.J. (1998). Combining Writing and the Electronic Media in Sales Management Courses. *Journal of Marketing Education, 20,* 226-235.

Maier, M.H., & Keenan, D. (April, 1994). Cooperative Learning in Economics. *Economic Inquiry, 32,* 358-361.

Manicas, P. (1998). The Radical Restructuring of Higher Education. *Futures, 30*(7), 651-656.

Manning, L. (1996). Economics on the Internet: Electronic Mail in the Classroom. *Journal of Economic Education, 27,* 201-204.

Monahan, B.D., & Dharm, M. (1995). The Internet for Educators: A User's Guide. *Educational Technology, 35,* 44-48.

Moncrief, W., & Shipp, S. (1994). *Sales Management Role Plays.* Addison-Wesley Publishing Company.

Moore, R.L. (1998). Teaching Introductory Economics with a Collaborative Learning Lab Component. *Journal of Economic Education, 29,* (Fall), 321-329.

Murphy, H.L. (2000). Long-Distance Makes Connection for Educators. *Marketing News, 34*(16), 12-13.

Natesan, N.C., & Smith, K.H. (1998). The Internet Education Tool in the Global Marketing Classroom. *Journal of Marketing Education, 20,* 149-159.

Rea Jr., A.I., Hoger, B., & Rooney, P. (1999). Communication and Technology: Building Bridges Across the Chasm. *Business Communication Quarterly, 62*(2), 92-96.

Roberts, R.D. (1994). *The Choice: A Fable of Free Trade and Protectionism.* Prentice Hall Business Publishing.

Rodgers, Y. van der Meulen, (1996). Role-Playing Exercise for Development and International Economics Courses. *Journal of Economic Education, 27* (3), 217-23.

Ronchetto, J.R., Buckles, T.A., Barath, R.M., & Perry, J. (1992). Multimedia Delivery Systems: A Bridge Between Teaching Methods and Learning Styles. *Journal of Marketing Education, 14,* 12-21.

Saunders, P., & Welsh, A.L. (1990). Lectures as an Instructional Method. In P. Saunders, & W.B. Walstad, (Eds.), *The Principles of Economics Course: A Handbook for Instructors*, (pp. 111-126). New York: McGraw-Hill, Inc.

Schibrowsky, J.A., & Peltier, J.W. (1995). The Dark Side of Experimental Learning Activities. *Journal of Marketing Education, 17*, 13-24.

Siegel, C.F. (2000). Introducing Marketing Students to Business Intelligence Using Project-Based Learning on the World Wide Web. *Journal of Marketing Education, 22* (2), 90-98.

Siegel, C.F. (1996). Using Computer Networks (Intranet and Internet) to Enhance Your Students' Marketing Skills. *Journal of Marketing Education, 18*, 14-24.

Smart, D.T., Kelley, C.A., & Conant, J.S. (1999). Marketing Education in the Year 2000: Changes Observed and Challenges Anticipated. *Journal of Marketing Education, 21* (3) 206-216.

Sosin, K. (1997). *Economics and the World Wide Web: Economics Information, Teaching, Resources, Organization, and Women's Issues.* CSWEP Newsletter [Online]. Available from World Wide Web: (http://ecedweb.unomaha.edu/webs4econ.htm),(May).

Suranovic, S.M. (1998). International Trade Theory & Policy Analysis. [Online]. Available from World Wide Web:(http://internationalecon.com/v1.0/index.html)

Thomchick, E. (1997). The Use of Collaborative Learning in Logistics Classes. *Journal of Business Logistics, 18* (2), 191-205.

Vygotsky, L.S. (1978). *Mind in Society: The Development of Higher Psychological Processes.* Cambridge, MA: Harvard University Press.

Walbert, M.S. (1989). Grading Software for Economics Principles Texts. *Economic Inquiry, 27*, (January), 169-77.

Webster, J., & Hackley, P. (1997). Teaching Effectiveness in Technology Mediated Distance Learning. *Academy of Management Journal, 40* (6), 1282-1309.

Wellington, W.J., & Faria, A.J. (1996). The Use of Simulation Games in Marketing Classes: Is Simulation Performance Due to Skill or Luck? *Journal of Marketing Education, 18*, 50-59.

Wright, L.K., Bitner, M.J., & Zeithaml, V.A. (1994). Paradigm Shifts in Business Education Using Active Learning to Deliver Services Marketing Content. *Journal of Marketing Education, 15*, 5-19.

Zack, M. (1995). Using Electronic Messaging to Improve the Quality of Instruction. *Journal of Education for Business.* (March/April), 202-206.

Interactive Case Studies – Enablers For Innovative Learning

Stefan Haaken & Gunnar E. Christensen
Norwegian School of Economics and Business Administration, Bergen, Norway

1.   INTRODUCTION

In 1921, Wallace Donham, Dean of the Harvard Business School advised his teachers to use student discussion based on case studies in addition to lectures (Erskine & Leenders, 1989, p. 13). This experiment proved to be one of the most successful in the field of teaching methods and today, teaching with cases is the most popular teaching method in business schools around the world.

However, the question evolves if teaching with article-based cases is still state-of-the-art. Through the use of multimedia technology, case studies may be presented more vivid and realistic and one may assume that interactive multimedia case studies support learning processes better than article-based cases.

This article describes the development of interactive case studies, focusing not only on technological requirements, but especially on didactic aspects. These are summarized in the concept of learning environments which give a comprehensive overview of all relevant factors which have to be regarded when designing an interactive case study. Furthermore, a general model for the design and production process is presented.

T.A. Johannessen, A. Pedersen and K. Petersen (eds.),
Educational Innovation in Economics and Business VI, 127–145.

2.   INTERACTIVE CASES: ADDING EDUCATIONAL VALUE

In general, there is no doubt that case studies are an appropriate tool to support learning in business and economics (Erskine, Leenders and Mauffette-Leenders, 1981, p. 17). However, interactive multimedia cases in contrast to traditional article-based case studies have the following advantages:

- Facilitation and acceleration of knowledge transfer through multimedia components: The user-friendliness and the customization implicit of the new learning technologies/approaches also support the diffusion of interactive cases among users who are not confident with technical approaches.
- Reach new types of potential users: New ways of knowledge transfer using new technologies can reach new types of potential users, such as SMEs, which cannot afford to attend traditional events (courses, conferences, consultants) related to technological transfer.
- Flexible medium without constraints regarding time and place: The case studies can be used on-demand in the office, in seminars, at home etc., whenever people have time and motivation to learn. Furthermore, they can be used for real-time problem solving, which means that a person (manager, specialist, change agent, ...), who has to innovate a process or an organization in a certain situation, can first try to find a case study that fits best to his problem situation.
- Topics have not to be learned sequentially.

As a conclusion, there are numerous reasons to research into interactive case studies. On the other hand, existing interactive cases do often not comply with these opportunities, and we still lack guidelines and tools to design and develop such multimedia applications (Bieber & Isakowitz, 1995, p. 26). One reason for that might be that multimedia development often focuses too much on attractive interface design, neglecting psychological and didactic aspects. Therefore, this article stresses the importance of those factors and builds up a generic framework for the educational design of interactive cases.

3.   LEARNING ENVIRONMENTS

A learning environment contains all relevant factors involved in learning processes with interactive cases and the relationship between them. Its key elements are related to the key questions of all learning processes:

1. Who are the learners (the target groups)?

2. What are the learners supposed to learn (the learning objectives)?
3. How is the learning process conducted (the context factors)?

These factors have to be taken into consideration when designing and developing an interactive case study. The interactive case itself is tightly connected with them and therefore also belongs to the learning environment.

3.1 Target group characteristics

The learners as the target group should be the starting point when planning and defining a learning process. The learning objectives as well as the methods and techniques applied in learning processes are dependent on the learner's situational, emotional dispositions and the dispositions related to his or her own capabilities and knowledge (Huitt, 1996).

3.1.1 Capabilities and knowledge related dispositions

These dispositions are related to the cognitive capabilities and knowledge of the learner. They could be characterized by learning-process related capabilities and habits like the style of learning (passive or active), preferred perception (abstract or concrete), information processing capabilities (integration of new information into one's mental models) and the previously acquired knowledge on the content and methods of the learning process.

3.1.2 Emotional dispositions

Emotional dispositions are describing the attitudes and opinions of the learners to the content, methods and technologies offered in the learning process. They include for instance the acceptance to multimedia and Internet based learning technologies, emotional vs. rational oriented learning and emotional relationship to the content (e.g. working in the domain).

3.1.3 Situational dispositions

The situational dispositions are describing the socio-economical context of the learner. They can be characterized by profession, family, school, culture etc. The situational dispositions of the learner could give information about the capabilities, knowledge and motivation of the learner. For instance, the profession could give decisive information on the capabilities and motivation of the learners. Executives and part time students may have a totally different view on certain issues than graduate students because of their experiences they have made in business. For the teacher it is important to address the current and future "real life" of the learner in order to spur his or her attention and motivation to learn.

3.2   Learning objectives

From a case-oriented view, acquiring cognitive skills (by learning specific contents), is the core learning objective as all cases are content-related (Winterburn, 1990). While learning with the contents, important basic skills may be trained. These include planning & problem solving skills, communication & presentation skills and information retrieval & handling skills (Masoner, 1988).

An essential enabler for the acquiring of all these skills is motivation, i.e. the learner's mental attitude towards the knowledge he has to acquire and to the learning process in total. This has to be addressed explicitly in the design of multimedia cases and learning processes (cf. Figure 1).

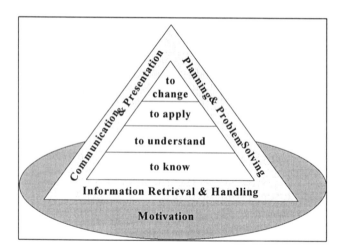

Figure 1: Learning objectives.

3.2.1   Cognitive skills

The cognitive skills have been adapted from Bloom's learning taxonomy (Bloom, 1984) and include (1) to know facts, (2) to understand concepts, (3) to apply these concepts, and (4) to change them. Thus, success on one level is a precondition to achieve the next one. While proceeding through these learning levels, the individual gets a deeper and deeper insight into the learning issue which may be used as a measure for evaluating the learning process.

3.2.1.1   To know (facts)

The easiest way of learning encompasses just the learning of explicit knowledge, such as facts or figures ("learning by heart"). In most situations this is just done to enable the learner to advance on higher learning levels, although there may be issues where knowing facts alone provides the deepest insight possible into a specific learning issue, such as a company profile.

3.2.1.2   To understand (concepts)

Understanding facts involves intense cognitive reflection and analysis, leading to the creative act of building a mental model about the learning issue. This involves system-building by identification of specific elements and relations between them.

3.2.1.3   To apply (implementation)

Even more sophisticated than understanding something and thus demanding further learning processes is the implementation of learned and understood material in a real-world environment. This step establishes the crucial link between mental models and individual action driven by these models.

3.2.1.4   To change (manipulation)

The highest level of learning has been reached when the learner has accomplished an insight so deep that he is able to manipulate and change the learning issue, e.g. to adjust it to his specific needs or to improve it generally. This involves bringing together experience from the implementation level with knowledge from other contexts, which results in an enrichment of the individual's mental models.

3.2.2   Motivation

In this context, motivation as a learning objective has two meanings: One is related to the cognitive skills the learner has acquired and may be defined as *having a positive personal attitude towards learning issues (to trust learning issues, e.g. "I like the electronic business")*. Without such motivation, knowledge will not lead to effective action (Fuchs, 1990).

Furthermore, motivation may be related to the learning process as a whole, meaning *the learner's drive to undergo the learning process being an enabler for the achievement of all other learning objectives (e.g. "I have fun participating in the case course")*. Concerning this second meaning, psychology distinguishes a variety of motivation types, in particular:

- **Altruistic vs. egoistic motivation**
  Egoistic motivation is aimed at the well being of the individual alone, whereas altruistic motivation is related to the group or organization the learner is embedded in. As some authors argue, most motives are egoistic, but nonetheless it should be an objective of learning process design to generate altruistic motivation, as this is an essential enabler for group learning.

- **Intrinsic vs. extrinsic motivation**
  It is a common understanding that intrinsic motivation – motivation based on internal, personal reasons – is more desirable than extrinsic motivation, which arises from external reasons. In the context of case-based learning, intrinsic motivation should be stressed, though some extrinsic measures may be taken into account to support further motivation.

3.2.3   Information retrieval and handling skills

These skills enable the learner to seek, describe and interpret information within the context of his disciplines.
In particular, information retrieval and handling involves:
- Identifying information needs resulting from a specific problem;
- Identifying appropriate sources of information;
- Scanning sources for relevant information;
- Analyzing and structuring data, combining data from various sources;
- Using appropriate IT resources to support the above tasks.

3.2.4   Communication and presentation skills

These skills address all issues related to exchanging information between individuals and contain both technical and social aspects:

3.2.4.1   Technical Skills
- Express his own thinking both orally and on article, distinguishing between ideas, facts, opinions and judgments;
- Choose style and structure of oral and written contributions in relation to its target audience;
- Use appropriate communication and presentation media, such as e-mail, newsgroups and presentation software.

3.2.4.2   Social skills
The learner should be able to:
- Co-operate with others and contribute to a common goal;
- Formulate and implement effective strategies for achieving goals when working with others;
- Give and receive constructive feedback.

3.2.5   Planning and problem solving skills

The learner should be able to choose and apply appropriate methods and tools to solve a given problem and to organize the process of problem solving typically given in the context of business managers. This includes:
- Analyzing given problem situations;
- Formulating and implementing action plans for solving the problem;
- Managing time and resources effectively in order to achieve intended goals;
- Identifying criteria for success and evaluating performance against them.

3.3   Course context

Most authors of books and articles on the case study method stress the importance of accompanying course events when using case studies in courses. For most of the authors the case study method as a basic element includes the classroom discussion on the case (e.g. Barnes, Christensen & Hansen, 1994). For that reason the accompanying measures in the course context of the case study are part of the learning environment as well. They may be described with the following attributes.

3.3.1   Organization of course

The organization of the course describes the kind of course activities as well as the sequence of them. In particular, the role of the multimedia case study is outlined as its role has significant influence on the design of the case. In relation to other course activities the case could be used as:
- Basis for giving lectures;
- Basis for writing reports and presentations;
- Basis for the classroom discussions;
- Basis for working in groups;
- Basis for role games/business simulation.

3.3.2   Virtuality level

This section describes the level of "virtuality" of the course. It includes the way the case study is delivered (on hard-medium like CD-ROM or via networks like Inter-/Intranet) and a description of the usage of net-based communication means for the interaction between teachers and students or among students. In this section the characteristics of the target group set the constraints for defining learning environments. For example, network connections of executives working in companies are often faster than network connections of students working at home.

Principally, the course context could play two roles: as a constraint which has to be taken into account when designing multimedia cases or as an characteristic of the learning process which can also be designed and developed. Practically, there will be always a mixture of exogenous and endogenous elements of the course context. For instance, the realization of cases in "virtual" learning environments is heavily dependent on the availability of the appropriate IT-Infrastructure (which is a constraint). Nevertheless, the IT-infrastructure could also be a part of the design of the course context e.g. by integrating innovative communication software (like NetMeeting etc).

3.4   Interactive case study

The architecture of the interactive multimedia cases may be divided into the content, instructional and presentation & delivery level (cf. Figure 2).

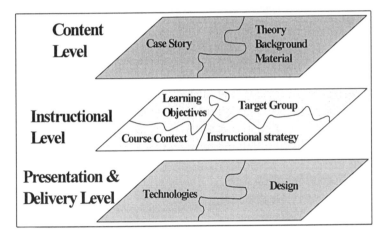

Figure 2: The three levels of interactive case studies.

3.4.1   Content level

The main part of the content of the case is the case story. Beyond that, the theoretical background material which is necessary to analyze the case is part of the content. The theoretical background consists of tutorials, frameworks, glossaries, references and tools. The extent of given case story and background information is dependent on the instructional strategy. For instance, some of the innovation of the case could be hidden in order to stimulate own problem solution processes.

3.4.2   Instructional level

The instructional level presents the instructional objectives of the case and the instructional strategy to reach the objectives. All information about the instructional level should be included in accompanying teaching notes of the cases.

The first three elements of the instructional level (target groups, learning objectives and case context) are already described in previous chapters. The fourth element, the instructional strategy, is characterized by: Case difficulty

Adapted from Erskines and Leenders' difficulty cube (Erskine and Leenders 1989, p. 116), we distinguish the following dimensions of difficulty levels in case analysis:

- The problems and solutions are given. Students should get an insight into the specific process and context of decision making, evaluate the decisions which have been made and, eventually, propose alternative solutions.
- The problems are described, the students have to evaluate different approaches for solving the problems.
- Hidden problems have to be detected and analyzed, situations have to be evaluated and decisions to solve the problems have to be found.
- The case is given with incomplete information, the information needed for decision making has to be acquired from various information sources.

The appropriate level of case difficulty should be selected depending on the learning objectives and the target group.

3.4.2.1   Level of interactivity

The following basic types of interactivity can be distinguished:
- Access to information (navigation).
- Yes/No-Response.
- Free dialogue and interaction with the computer.

Principally, it is preferred to have a maximum of interactivity. Restrictions are personnel and technical constraints which often prevent the development of advanced interactive applications.

3.4.2.2   Level of guidance

The cases could have an instructional structure guiding the learner through the case by giving directions, asking questions etc. The extreme opposite to this is a case whose function is only to serve as a collection of information for extraction and analysis and which gives no guidance neither by a virtual agent nor by a teacher. The analysis of the case is then driven by the learner. The selection of the level of guidance depends on the skills of the target group (e.g. more guidance for undergraduate students) and the learning objectives (e.g. a collection of information for the improvement of information handling skills).

3.4.2.3   Organization of content

The content or parts of the content could be structured either sequential or with hyper linked modules. Similar to the level of guidance, the decision on how to organize the content is dependent on the skills of the learners and the learning objectives. Generally speaking, the benefits of modularizing the content should be exploited by separating the content into didactic meaningful modules. Nevertheless, it should be avoided to "over-modularize" because hypertexts with deep hierarchies which could confuse the learner.

3.4.2.4 Modules and the structure of modules

The case modules and a structure of modules are designed and developed according to the learning objectives. Modules are multimedia units which fulfill a certain instructional purpose and consist at least of one type of media (text, diagram, etc.). Activities in modules can be (Hall, 1997, p. 239):

- Pre-instructional (e.g. course overview, information of prerequisite skills required, objectives, navigational instructions, etc.).
- Information presentation.
- Student participation (e.g. click and drag exercise, systems simulation etc.).
- Testing/assessment (multiple choice, story-based questions etc.).

3.4.3 Presentation and delivery level

This view describes how the content is presented and delivered according to the instructional strategies presented above.

3.4.3.1 Level of multimedia usage

The presentation of the content of the cases may be rather text-based with less multimedia content and small multimedia components or aim to increase the media-richness by using advanced multimedia components like video or programmed animations. The usage of multimedia is dependent on the preferred cognition of the target group, the learning objectives and the instructional strategy. Multimedia elements to be used are for example text, images, diagrams and animations.

3.4.3.2 Carrier technology

Both the Internet, a hard medium or a combination of both could serve as a delivery medium for interactive cases. The selection of the delivery medium is mainly determined by financial and technical constraints of the learners, the educational institution, the case producers as well as the case publisher.

4.   DESIGN AND PRODUCTION PROCESS

4.1   Overview

The starting point for the design and production process should be a compilation of the case data called the analytical case. It represents the output of the data collection and case analysis phase. Additionally, some multimedia modules like videos of interviews, company movies and pictures might have been collected. The third outcome of the analysis is a description of the learning perspectives from which detailed learning objectives are derived.

A general model for the design and production process is depicted in Figure 3. Even if the general model looks very sequential, many of the activities could be run in parallel. Critical parts of the multimedia case should be developed in iterative cycles while using the prototype approach. The development process should especially consider several iterations between design, prototyping and evaluation.

4.2   Define case setup

The case setup is a requirements analysis adapted to the special needs of the development of multimedia case studies. Consequently, it is oriented towards the structure of the learning environment. It describes the target group, the learning objectives, and the case context and outlines the structure and technology of the multimedia case. During the development process, the case setup is refined and serves as an input for the definition of the teaching notes of the case at the end of the process. In the case of text-based case studies teaching notes are usually giving information on how to apply the case in courses. When developing an interactive case, the teaching notes also cover other aspects like requirements for the technical infrastructure, technical specifications etc.

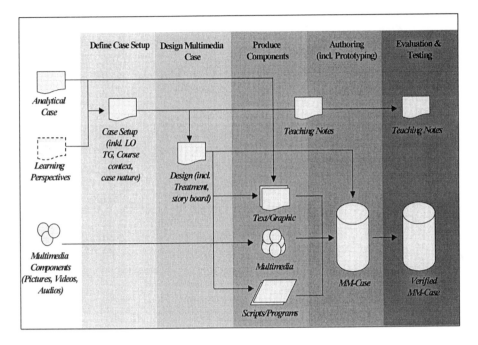

Figure 3: Design and production process.

Thus, the case setup has two purposes: Firstly to create a basis for the following design phase and secondly to give input for the accompanying teaching notes which should be delivered with cases.

4.3 Design multimedia case

Based on the case setup the modules, structures and user interfaces of the multimedia case are outlined and the technical standards and formats of the case are determined. The main objective of this phase is to give the producers a clear description of the process of learning and what should be produced. In how far these methods are applied is heavily dependent on the learning scenario and on how many different people are involved in the project. The main purpose of the design methods is to visualize and, thus, to anticipate the future case study in order to give designers, programmers and media producer a concrete basis for their work. The following design methods and tools can be useful:

- Treatment.
- Flowcharts.
- Storyboards.
- Scripts.

Using a certain method in the production process does not necessarily mean to apply this method to all parts of the case study. Depending on the complexity and the level of interactivity of the different modules, some methods are more applicable than others.

4.4   Produce components

According to the design of the case, the required text and multimedia components are produced. The general components that may be used in multimedia case are:

4.4.1   Text

In theory, plain text on a computer screen should be prevented as much as possible because it is static and a computer screen is not the best medium to read text from. However, text has some advantages as it is easy to produce and change and requires low bandwidth if the case is provided over networks.

Students are used to collecting information by reading. Thus, information gathering and structuring skills are addressed by using text. However, they are still used to sequential reading and not to moving in hypertext structures. Thus, it cannot be assumed that the students have read something prior to the page they are looking at the moment. Text is also a way to train students' abilities to structure unstructured information, although they will then most likely just print the pages with the information.

4.4.2   Images

Images form a large part of the look and feel of the case. Examples are buttons that enhance the navigation or images illustrating which information the participant is looking at.

The other usage of images is directly related to illustrate the case subject: photographs of people involved, equipment used, buildings, processes, etc. This can be shown in one photo or a photo strip in which a sequence is illustrated. The general purpose of these photos is to give students a realistic impression of the described company. Not every image that looks good on article also looks good on a computer screen. Furthermore, images require more bandwidth and are more difficult to develop in respect to text.

4.4.3   Animations

An animation is a sequence of different images. Typical animations are: sequences in an organization, future business processes, and other future changes. It can also be used for showing (digital) information and physical flows.

One should keep in mind not to oversimplify the issue. Animations can also be very useful to train students if they employ user-interventions to walk through the sequence.

4.4.4   Video

Video is usually more expensive than animation. The object filmed is an existing situation, not just a model for simplified presentation. It is therefore important to prepare the set as much as possible. It requires high bandwidth (or CD-ROM) and an "advanced" computer. The advantage is that it transfers the learning issue more vivid and gives the users the illusion of being close to the matter.

People are very used to looking at video. On the other hand it is harder to process information acquired by videos. Therefore should not contain an overflow of information (i.e., it should not be too long especially, if it only contains a "talking head" like in a interview).

4.4.5   Authoring

In the authoring phase the multimedia components are integrated into modules which are then assembled into the multimedia case-study. The concept of modules allows an efficient reuse of parts of the case for different kinds of learning processes. Thus, the modules can be recombined according to another learning scenario without reproducing the whole case.

Besides the multimedia modules the related teaching notes are written. They can be derived from the case setup where the target group, the learning objectives, course context and instructional strategy are already described.

The choice of an appropriate *authoring platform* really depends upon the requirements of the system. Is it a system which should be able to run without the users having any special programs on their computer? Is it an educational system, a distance learning system, a presentation system? It is always very difficult to actually name products, which are good for one purpose or the other, because of the dynamic of this field. In general authoring systems like Authorware and Director from Macromedia and Toolbook from Asymetrix are some of the more well-known platforms for systems, which will run on your computer, without any other support than maybe a video-player (like the MediaPlayer or Quicktime).

4.4.6   Testing and evaluating

In the testing and evaluation phase there is a fluid transition to the learning processes where the multimedia cases should be applied. The following steps may be distinguished (cf. Figure 4):
- Technical and functional testing.
- Quality review.
- Didactical testing.

Testing is related to the *functional and technical* check of the case study. Usually, this check will be done immediately after authoring by the developers of the case and, if necessary, they will step back to the authoring phase. Obviously, the following phases can only start when the functional and technical testing has been completed successfully.

The quality review includes the evaluation of the case-study according to selected quality criteria. The main criteria for quality assessments are (Alessi, 1991, p. 364):

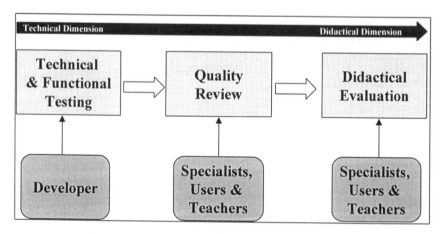

*Figure 4:*Testing and evaluation steps.

4.5   Presentation

- Graphical User Interface (look & feel of the surface, appropriated visualizing of content, consistency of the usage of symbols, colors etc.).

- Information presentation (right amount and quality of information, appropriate structure of the content according to the needs of the learners, etc.).
- Language and Grammar (consistency in conventions and wording, appropriateness of language to the target group etc.).

4.6   Interactivity and motivation

- Questions & Assignments (multiple choice or open questions, adequacy of questions to content and learning objectives, etc.).
- Feedback (constructive feedback, adequacy to the former question/action, etc.).
- Encouragement (interesting introduction, usage of motivational components, motivational feedback etc.).

4.7   Navigation and guidance

- Controllability (cancellation of programs, self-pacing etc.).
- Transparency (existence and clearness of navigation symbols, navigation bars/maps and menus).
- Other criteria (printing facilities, saving of intermediate results etc.).

4.8   Additional material

- Teaching Notes (description of target group, learning objectives, degree of detail, description of all relevant aspects for the application of the case, providing of solutions etc).
- Background material (description of theories, models to understand the case study, glossaries etc.).

The usage of these criteria is dependent on the intended "nature" of the case. For instance, if it was planned to construct a pool of information with an intended renunciation of interactivity the employment of interactivity related criteria would be misleading. Thus, by reviewing the quality of the case, the underlying target group, learning objectives and course context should be taken into account. Independent experts and users should do the quality review.

The didactical evaluation can only be done in learning processes, either real or "simulated". Here the achievement of intended learning objectives is measured and evaluated. The tools for evaluating the student are usually tests or assignments in the case study or in the course where the case study is applied. Although the results of these tools may give information on the student's performance it is even more difficult to evaluate the effectiveness and the efficiency of the multimedia case-studies against other didactic instruments. In order to get reliable results on effectiveness one should use different didactic instruments (e.g. a multimedia and a article-based case study) with fairly identical students (in terms of knowledge, motivation and intellectual capabilities) in courses with identical content and learning objectives.

5.   CONCLUSIONS AND FURTHER RESEARCH

This article has presented the concept of learning environments which embraces all relevant factors for the educational design of interactive multimedia case studies. Target groups, learning objectives and the course context are essential variables for user-centered learning processes and have to be analyzed thoroughly prior to the production of the case.

For the process of design and production, a general model has been outlined which also stresses the importance of the learning environment. Its most critical step is the didactical testing as the final review if the case really supports learning. With regard to this, further research has to be carried out to compare the effectiveness of interactive case studies compared to other educational tools, esp. article-based cases. This will be both costly and time-consuming, but it is essential to prove that interactive multimedia case studies really add educational value to learners.

REFERENCES

Alessi, S.M. (1991). *Computer-Based Instruction*. Englewood Cliffs, N.J.: Prentice Hall.
Barnes, L.B., Christensen, C.R., & Hansen, A.J. (1994). *Teaching and the Case Method*. Boston, Mass.: Harvard Business School Press.
Bieber, M., & Isakowitz, T. (1995). Designing Hypermedia Applications. *Communications of the ACM, 38*(8), 26-29.
Bloom, B.S., & Krathwohl, D.R. (1984). *Taxonomy of Educational Objectives*. Handbook I: Cognitive Domain. New York, N.Y.: Addison-Wesley.
Erskine, J.A., Leenders, M.R., & Mauffette-Leenders, L.A. (1981). *Teaching with Cases*. London, Ontario: University of Western Ontario.
Erskine, J.A., & Leenders, M.R. (1989). *Case Research: The Case Writing Process*. London, Ontario: University of Western Ontario.
Fuchs, R. (1990). Change in Motives and Attitudes Induced by Instruction Method. In E.A. Stuhler, & M. Ó Suilleabhain, (Eds.), *Research on the Case Method – in a Non-Case Environment* (pp. 71-128). Cologne, Germany: Boehlau.
Hall, B. (1997). *Web-Based Training Cook Book*. New York, N.Y.: John Wiley & Sons.

Huitt, W.G. (1996). *Systems Model of Human Behaviour.* Available from World Wide Web:(http://www.valdosta.edu/~whuitt/psy702/sysmdlhb.html).

Masoner, M. (1988). *An Audit of the Case Study Method.* New York, N.Y.: Praeger.

Winterburn, R. (1990). The View from a Different Perspective – Some Other Thoughts and Suggestions about Teaching and the Case Method. In E.A. Stuhler, & M. Ó Suilleabhain, (Eds.), *Research on the Case Method – in a Non-Case Environment* (pp. 219-234). Cologne, Germany: Boehlau.

The Role of Problem Based Learning and Technology Support in a 'Spoon-Fed' Undergraduate Environment

Frank P. Forsythe
University of Ulster, Jordanstown, Northern Ireland

1.   INTRODUCTION

This article assesses the impact of introducing change to the method of teaching a 12-week introductory economics module within an inter-disciplinary undergraduate program at a United Kingdom higher education institution. The primary aim of the change in teaching methods was to encourage a more active involvement by students in the learning process and to give less emphasis to the traditional lecture/tutorial format that had been employed previously. It was hoped that the new approach would promote greater satisfaction among students and generally enrich the learning experience for both teachers and students.

In an effort to promote active student participation in the learning process and develop independent learning skills a PBL format was adopted in both modules (Barrows, 1986; Albanese & Mitchell, 1993), along with a greater utilization of technology support measures than had been undertaken previously. The primary problem in implementing the new approach was the considerable planning required to organize physical resources that were geared towards large group traditional teaching methods and, where a number of staff were involved with the module, to retain the support of teaching staff more experienced in transferring information to students than facilitating small group interaction.

T.A. Johannessen, A. Pedersen and K. Petersen (eds.),
Educational Innovation in Economics and Business VI, 147–161.
© 2002 *Kluwer Academic Publishers. Printed in the Netherlands.*

2. CHANGING MARKET FOR UNDERGRADUATE ECONOMICS

In a broader context, there can be no denying that the undergraduate market for economics is changing. The fall in popularity of economics in the 1990's appears to be a general phenomenon. The decline in applications for single discipline economics programs that is evident within the UK university sector (Abbott & Williams, 1998), is also a feature within the USA (Siegfried, 1997; Siegfried & Scott, 1994; Willis & Peiper, 1996) and Australia (Lewis & Norris, 1996). In the case of the USA it is suggested that teaching methods dominated by traditional 'chalk and talk' lectures with rare use of small group, interactive teaching techniques may be a contributing factor in causing the decline in applications for single discipline economics (Becker & Watts 1996; Becker, 1997).

Within the UK the plight of economics is not ignored by the quality media (Financial Times, 1995a, 1995b Times, 1995, Economist, 1997) which emphasize the technically difficult and abstract nature of the analytic method of economics and its tendency to be perceived as boring by many of those who study it. The falling popularity within the UK is also reflected at A-level, with the number of A-level economics candidates falling significantly in recent years (Times, 1995). The latter trend suggests that future applications for single discipline undergraduate economics will continue to fall in the UK (Finch & Frederiksen, 1998).

The decline in numbers applying for single discipline economics programs has prompted many UK universities, particularly the vocationally orientated new universities established after the ending of the university-polytechnic divide in 1992 (Forsythe, 1996), to offer economics within inter-disciplinary programs along with business studies, accounting, politics, law, public policy, computing etc.

The interdisciplinary context of economics teaching within many UK universities poses a problem if students perceive that economics is more difficult, abstract and boring relative to the other disciplines studied (perceptions also identified by Abbott & Williams, 1998, particularly within the new universities). Failure to respect and resolve these student perceptions will lead to disillusionment with economics and, ultimately, 'switch-off' by students within the program.

'Spoon-feeding', in the sense of over-teaching at the expense of teaching methods that encourage active student participation in the learning process, represents a short-sighted response that fails to resolve negative student perceptions of the learning experience. 'Spoon-feeding' typically involves 'more of the same' from the student viewpoint and fails to stimulate student interest and enrich the learning process.

3.   MOTIVATING STUDENTS IN ECONOMICS: SOME EXPERIENCES AT UUJ

The 130 first year students taking the introductory economics module at UUJ represent a very diverse student body, with only 40% registered on a single or joint discipline program involving further full time (FT) study in economics (the 'specialist' group). These students require a minimum level of economics before taking more advanced economics modules in second year. The remaining 60% 'non-specialist' students are registered on a joint discipline program in law and government, and do not take further study in economics after the introductory module. Around 20% of the non-specialist group are part-timers in full-time employment.

Students have one 2-hour lecture and a 1-hour tutorial per week over a 12-week semester. There are seven tutorial groups (3 specialist FT, 3 non-specialist FT and one non-specialist PT), each comprising 18-20 students. Tutorial rooms accommodate 24 students and the lecture theatre 250 students. Attendance at tutorials is compulsory, but not lectures and, invariably, lecture attendance by non-specialist students begins to deteriorate after 5 weeks. Providing separate specialist and non-specialist modules in economics is not an option available to the subject team. The different characteristics of the student body are summarized in Table 1.

Table 1: First year module in economics: student characteristics.

Student Group	Median A-Level Entry Score	Economics at A-Level	Numerate Subjects at A-Level	Arts only at A-Level (no economics)
	Proportion of Students with Given Characteristics			
Specialist (FT)	20	51	30	32
Non-specialist (FT)	22	5	6.5	77
Non-specialist (PT)	n.a.	0	0	100

3.1   The old regime

Although the students are well qualified in terms of pre-entry A-level scores[1], the experience of the subject team in economics is that Arts-based students tend to find the analytic method of economics (concepts, abstract

---

[1] The average A- Level entry score for the specialist group (20) is marginally below the average economics entry grade at traditional universities (22) and significantly above the average economics entry grade at new universities (12-13). See Abbott & Williams (1998). UK students typically take three A-Levels prior to university entrance. For each A-Level, points are awarded as follows: Grade A=10 points; Grade B=8 points; Grade C=6 points; Grade D=4 points; Grade E=2 points. Grade F is a failure at A-Level.

models and diagrams) extremely difficult to handle. Since graphs are the primary method of representing economic ideas at the introductory level, difficulty in handling or 'reading' graphs will adversely affect one's understanding of the underlying concepts and, consequently, inhibit examination performance. Although one-third of the specialist group has an Arts based background with no prior knowledge of economics, it is the non-specialist students with these characteristics (who have no long-term commitment to the discipline) who pose a significant teaching challenge to the subject team.

The challenge for the subject team is to provide sufficient analytic content for the specialist group while retaining the interest of the non-specialists. The latter tend to exhibit extremely negative perceptions regarding 'traditional' economics and under conventional teaching methods have been difficult to motivate. Tensions within the subject team related to the minimum level of analytic content to be contained in the module to satisfy the second level requirement of specialist students. Tensions between the subject team and Faculty arose from the contrasting perceptions of the learning experience and examination performance of non-specialist students relative to the other disciplines.

Previous responses by the teaching team had been to reduce the analytic content of the module and to over-teach the remainder. The consequences of over-teaching represent the antithesis of a sound undergraduate learning environment. Tutorials tended to degenerate into mini-lectures with minimal student participation. Overall, the teaching approach was primarily one of information transfer from teacher to student. There was no management of non-contact time and student input was based on one written assignment to be submitted near the end of the teaching period. The emphasis on the transfer of information from teacher to student created an environment where students generally received rather than generated information. Teacher-student communication was one-way with teacher-student interaction minimal and student-student interaction non-existent. Within such an environment, students tended to lack confidence in respect of decision taking and, despite having tutorial sessions, had little opportunity to work in small-group situations requiring interactive skills. These negative outcomes associated with over-teaching impacted negatively on other modules owing to a poor development of independent learning skills. Despite the existence of diverse technology support systems within the Faculty, incorporating free and easy access to a comprehensive range of networked software packages, the Internet and personal email account, the full information-generating potential of these systems was not integrated formally within the teaching program and, consequently, was under-utilized by students.

3.2   The new regime: main features

The primary aim of the new regime was to promote student participation in the learning process and to develop independent learning skills in students. To achieve these aims a radically new teaching approach was adopted within the administrative, timetabling and teaching resource constraints that were beyond the control of the subject team. The new approach involved both contact and non-contact learning periods.

- The 2-hour conventional lecture, with its emphasis on the transfer of information from teacher to student, was replaced with a 'workshop' approach in which teacher-student and student-student interaction dominated. During these 2-hour large group sessions, initial teacher-led 'information' sessions would give way to student-centered activity in which worksheets containing simple tasks had to be completed by each student and submitted to the teacher at the end of the session (providing feedback to the teacher). Students were encouraged to work in pairs or in units of 3-4 when completing the worksheet. The aim of these sessions was to promote confidence and familiarity with key analytic concepts and graphs within an informal 'shared' workshop environment – activities included the manipulation of diagrams, simple numerical calculations, identifying real-world applications etc (see Cohn & Cohn, 1994). The primary role of the lecturer during workshop sessions was to provide general assistance as the need arose; the size and layout of the lecture theatre permitted easy access to any particular group of students.

- Tutorials followed a PBL format. Each of the original seven tutorial groups of 20 students was split into two smaller 'discussion' groups that shared the same seminar room. Each discussion group operated independently throughout the 12-week semester. Since discussion groups were time-tabled to meet for one-hour only per week it was decided to adopt the format depicted in Fig. 1, which was repeated every 2-weeks.

The usual PBL group structure and procedure were adopted. For each task there was rotating responsibility for discussion leader and recorder, initial discussion and identification of learning objectives, delegation of study tasks to be undertaken by group members during non-contact hours and feedback discussion one-week later. Discussion groups had two 40-minute sessions to organize and assimilate a response to each task. Finally, at the end of their respective feedback sessions, groups were required to present their response to both the tutor and the other discussion group (20-minutes). The latter feature provided an opportunity for general class discussion and tutor feedback. The tasks required students to apply the economic ideas met during the large group session to real world situations (i.e. housing markets, market failure, labour markets etc). Discussion groups also had to identify relevant Internet sources used to complete the task.

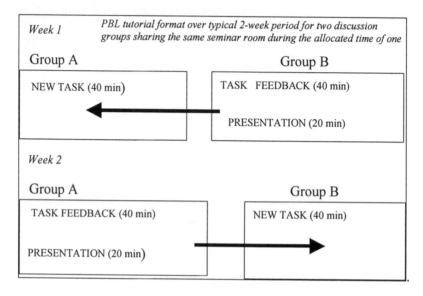

Figure 1: First year module in economics.

In addition to the necessity of operating within strict time-scales, a second potential difficulty with the new tutorial format was that five of the six tutors responsible for tutorial sessions had no previous experience with PBL. Each tutor was fully briefed on the potential benefits of group tasking and of adopting a facilitating role rather than dominate group discussions. Tutors were specifically requested to avoid resorting to mini-lectures during tutorial sessions (we return to the staff issue in relation to Table 3 below).

- The computer-aided learning package, WinEcon[2], was adopted for the first time by the teaching team. The software allows teaching staff to monitor how the package is being utilized by individual users. Both these attributes - customization and monitoring- are crucial properties if computer-aided learning is to be fully integrated within the learning regime. Students were expected to use the package in their own time and could earn up to a maximum of 10% of the module assessment marks for

---

[2] WinEcon is a computer-based learning package covering the whole syllabus of a first year undergraduate economics course. It has won a variety of awards in Britain and Europe. The software was developed by a consortium of UK university economics departments and is supported by over 150 associate member institutions world-wide. See the WinEcon website at http://sosig.ac.uk/winecon and Soper & Hobbs, (eds.) (1996); Hobbs & Judge, (1996); Sloman, (1995).

working through the interactive tutorials and completing a series of self-assessed tests

- Other technology support measures included the on-line availability of all teacher- generated information that was to be used in the large-group sessions (this material was produced in Microsoft Powerpoint format to aid the explanation of key economic concepts and graphs); general advice on how to structure answers to economic questions was also available on-line and students were encouraged to e-mail tutors with individual queries etc. Students were also encouraged to use the Internet to access information relevant to the module.

3.3   The new regime – evaluation

Student views on the new learning regime (Table 2) were obtained from responses to a questionnaire sent to students after the final examination. The questionnaire was used to obtain detailed comments from students on all aspects of the learning regime in addition to simple yes/no quantitative responses. The qualitative information provided by the detailed comments allowed one to fully assess student experiences with the PBL tutorial format, WinEcon and the other technology support measures associated with the module. The response rate was high and the composition of questionnaire respondents closely matched that of the full student cohort. Students failing the final module examination had additional questions to answer and this provided the subject team with a more comprehensive feedback on the views of this particular group of students.

Table 2: First year module in economics: student views.

ATTITUDES of questionnaire respondents taking introductory economics module	Specialist (%)	Non-specialist (%)
Questionnaire Response Rate:	63	72
Proportion of respondents agreeing that:		
PBL tutorial format should be continued:	73	69
Economics was relevant to other modules studied:	85	64
Economics was more difficult than other modules:	31*	86
Students failing final module examination		
After how many weeks did failure seem inevitable?:	n.a.	4-5
Views Concerning Technology Support		
(i) *WinEcon found to be generally helpful*:	81	83
(ii) *Web used regularly for information*:	62	50
(iii) *on-line lecture availability helpful?*:	88	92
(iv) *other on-line help utilized?*:	54	61

* This result reflects the experience of joint discipline students.

3.4   The new learning environment: student views

Table 2 shows that students had a generally positive view of the learning experience. A clear majority of respondents recommended that the PBL tutorial format should be continued and, in respect of technology support, both WinEcon and the on-line teacher information source were found to be particularly helpful. Surprisingly, only a handful of students used the e-mail facility to access staff directly, though the regular use of the Internet by 50% of non-specialist and 62% of specialist students was regarded as a successful outcome by the subject team. The range of information sources accessed by regular Web users was quite impressive (the significance of WinEcon and Web use in relation to assessed performance is discussed below).

Regardless of performance in the final examination, the vast majority of non-specialist students (and a significant number of joint discipline specialist students) felt that economics was more difficult than other modules taken in the first semester (government and law); a majority of these students did feel, however, that the content of the introductory module had relevance within the overall context of the particular undergraduate program undertaken. These two particular attributes – difficulty and relevance – provide important feedback information to the subject team on the overall academic content of the module: a high difficulty rating suggests that the analytic content has not been pitched too low, while a high relevance rating suggests that the module has gained acceptance from students. There is no doubt that an element within the non-specialist group are still prone to 'switch-off' after a relatively short period; non-specialists who failed the final examination felt that they would do so only after 4-5 weeks into the semester. A small number of non-specialist students did find the PBL format frustrating. These students tended to have negative views across all categories listed in Table 2 – PBL, module relevance and difficulty, WinEcon, Web, on-line facilities etc. Unfortunately, the experience of these particular students (involving the same 2-3 discussion groups) would appear to have suffered from poor tutor-student interaction as this was the dominant reason given for their PBL criticisms. It is very possible that a better tutor-student interaction for these particular groups may have generated a more positive view of the PBL experience and a higher relevance rating. This emphasizes the key role of tutors as facilitators within a PBL small group context, particularly where first year students are concerned. Although tutors should not dominate student discussions, a good facilitator still has a vital role to play to ensure the process continues smoothly.

The qualitative feedback of respondents identified very clearly the perceived benefits of PBL and the impetus given to the learning experience when one is a member of a small group with responsibility for contributing to the knowledge base of the whole group. Other positive features of PBL group activity emphasized by students were the sharing of views and getting acquainted with one's peers – valuable attributes for newcomers to a university environment.

Respondents also noted the general benefits, and pressures, from working within a PBL small group context - working to deadlines, coping with group responsibilities and commitments, open to new ideas, more in-depth discussions of syllabus content, work sharing and being better prepared for the final examination because the PBL format obliged students to work throughout the semester. These represent the 'direct' benefits of PBL that enhance the learning experience within the PBL module itself.

A number of respondents made explicit reference to additional 'externality' effects that aided their studies in other modules. The positive externality effects emphasized by students related to improved study skills, the discovery of valuable Internet sources, and the development of problem solving skills, all of which were perceived to improve performance in other modules. The externality effect suggests that the benefits of PBL are wider in scope than the direct benefits noted above, whereby the improved learning 'ethos' extends to other areas of the curriculum. This important result is discussed below.

3.5　　Examination performance

The examination performance of students (Table 3) is based on the official results of all students taking the final 'closed book' examination for the module. In terms of examination performance, the impact of the new regime is most evident on non-specialist students. The median score of non-specialist students in 1999, the first examination following the new teaching regime (a) matched the specialist group and (b) represented an improvement over the previous year under the old 'spoon-fed' environment. In addition, the failure rate for non-specialists in the final examination not only matched that of specialist students, but was also significantly lower than the corresponding rate the previous year. Table 3 also shows that this outcome was repeated in 2000, the second year following the new teaching methods. Overall, the examination performance of non-specialist students under the new regime is encouraging.

Table 4 also shows the results of linear regressions undertaken in an effort to identify possible influences on final examination performance in economics (EXAM)[3]. All regression results are based on the 1999 cohort of

---

[3] The results depicted for each model represent the final regression after insignificant variables had been excluded. Variables used in the regressions:

students. Models 1 & 2 are based on the full data available for all students taking the introductory economics module; Model 3 is based on questionnaire respondents only (i.e. those students discussed in Table 2), giving access to additional information that could be incorporated in the regression tests. All models use the single discipline economics specialists as the control group, making the constant statistically significant in all the results.

Table 3: First year module in economics: examination performance under the new system.

The new teaching regime was introduced in 1999	Specialist (%)	Non-specialist (%)
Final 'closed book' examination (under new system, 1999) (median score):	53	52
minimum-maximum scores:	(3-74)	(5-82)
Failure rate	(20.0)	(21.6)
Final 'closed book' examination (under new system, 2000) (median score):	56	55
minimum-maximum scores:	(20-76)	(19-68)
Failure rate:	(12.1)	(12.8)
For comparison Final 'closed book' examination (under old 'spoon-fed' system, 1998) (median score):	54	46
minimum-maximum scores:	(20-70)	(8-67)
Failure rate:	(23.0)	(35.0)

The single most important explanatory variable on EXAM is whether or not the student failed another module (FOTHER); poor performers in economics tended to perform poorly elsewhere, with 76% of those failing economics also failing at least one other module. This suggests that poor

---

EXAM (dependent variable in all regressions): examination score (maximum 100)
FOTHER: student failed at least one final examination in another module;
WINECON: score awarded for using Winecon (maximum 100%);
MSCORE: score awarded in multiple choice test three weeks before final examination;
PTIME: mature student attending university on a part-time basis;
AESCORE: grade attained in A-level economics, if applicable;
WWW: dummy variable indicating that student made use of internet for information.
Two additional variables mentioned in the text which were not significant in any of the regressions were:
ARTS: students with an Arts A-Level background, with no economics, pre-university entrance;
ALECON: dummy variable indicating whether students had taken A-Level economics regardless of grade prior to university entrance.

examination performance in economics is not due to any inherent inadequacies of the new regime. Although FOTHER may be regarded as a proxy for the general pre-examination preparedness of a student, it was omitted from subsequent analysis in an effort to identify potentially poor examination performers using information that is available prior to the final examination. In this respect the influence of WINECON, the second most significant explanatory variable overall after FOTHER, is of particular importance from a monitoring viewpoint. WINECON, the score earned from using WinEcon, could be regarded as a proxy for hidden student qualities such as 'self-discipline', 'diligence' or 'independent study skills', since students earned their score by working at their own discretion and convenience during non-contact time throughout the 12-week teaching period. All regression models show that EXAM is positively related to WINECON; indeed, 60% of poor performers in the economics examination (i.e. EXAM W 45) did not use WinEcon. In terms of identifying potentially poor performers in economics, the possible link between WINECON and EXAM is very important, since the WinEcon package allows one to identify with confidence problem-users as early as four weeks into the module. Given the observation noted in Table 2 that poor performers tend to 'switch-off' after 4-5 weeks, the value of computer-aided packages with a monitoring facility such as WinEcon, cannot be overestimated.

Table 4: First Year Module in Introductory Economics: regression analysis of 1999 student cohort.

Estimating possible influences on examination performance (EXAM) under the new system			
Variable	Model 1 (All Students)	Model 2 (All Students)	Model 3 (Q-Respondents only)
FOTHER	-17.9 (-6.7)	-	-
WINECOM	1.5 (5.5)	1.8 (6.1)	2.0 (4.6)
MCSCORE	0.24 (3.1)	-	-
PTIME	-	15.2 (3.42)	-
AESCORE	-	1.94 (4.4)	-
WWW	-	-	16.6 (4.4)
Constant	33.7 (8.03)	33.8 (15.1)	26.1 (6.7)
Adjusted R2	0.52	0.39	0.38
F-value	41.5	24.6	19.1

Note: all regression coefficients and F-values significant at 0.01 significance level. See Note 3 for variable definition.

Model 2, with FOTHER omitted, also suggests that having A-Level economics per se does not explain EXAM (i.e. ALECON was not significant), whereas having a high grade in A-Level economics (AESCORE) does contribute to EXAM. The superior performance of part-time students within the non-specialist group is also highlighted in Model 2. In previous years the part-timers had extreme difficulty with economics and had argued for the module to be omitted from their particular undergraduate program.

Model 3, also omitting FOTHER, contained the same variables as Model 2 but incorporated additional information derived from questionnaire respondents that could not be included in the other regressions (WWW use, for example). The importance of technology support, namely WINECON and WWW, on EXAM is highlighted in Model 3. Only these two influences exerted a significant explanatory influence on EXAM. Similar to WINECON, use of the Internet during non-contact time to generate information also suggests the presence of hidden qualities that enhance examination performance. The significance of this result is discussed below.

It should be noted that the final examination in economics did not require specific information from either WinEcon or the Internet, and in this respect use of these technology support facilities could not exert a direct influence on EXAM. Rather, these variables are highly correlated with EXAM because their successful use requires the same hidden student attributes noted above that are also needed for a good examination result.

3.6   The new learning environment: conclusions concerning examination performance

It is viewed as a measure of success of the new regime that variables such as ARTS (Arts A-levels with no economics) and ALECON (possession of A-level economics per se, regardless of grade) appeared to have no significant influence on examination performance. Since these variables emphasize basic differences in the characteristics of students that might be expected to account for differences in exam performance, the new regime may represent a fairer teaching system relative to the conventional lecture format. Arts-based students were likely to do as well (or as bad) as those students with economics related A-Levels.

As already noted, WINECON and WWW may be regarded as proxies for hidden qualities within students that are difficult to identify, but which are clearly important for examination performance. Hidden qualities such as 'self-discipline', 'diligence' and 'independent learning' need to be encouraged and developed in first year students so that each cohort of students get the maximum gain as they progress through successive years of the undergraduate program. If the absence or lower development of such qualities can be identified via the use of technology support facilities, as the above regressions suggest, technology support becomes a crucial element in terms of managing the learning environment. Similarly, by obliging students to generate information during non-contact time, PBL group-work is helping to develop these same vital qualities in students.

Certainly under the old spoon-fed and over-taught regime, it would have been impossible to identify poor performers until after the final examination. In this sense the element of randomness in final examination performance that characterized the old regime has been reduced. Overall, the subject team regarded the new regime as a significant improvement over the previous over-taught approach.

3.7 Benefits of PBL from teaching viewpoint

There was no reduction in syllabus content from the previous year and student coverage of individual topics tended to be more comprehensive and varied relative to the conventional lecture-directed approach.

PBL obliged students to work continuously throughout the 12-week semester, covering the whole syllabus rather than focus on a few areas for examination purposes. The 'work-sharing' aspect of PBL requires students to work for the group during non-contact time with specific outcomes to attain. Much of this time is wasted by students working under a conventional teaching format. Work-sharing represents a key property of PBL that generates dual benefits for those participating in the learning environment: students gain from sharing of the work load to complete a task, while staff can exercise more control over non-contact learning periods.

Finally, there can be no greater pleasure for a teacher than to experience the synergy that results from a successful grouping. Such groups become extremely efficient at organizing the learning environment, via additional meetings during non-contact periods and the transfer of information via summary reports, photocopies, fax, email etc. The final year PBL experiment was particularly fortunate in this respect with the emergence of a number of dynamic groupings.

4. CONCLUSION

In the context of teaching economics within an interdisciplinary program, the adoption of teaching methods that incorporate a PBL format produced very favorable results. Although a positive outcome of PBL is dependent on a number of factors – not least the willingness/ability of staff to act as an effective facilitator – given the right conditions, PBL was found to be an excellent teaching method, generating both direct and indirect outcomes that benefit the whole program. The potential benefits of PBL are not confined to those elements of the curriculum using PBL. The direct 'immediate' benefits that accrue within the module using PBL methods include a broader coverage of the syllabus, effective use of non-contact hours, and the hidden benefits generated by the dynamics of a successful group (extra meetings, more formal/useful transfer of information via photocopies, summary reports etc). Positive externalities that generate benefits elsewhere on the curriculum include the development of independent learning and study skills. In this context where PBL can be adopted, to maximize the 'external' benefits PBL should be implemented sooner rather than later in the curriculum.

However, in terms of using PBL in first year modules, careful monitoring of groups throughout the semester is imperative. With first year students there is a greater likelihood of poor self-discipline, which can lead to a breakdown of the group. In this respect staff play a crucial role.

As for technology support, availability of the necessary technology does not guarantee its use. However, as with PBL, when it is used effectively in this role it can also generate widespread 'external' benefits throughout the curriculum. This article suggests that, particularly in the case of first year students, a very desirable attribute of technology support where it is used by students as a source of information is that its use can be monitored, as is the case of WinEcon, This allows identification of students with poor self-discipline skills during non-contact time: such students are highly likely to exert a negative influence within a group. In the case of WinEcon, after four weeks it was possible to identify those most likely to perform poorly in the examination. This aspect of WinEcon was just as important as its usefulness in explaining key economic concepts. Mechanisms for monitoring student use of Internet sources is also recommended as a means of facilitating early identification students with weak independent learning skills.

REFERENCES

Abbott, A., & Williams, R. (1998). Recent trends in enrolments for UK economics degrees, discussion article, Economics Division, Sunderland Business School, University of Sunderland, May 1998. This article was included as a supplementary item at the Royal Economic Society Conference of Heads of University Departments of Economics (CHUDE), University of Nottingham , 1999.

Albanese, M., & Mitchell, S. (1993). Problem-based learning: a review of literature on its outcomes and implementation issues. *Academic Medicine, 68*, No. 1, 52-81.

Barrows, H. (1986). A taxonomy of problem-based learning methods. *Medical Education, 20,* 481-486.

Becker, W. (1997). Teaching economics to undergraduates. *Journal of Economic Literature, 35,* 1347-1373.

Becker, W. & Watts, M. (1996). Chalk and talk: a national survey on teaching undergraduate economics. *American Economic Review, 86,* No. 2, Articles & Proceedings, 448-453.

Cohn, E., & Cohn, S. (1994). Graphs and learning in principles of economics. *American Economic Review, 84,* (2), Articles & Proceedings, 197-200.

Economist (1997). The puzzling failure of economics. *Economist, 23* August, p. 11.

Financial Times (1995). Decay of the dismal science. *Financial Times,* 28 March.

Financial Times (1995). Pupils abandon dismal science. *Financial Times,* 20 March.

Financial Times (1999). Britain's top 100 universities: indicators of performance. *Financial Times,* 1-5 April, 1999.

Finch, J., & Frederiksen, M. (1998). *Report on a survey of economics graduates, 1982-1996.* Department of Economics, University of Aberdeen.

Forsythe, F. (1996). Viewing the university gap. *Education Economics, 4,* No. 1, 45-63.

Hobbs, P., & Judge, G. (1996). WinEcon: a new generation computer based learning package. *Social Science Computing Review, 14.*

Lewis, P. & Norris, K. (1997). Recent changes in economics enrolments, *Economic Articles, 16,* No. 1, 1-13.

Siegfried, J. (1997). Trends in undergraduate economics degrees: an update. *Journal of Economic Education, 28,* No. 3, 279-82.

Siegfried, J., & Scott, C. (1994). Recent trends in undergraduate economics degrees. *Journal of Economic Education, 25,* No. 3, 281-86.

Sloman, J. (1995), WinEcon: software review, *Economic Journal, 105,* 1327-1346.

Soper, J. & Hobbs, P. (Eds.), (1996). *The WinEcon Workbook: Interactive Economics.* Oxford: Blackwell Publishers. [also Cambridge, Massachusetts, USA].

Times (1995), A-level economics falls from favour, The Times, 27 March.

Willis, R. & Pieper, P. (1996), The economics major: a cross-sectional view, *Journal of Economic Education, 27,* No. 4, 337-349.

From Information to Knowledge: Teaching and Learning Online

Herb Thompson
Murdoch University, Murdoch, Australia

1.   INTRODUCTION

"Computer-based learning has not been immune from the missionary zeal so characteristic of applications of hypertext and hypermedia. Claims and counterclaims of the supposed effectiveness of hypertext and multimedia abound, usually pregnant with unstated assumptions about the nature of learning". (Hammond, 1993, p. 51)

There are a number of forces driving the transformation towards a knowledge-based global economy. The growing role of information and communications technologies, a continuing shift towards services, and the globalization of markets and social formations are just some of the key ones (Pilat, p. 5). Within this environment an increasing number of firms now see themselves, in the first instance, as creators, organizers and developers of knowledge (Drake, p. 24). This is combined with devolution of managerial responsibilities, more flexibility and outsourcing, and a renewed emphasis on networking within the firm to enhance the efficiency of information flow (Vickery & Wurzburg).

The primary argument pursued herein is that it is not "knowledge" which "travels fast, through a variety of distribution channels, many of which were unknown only a few years ago", which has been stated as the opening premise of this international conference. Rather, it is information that travels fast. Knowledge advances very slowly and continues to remain a very scarce commodity in economics (the word 'commodity' is used advisedly).

T.A. Johannessen, A. Pedersen and K. Petersen (eds.),
Educational Innovation in Economics and Business VI, 163–177.

Information is not knowledge. We mustn't confuse the thrill of acquiring or distributing information quickly with the more daunting task of converting it into knowledge and wisdom. Regardless of how advanced our computers become, they are not (yet, in any case) a substitute for our own basic cognitive skills of awareness, perception, reasoning and judgment.

"Information is a descriptive term for an economically interesting category of goods which has not hitherto been accorded much attention by economic theorists" (Arrow, p. 138). Knowledge, on the other hand, "is a complex structure of heterogeneous thoughts, each available at zero marginal cost but useable only together with resources available only at positive, and often very high cost" (Machlup, p. 8 & p. 10). One delineation (drawn heuristically) between the business and academic communities is that information is the lifeblood of business whereas knowledge is the *raison d'etre* of the academy. This is not to demean either community, but simply to underline the difference between them. Therefore, questions that should be the focus of attention include:

1. Are teachers/learners in the academy any more capable of transforming information into socially meaningful and equitably distributed knowledge via computer-mediated-communication than they have been through alternative mediums in the past?
2. If the capability exists, how exactly might this be accomplished?
3. Do members of the business community truly want knowledge which is open-ended, boundless, and continually under examination, critique and contestation; or are they, as one might expect, desirous of cheaper, measurable and more efficiently produced data sets, in the essential quest for market share and profit-maximization?

Although knowledge is partially constructed from information, and informative understanding may be gleaned from various knowledges, it is not requisite that ever the twain shall meet. The cynosure of this paper will be to examine the interrelation of the first two questions. An un-dogmatic agnosticism is professed with reference to question three and therefore, it will be set-aside in this instance.

The following section proceeds with a specification of the main argument: that is, computer-mediated-communication provides the potential but not the actuality of the development of knowledge. With particular reference to web-based teaching/learning in economics, the legitimation of knowledge continues to be under-theorized, particularly with regard to electronic transmission. The determinism of the "progressive narrative" within and around the "hypertext revolution" deserves careful scrutiny, particularly in its application to pedagogy. The "progressive narrative", to which we allude, is that which represents hypertext as the latest flowering in a long march of democratic progress originating in the displacement of Platonic authority by the lesser authority of the written word. (See for instance, Landow, p. 13).

Section three puts forward the argument that much economic education is based upon the pursuit of a particular form of ignorance, rather than knowledge. If the utilization of the newest forms of technology are used to continue this process of increasing and enhancing ignorance, then the narrative should be viewed as one of regressivity, irrespective of the most powerful software and hardware that is electronically available. Both the technology used, and the manner in which it is used, arises from social contestation and struggle. The production, exchange and distribution of knowledge will partially be a result of this social process. The computer provides a new medium of struggle, and in that sense has the potential to advance knowledge. But the actuality of the production, exchange and equitable distribution of knowledge is determined socially, not technologically.

Attention is given in section four to the praxis of teaching/learning economic knowledges via computer-mediated-communication. The author has, for the past three years, been teaching courses in economics via the Internet. Except for the provision of a textbook and the necessity of a proctored final exam, all work and communication takes place via computer. As will be described below, the two most important elements in teaching/learning online include the hypertext medium and the discussion forum. The courses were constructed with epistemological principles informed by Vygotsky and Scribner (Vygotsky; Tobach, E., et al.); and in turn these principles are continually re-examined based upon collaborative 'learning-by-doing'. Conclusions are then drawn based on the dialectical interaction between theory and praxis.

2. INFORMATION OR KNOWLEDGE

"Professor Reed saw an alarming example of reduced quality of thought when he assigned his students several chapters in a recent and respected biography on Samuel Coleridge. Rather than do the assignment, a student went to Web pages and came back with odd bits and pieces of information, some of them trite, some of them repetitious, many wrong. The technology can sometimes reduce knowledge to information, forget about wisdom." (The Australian 19/8/97, p. 14)

One of the most important advantages of Web-enhanced teaching is access to huge quantities of current information. Web sites that provide economic data are, or can be, updated much more frequently than the printed materials; and a web-based course can be updated even while the course is in progress. Online journals and working paper series are most convenient and, for universities with small libraries, very important sources of information. However, access to information does not imply either the ability to use it, nor a cause-effect relation between the amount of information and the amount of knowledge generated. In fact, "information overload" is a commonly recognized aspect of online studies, suggesting diminishing returns with respect to knowledge production. E-information (i.e., the application of electronic technologies to the creation, classification, synthesis, storage, retrieval and display of data) has given rise to a need for people to certify, calibrate and analyze the information glut (Cunningham, et al. 1998, Gartner, p. 43).

Economic knowledge is social knowledge. It is knowledge that is comprised of a society's pre-existing procedures for theorizing about, understanding, and solving the problem of human relationships with respect to a shared material environment. Thinking about economics requires metacognitive skills; that is, pre-existing ways of thinking about social knowledge that generalize beyond the specific information making up any particular economic experience. Hence, economic information and economic thinking are separate, but interrelated, elements of the learning process. Acquisition of economic information is tied to particular ways of economic thinking. Moreover, strategic learning may be either empirical (systematic observation and comparison of the features of economic systems as they are phenomenally represented); or theoretical (application of a priori models and deduction to determine, ceteris paribus, the generalities of economic relationships). To some degree, this defines a perceived difference in academia between departments of business (more empirical) and departments of economics (more theoretical).

However, the difference is just that – perceived. Empirical work always presumes some theoretical positioning, irrespective of how explicit the theory is to either teacher or learner. And the theoretical, if it is not to cross the boundary of metaphysics, must contain the elements of its own falsification, which is largely an empirical exercise. On the one hand, individuals arrive at everyday understanding in a bottom-up fashion through experiential or empirical investigation. Human learning, via various forms of socialized instruction, allows the individual to generalize, theories, in sum to think about the variegated relationships embedded in his/her everyday understanding. Thus individual empirical knowledge is tied to particular forms of socialized theoretical instruction (usually deemed "common-sense"). On the other hand, theoretical instruction should enable the individual to view the objective world with a refined sensory perception by challenging and re-conceptualizing the phenomena of "common-sense".

Hypertext can play a major role in both the provision of information (empirical knowledge) and, with thoughtful design and interaction, the theoretical reconceptualization of empirical knowledge. Hypertext (an electronically organized information system for linking, what are seemingly, unrelated materials via the Internet) is concerned with engineering complex learning environments containing innumerable data sets. The attention to design issues, in this environment, by educators aims to afford learners a degree of "self-directed access" over the "pathway they want to explore"; as well as an egalitarian environment in which the teacher's voice recedes, thereby empowering learners (Brown & Thompson, p. 75).

However, other educators (Walkerdine; Valsiner; Valsiner & Voss; Van Oers; Cole & Engestrom; & Moll and Greenberg) warn against the overemphasis on questions of design and argue that effective learning depends upon the concepts of learning we hold, and the social goals of education. Given this social construction of learning, it is necessary to pay more attention to the way in which teaching practice and values interact to create the contexts of use (Pickering; Turkel & Papert & Turkle). Thus, technological design must be extended beyond simply designing "pathways of exploration", in order to incorporate pedagogical values and social contestation. For instance, until recently, November, 1998, it was illegal in Tasmania, Australia to discuss or distribute materials referring to homosexuality. In this sense, "pathways of exploration" can be blocked, given socio-historical circumstances, irrespective of how 'revolutionary' the form of transmission at our disposal.

Hypertext pedagogy must be based on epistemological principles and understandings of what it is to know, teach, and to learn (Cunningham, et al., 1993). While it is often presumed that the basis of knowledge is located in the subjective reconstruction of the objective world by the individual learner (Gardner, pp. 38-45), the position taken here is that knowledge requires teacher/learner collaboration. Both teacher and learner begin with a specific experiential awareness of the material world. The computer mediates this empirical understanding. From empirical beginnings, both teachers and learners through a hypertext medium approach the dominant and subordinate disciplinary knowledges. Their theoretical representations are then communicated and tested via the discussion forum.

Information gathered in the process is important only as the first step for purposes of theorizing and constructing models. Definitions of problems, a priori generalizations, working assumptions, reliability of data sets, hypotheses, tests and conclusions are all separately and jointly subject to criticism and the suspension of belief. In this manner, knowledges are contextualized, questioned, replicated, re-tested and put forward as part of a process of becoming, rather than being subsumed under some fixed mantle of truth. Socially, expectations are challenged, biases and beliefs are openly questioned, humility is essential, awareness of, and respect for, the a priori beliefs of others is demanded, and any resulting truths are put in context.

Most of the technologies that create and feed hyperspace are intended to make information accessible, not to help people understand it. The question results: does business want a person who is capable of manipulating, organizing and collating ever-increasing sources and quantities of information, a most important skill in its own right; or a person who, in the spirit of the search for knowledge, begins by questioning the importance of the very problem for which the information is required?

What the representative of business must realize is that for an academic, knowledge never "is" – it is always becoming. What the academic must comprehend is that the entrepreneur requires the best information at hand for the problem as presently defined. It is calculated that companies in the United States produce 5.5 billion documents annually, most of which are being accessed and retrieved manually. "The Internet has been the catalyst. It's created more unstructured data, as knowledge workers go out on the Web and bring in documents. That results in an overload of unstructured data" (Moad, pp. 112).

3.   PURSUIT OF IGNORANCE

Knowledge is constructed trilaterally, i.e., via the individual's empirical awareness, the social collaboration of generalization and theorization, and the social relations of technology embodied in artifacts. More importantly, for the thesis at hand, is that ignorance is constructed in the same manner.

For representations of both knowledge and ignorance, we increasingly rely on the pronouncements of experts. The volume of information, the complexity of modern technologies, and the sophistication of analysis required, give the experts (both self-styled and nominated) a weighty control over both learning and knowledge (Coleman, p. 63). Yet biologists cannot even say, within an order of magnitude, how many species there are with which we share the planet (Thompson & Kennedy, p. 172). Economists are unable to say conclusively what processes supported the emergence of the Asian economic tigers, and are now fumbling to agree on why they collapsed in 1997. Several weeks before the 1929 stock market crash, Yale's respected monetary theorist, Irving Fisher, pointed out confidently that "stock prices have reached what looks like a permanently high plateau" (Coleman, p. 64). The fact is that each generation gains amusement from the dated forecasts of its parents, given the unexpected, and debunks old concepts and knowledge with new scientific and technical insights.

In January 1996, Anne Mayhew, editor of the *Journal of Economic Issues*, made a presentation to the publishing Committee of the American Economics Association responsible for the *American Economic Review*, *Journal of Economic Literature*, and the *Journal of Economic Perspectives*. Speaking before the Committee, she cogently argued that a small group of economists have "captured" these journals to promote mathematical complexity at the expense of issues, which incorporate "history, institutions and power". Further, the prestige of the Association and the journals is used, she said, "to narrow the discipline, to reward the excessive technical training of the prestigious graduate schools, and to stifle the advance of heterodox approaches to economics" (Mayhew).

The stated concern is that neoclassical economists, as traditional intellectuals, cultivate the social production of ignorance in the struggle for ideas. This is done through narrowing the pedagogy (mathematical modeling), delineating research parameters (excluding institutional analysis as non-economic), and by constraining the production and presentation of non-neoclassical knowledge (excluding most of the forms of heterodox economics). Examination of an empirically defined problem, such as unemployment will likely reflect irreconcilable differences in the frameworks or worldviews with which these problems are analyzed. Those who believe that the free market is internally stable and coordinated, with instability only the result of exogenous shocks, largely fall into the neoclassical camp and will view the problem as fundamentally one of inflexible markets. Those who see factors, such as uncertainty or exploitation at work promoting instability, will normally be those working in a tributary of the discipline, and will be concerned about the inequity and lack of coherent government policy (Brown, pp. 457-58). With reference to instability, the basic difference between the groups will most likely be whether equilibrium or des-equilibrium is the normal state of affairs within capitalist markets.

(Arthur) divides up the profession into groups with two world views, the neoclassical and the 'new' non-linear economics: neoclassical economics is based on diminishing returns; 19th century deterministic dynamics approaching equilibrium; homogeneous factors; no externalities; and is structurally simplistic around the concepts of supply and demand. Alternatively, 'non-linear' economics introduces increasing returns; is evolutionary; focuses on heterogeneity and externalities; and is structurally complex and ever changing (Waldrop, p. 38; Bak & Chen). Most students graduate, only having come into pedagogical contact with the former worldview. Therefore, irrespective of the phenomenal (albeit excellent) design of the hypertext, the content may or may not be expanding knowledge. If hypertext is solely used to pursue the limited neoclassical vision of homo economicus, then nothing, from an academic perspective, has been gained that couldn't have been gained in a more traditional manner. If however, the goal is to gather information more efficiently in order to pursue the neoclassical worldview (for instance, updated, disaggregated census, employment, or monetary data), then the business community may be very satisfied with the exercise. In other words, the difference between information and knowledge (ignorance) must be recognized before the progressive or regressive narrative is written with respect to hypertext.

If, through the use of hypertext, students are left with technically elegant tools, learning how to replicate non-existing equilibrium conditions based on a large set of assumptions (Mueller, p. 159), what has been achieved? Simultaneously, affording learners a high level of access and choice over information pathways, may have little if anything to do with the generation of new knowledge, or 'deep learning' or 'learner-contredanses' or what ever else makes up the progressive narrative of electronic teaching/learning. Instead, it may simply provide for a larger, and more accessible information base to solidify the pursuit of ignorance embellished by elegant techniques (see Thompson, 1997). Specifically, engineering the environment to make it more appropriate for autonomous empirical investigation is to effectively opt out of the teaching/learning process. It is new information, not new knowledge; empirical awareness, not critical learning; and learner-myopia rather than learner-contredanses that are likely to be advanced.

A student may actually accept what s/he is taught as normal, even justifiable, as part of the social order. Another may reject the information as "unreal", "incomplete", "too abstract", "not relevant", or "not falsifiable" and yet have no "realistic" option to present as a critical counter-claim. In either case, whether via hypertext or textbook, to survive, to pass the course, to increase their potential material enhancement upon graduation, both types of student must internalize and become technically proficient with what is served up. At the level of ideas, this symbolic production and re-production of ignorance is replicated, with or without a computer (Gramsci, *passim*).

4.   ECONOMICS ONLINE

How might thinking, theorizing and knowledge building be taught. Economic knowledge cannot be acquired via hypertext alone, although economic information is phenomenally embedded in hypertext. Many developments in online course formats are little more than an electronic repackaging of information transmission, characterized by a continuation of the one-way flow of information from lecturer to students, (telling students: "there's the information, go read it") and rudimentary levels of interaction ("see references at the end of the page" or "you might find some interesting stuff at the Resources for Economists site"). In this manner, computer mediated delivery is used as just another information source, replicated from that which already exists, with little imaginative concern as to the potential of computer mediated teaching/learning. The hypertext that is used refers to materials supplementary to, but outside the linear flow of the document itself. The underlying premises with this type of design are that information equates to knowledge and that providing information equates to teaching (Brown & Thompson, p. 74).

The practical implication of teaching/learning "online" is that the notion of collaborative learning should provide a dialectical framework that acknowledges a division of labour in the teaching/learning endeavor. Asymmetrical differences between learners and teachers may be theorized in terms of the differences between empirical life experiences and theoretical understandings. Both approach the interaction from different empirical and theoretical experiences, and right from the beginning there should be no apriori presumption that one individual or the other has a more sophisticated or correct position. The fact that one has studied the subject for a longer period or in greater depth does not, in violation of expectations, imply more useful or correct knowledge. In other words the dichotomy between teacher/learner is immediately blurred, if not dismissed. The teacher is in the socially constructed pedagogical position of initiating the presentation of "knowledge". This will normally consist of an introduction to the "already existing systematic understandings achieved by the culture" and will make up the bulk of the "topic notes" (Becker & Varelas, p. 442).

All concepts are mental constructions, and these mental constructions approach reality circuitously. Socially shared concepts are those which are, in some way, functional in solving certain problems. For instance, micro-economic models of price are more useful in understanding the exchange of commodities in a market economy than they are in understanding the workings of a subsistence economy where markets are limited or non-existent (Thompson 1987; Thompson 1991). Given the contextualized usefulness of micro-economic models, one might safely assume that they would be more relevant to Australian university students than they are to peasants in northern India or sago producers along the Sepik River in Papua New Guinea. If these are acceptable presumptions then it seems reasonable to ask rhetorically: is economic thinking an exercise in "pure thought" establishing universals; or is our thinking and theorizing about reality in some way mediated by cultural understandings? Either way, hypertext teaching/learning will be approached differently, and is on its own terms, pedagogically manipulable.

The online courses prepared by the author are deliberately designed, as a preliminary step, to direct learners to the rich information base found on the WWW. The course is then structured around a series of topics, readings and activities exploring different schools of economic thought. Each topic is presented in a hypertext format thus allowing a degree of learner control as to what information will be gained and in what order. Relevant links to outside sources (many contrary to what is being argued in the course material) are built into the text itself. Thus the lecturer's voice is only one of many possible voices in the exploration of a topic and is often contradicted by other voices to which the students have access. Further, the links are made at the point where relevant information interconnects with other information, rather than the traditional add on "for further information" section at the end of a topic or lecture or set of notes.

A key difference between hypertext and linear text is the degree to which the hypertext document is constructed, in part by the teachers who create and place the links, and in part by the learners who decide what threads to follow, what to ignore, and serendipitously discovering what else may exist (Snyder, p. 27). The crux of teaching with hypertext is to prevent the reader-controlled environment becoming one in which the numbers of choices are overwhelming and the learner becomes lost. On the other hand, the learner must not be restricted to a rigid, hierarchically structured, navigation of choice that would be better placed in a textbook. Well structured hypertext must blur the boundary between learner and teacher without losing the focus of what is to be learned (Burbules & Callister, p. 34; Snyder, p. 30; Bolter, p. 17).

In the aforementioned courses, the structure of linking is as follows: there are the intra-linkages (the links between elements of various economic knowledges developed by one's colleagues and their courses); extra-linkages (showcasing general study skills or academic conventions); inter-linkages (highlighting connections between economic knowledges and other interdisciplinary knowledges (e.g., linking Claude Debussy to Karl Marx or Ludwig Wittgenstein to John Maynard Keynes); or hyper-linkages (identifying supportive, adjunct or contradictory elements of socio-economic and historical knowledges in the resource base of the Internet such as working papers or publications); and finally, what may be called the supra-links (sharing, through mutual agreement, online material with teachers/learners around the world involved in identical courses, and establishing linked international electronic fora for collaboration amongst teachers/learners).

Effectively, the important intellectual processes of making connections, actively transforming knowledges, understanding, plotting, navigating and recreating the ways in which knowledge is structured, all provide the essence of teaching/learning in any form. Simply disseminating information is not the point in hypertext learning. The point is to exchange, develop and evaluate ideas. A well structured collection, but heterogeneous matrix of learning spaces, gives to computer mediated teaching/learning what cannot take place in a set of lectures or a textbook. Teachers inadequately trained to take advantage of hypertext pedagogy subvert the technology's potential.

Computer-mediated-teaching/learning has the potential to open new vistas of knowledge construction. It is more than just a new way of organizing existing information; it influences the kinds of information it organizes. As the matrix of hypertext grows and evolves, the structure of the information itself changes. Since knowing anything depends upon the meaningful organization of information, new methods of organization imply changing forms of knowledge. Possibly, and more importantly, computer mediated teaching/learning challenges traditional distinctions between accessing information (the learner's job) and producing new knowledge (the teacher's responsibility) (Burbules & Callister, p. 25).

An electronic discussion forum enables asynchronous communication between the learners and teacher and between peers themselves. The aim is to provide a more egalitarian, learner-centered process in which reflection and feedback become important (Brown & Thompson, pp. 76-77). Preparation of the 'online' material should permit both teacher and learner to reflect on the new material, discuss tentative understandings with others, actively search for more information to throw light on areas of interest or difficulty, and build conceptual connections (Laurillard; Yakimovicz & Murphy, p. 203).

Having access to information, and then collaborating in the reformulation of information sources, interpreting the connections, sharing new discoveries with others, and building further insights through feedback from tutor and peers, becomes the core of the production of knowledges online. Practically, teaching should aim at providing the learner with the cognitive tools necessary to engage in social practice. Teachers provide the metacognitive skills (models, assumptions, and strategies) for thinking about economics. Learners bring their empirical understanding and skills to the exchange. The conceptual and empirical interaction forces each to reconstruct their relative positions. The learner uses the metacognitive skills to reinterpret spontaneous experience and the teacher uses the experience of the learner to redevelop the conceptual apparatuses. The application of the different understandings that result from the teacher/learner collaboration constitutes the production of economic knowledge. When this occurs we can move beyond the phenomenal experience of economic thought as it is represented in the information of hypertexts. By using the computer/hypertext as a tool of mediation, social interaction between teachers and learners is assisted with the production of new knowledges and the creative destruction of the old.

5.   CONCLUSION

How might the malleability of hypertext tools be exploited to make economic thinking socially useful and consequential? How might the abstract systems of economic thinking be pushed out into the world to shed light on concrete problems? What do the everyday experiences of teachers/learners contribute to this process?

The teacher brings to the collaboration the pre-existing concepts of economic thought and a profound knowledge of the laws, theories and methodologies that comprise the strategic tools of economic thinking. The learner brings a recognition and common sense understanding of the material problems. Computerization, hypertext, and electronic fora provide the tools for discovery, in the sense that its malleability encourages higher level cognitive processing. For instance, we could at the beginning use hyperlinks to model the concept of 'economics' for the learner by asking: Why do we often identify 1776 as the date of origin of modern economic thought? Why not 430BC, beginning with the book Oeconomicus by Xenophon; or 384BC with Aristotle; or 1225AD with Thomas Aquinas; or indeed 1332AD with Ibn Khaldun. Here we begin to scaffold the social, political and philosophical texts that give meaning to the concept of 'economics', moving the learner beyond a phenomenal experience.

Although traditional courses provide learners with the bare bones of economic models, they are less likely to encourage exploration of the relationships those models describe. With hypertext we can escape the authoritative presence of the textbook and more easily seek to educate critical users, those who know enough to use the system to find what they are looking for, but who realize that what they have found is not all that there is to know (Burbules & Callister, p. 49).

The use of non-linear hypertext may help the teacher/learner to see that economic models are not fixed either in text or hypertext, but dynamic systems for explaining material reality – and that they can be, and are changed. The goal should not be to legitimate economic knowledge through the one-way transmission of esoteric mathematical analyses, but to empower teacher/learners so that they may reinterpret social knowledge and themselves begin to effect change. Hypertext is the force that pushes 'economics' into the world by making it dynamic, a theoretically powerful tool for learners to use.

There is no doubt that computer-mediation and hypertext potentially enhances the capacity for the production of economic information and knowledge. The potentiality is not teleologically incontrovertible however, as the presentation must encourage the learner to take an active approach to learning. Learning will fall apart if knowledge continues to be confused with transmitted information, and ignorance will continue to be promoted, albeit in another medium.

REFERENCES

Arrow, K.J. (1984). The Economics of Information. Collected Papers of Kenneth J. Arrow, Volume 4. Oxford: Blackwells.

Arthur, W.B. (1990). Positive Feedbacks in the Economy. *Scientific American*, (February), 92-99.

Bak, P., & Chen, K. (1991). Self-Organized Criticality. *Scientific American*, (January), 46-53.

Becker, J., & Varelas, M. (1995). Assisting Construction: The Role of the Teacher in Assisting the Learner's Construction of Pre-existing Cultural Knowledge. In L.P. Steefe, & J. Gale, (Eds.), *Constructivism in Education* (pp. 433-446). Hillsdale, New Jersey: Lawrence Erlbaum Associates.

Bolter, J.D. (1991). *Writing Space: The Computer, Hypertext, and the History of Writing*. Hillsdale, N.J.: Lawrence Erlbaum.

Brown, A., & Thompson, H. (1997). Course Design for the WWW: Keeping Online Students Onside. In R. Kevill, R. Oliver, & R. Phillips, (Eds.), *14th Annual Conference Proceedings for the Australian Society for Computers in Tertiary Education, What Works and Why?* (pp. 74-81). Perth, W.A.: Curtin University of Technology.

Brown, E.K. (1981). The Neoclassical and Post-Keynesian Research Programs: The Methodological Issues. *Review of Social Economy, 39*. (2), (October), 438-459.

Burbules, N.C., & Callister, T.A. (1996). Knowledge at the Crossroads: Some Alternative Futures of Hypertext Learning Environments. *Educational Theory 46*. (1), (Winter), pp.23-51.

Cole, M., & Engestrom, Y. (1993). A Cultural-Historical Approach to Distributed Cognition. In G. Salomon, (Eds.), *Distributed Cognition* (pp. 1-46). Cambridge: Cambridge University Press.

Coleman, L. (1998). The Age of Inexpertise, *Quadrant 42* (5), (May), 63-67.

Cunningham, D.J., Duffy, T.M., & Knuth, R.A. (1993). The Textbook of the Future. In C. McKnight, A. Dillon, & J. Richardson, (Eds.), *Hypertext: A Psychological Perspective* (pp. 19-50). Chichester, UK: Ellis Horwood Ltd.

Cunningham, S.J., Holmes, G., Littin, J., Beale, R., & Witten, I.H. (1998). Applying connectionist models to information retrieval. In S. Amari, & N. Kasabov, (Eds.), *Brain-like Computing and Intelligent Information Systems* (pp. 435-460). London: Springer.

Drake, K. (1998). Firms, Knowledge and Competitiveness. *The OECD Observer, 211* (April/May), 24-27.

Gardner, H. (1995). *The Mind's New Science: A History of the Cognitive Revolution*. New York: Basic Books.

Gartner, G. (1997). Grappling with e-knowledge. *Computerworld, 32* (1), (December), 43-44.

Gramsci, A. (1971). *Selections from the Prison Notebooks.* Edited and translated by Quentin Hoare and Geoffrey Nowell Smith. London: Lawrence & Wishart.

Hammond, N. (1993). Learning with Hypertext: Problems, Principles and Prospects. In C. McKnight, A. Dillon, & J. Richardson, (Eds.), *Hypertext: A Psychological Perspective* (pp. 51-70). Chichester, England: Ellis Horwood Ltd.

Landow, G.P. (1992). *Hypertext: The Convergence of Contemporary Critical Theory and Technology.* Baltimore: John Hopkins University Press.

Laurillard, D. (1993). *Rethinking university teaching: A framework for the effective use of educational technology.* London: Routledge.

Machlup, F. (1982). Optimum Utilization of Knowledge. Knowledge, Information, and Decisions. *Society, 20* (1), 1-15.

Mayhew, A. (1996). *AEA Economics Journals.* Review of Heterodox Economics, (Winter), 1-2.

Moad, J. (1998). In Search of Knowledge: Growth of Knowledge Management Tools and Technology Information. *PC Week,* (December), 111-112.

Moll, L.C., & Greenberg, J.B. (1990). Creating Zones of Possibilities: Combining Social Contexts for Instruction. In L.C. Moll, (Eds.), *Vygotsky and Education: Instructional Implications and Applications of Socio-Historical Psychology* (pp. 319-348). Cambridge: Cambridge University Press.

Mueller, D. (1992). The corporation and the economist. *International Journal of Industrial Organization, 10*, 147-170.

Pickering, J. (1995). Teaching on the Internet is Learning. *Active Learning, 2*, 9-12.

Pilat, D. (1998). The Economic Impact of Technology. *The OECD Observer, 213* (August/September), 5-9.

Snyder, I. (1995). Reconceptualising Literacy & Hypertext. *English in Australia, 111*, (April), 27-34.

Thompson, H. (1987). Theorizing Simple Commodity Production in Papua New Guinea. *Journal of Contemporary Asia, 17* (4), 436-455.

Thompson, H. (1991). Economic Theory and Economic Development in Papua New Guinea. *Journal of Contemporary Asia, 21* (1), 54-67.

Thompson, H. (1997). Ignorance and Ideological Hegemony: A Critique of Neoclassical Economics. *Journal of Interdisciplinary Economics, 8* (4), 291-305.

Thompson, H., & Kennedy, D. (1996). Ecological-Economics of Biodiversity and Tropical Rainforest Deforestation. *Journal of Interdisciplinary Economics, 7* (3), 169-190.

Tobach, E., Falmagne, R., Parlee, M. Martin, L., & Kapelman, A.S., (Eds.). (1997). *Mind and Social Practice: Selected Writings of Sylvia Scribner.* Cambridge: Cambridge University Press.

Turkle, S. (1997). Seeing Through Computers: Education in a Culture of Education, *The American Prospect*, (March/April), 76-82.

Turkle, S., & Papert, S. (1990). Epistemological Pluralism: Styles and Voices Within the Computer Culture. *Signs, 16* (1), 128-157.

Valsiner, J. (1991), Construction of the Mental, *Theory and Psychology, 1* (4), 477-494.

Valsiner, J., & Voss, H.G. (1996). The Structured Nature of Learning: History Revisted. In J. Valsiner, & H.G. Voss, (Eds.), *The Structure of Learning Processes* (pp. 1-14). Norwood, New Jersey: Ablex Publishing Corporation.

Van Oers, B. (1996). The Dynamics of School Learning. In J. Valsiner, & H.G. Voss, (Eds.), *The Structure of Learning Processes* (pp. 205-228). Norwood, New Jersey: Ablex Publishing Corporation.

Vickery, G., & Wurzburg, G. (1996). Flexible Firms, Skills and Employment. *The OECD Observer, 202*, (October/November).

Vygotsky, L.S. (1930-1978). *Mind in Society: The Development of Higher Psychological Processes.* Cambridge, MA: Harvard University Press.

Waldrop, M. (1992). *Mitchell Complexity: The Emerging Science at the Edge of Order and Chaos.* Harmondsworth: Penguin.

Walkerdine, V. (1984). Developmental psychology and the child-centered pedagogy: the insertion of Piaget into early education. In J. Henriques, W. Holloway, C. Unwin, C. Venn, & V. Walkerdine, (Eds.), *Changing the Subject: Psychology, Social Regulation and Subjectivity* (pp. 153-202). London: Methuen.

Yakimovicz, A.D., & Murphy, K.L. (1995). Constructivism and Collaboration on the Internet: Case Study of a Graduate Class Experience. *Computers in Education, 24* (3), 203-209.

Learning Methods and the Use of ICT

Jakob Ravn
CBS Learning Lab, Copenhagen Business School, Copenhagen, Denmark

1.   INTRODUCTION

Pressure on higher education institutions has increased in many ways over the last decades: increased number of students, new kinds of students (part time students, mature students etc.), increased political and public focus on educational quality and increased competition between higher education institutions for the students. While struggling with all this, one of the solutions has been the use of Information and Communication Technology (ICT). As Diana Ravitch notes: *"This* (heavy investments in educational technology, author's note) *smells suspiciously like the latest miracle cure"* (Forbes; New York; 1998).

Almost every university and Business school in the western world are experimenting with and developing new technologies for educational purposes. The needs for using ICT in a variety of ways has in the last years been institutionalized as a matter of life or dead to higher education institutions.

ICT has become a pressure in itself and everyone has to jump on the fast moving train if they want to survive in the highly competitive world of higher education. One of the main drivers on ICT in higher education has become fear (of lacking behind and of the unknown) instead of real needs.

In the heat, it may be that some have forgotten that ICT is a *tool*; not an end in itself. Educational technology does not create better learning processes per se, but alone as a result of the changes in the design of the teaching methods. It is not the media, which is used to facilitate the learning

T.A. Johannessen, A. Pedersen and K. Petersen (eds.),
Educational Innovation in Economics and Business VI, 179–188.
© 2002 *Kluwer Academic Publishers. Printed in the Netherlands.*

process that improves learning, but what is put into it and how it is used (Owston, 1997).

2.   THE USE OF TECHNOLOGICAL TOOLS

It may sounds obvious but when was the last time you considered how, for example, your slides supported the chosen type of teaching? And how this matched the learning objectives for the course? You have probably done some thinking about how it supported the type of teaching: Slide use is best suited for face-to-face teaching and is most used in traditional lectures. They are less frequently used in case teaching and nearly never used in project-based teaching. Slides are a teaching technology suited to visualize an overview of a difficult subject, when transferring knowledge to the students. The problem is that this technology is often used for another purpose.

Take for example this slide, which could be a slide for the presentation of this Paper:

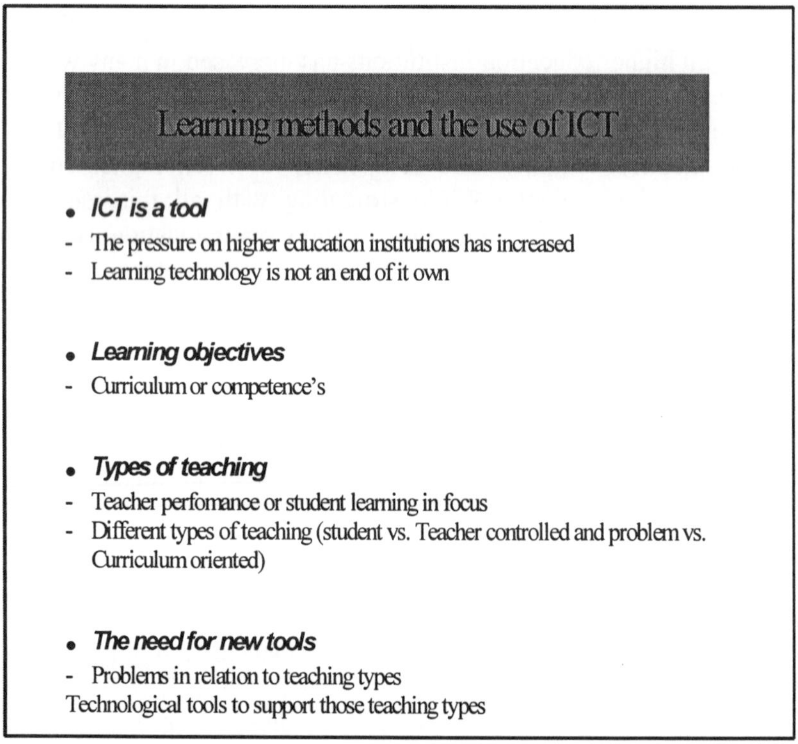

Figure 1: Example of a slide.

This slide is more a reminder to the teacher, than it is a learning tool for the student. Even though slides are a well-chosen technology for the purpose of visualizing an overview or to show a structure of the subject, it fails when used as a memorandum for the teacher. If used as such, and I believe they often are, slides are confused with another teaching tool, the manuscript. The teacher structures the lecture by the content of her slides. The problem in doing this is, that the lecture turns into a "Power Point show" in which the teacher perform very well but the students do not actually learn very much. They are busy looking at the show; not engaged in thinking.

3.   TEACHING- OR LEARNING TECHNOLOGY

The technology is in this case is a teaching technology, used on behalf of the teacher. A lot of the educational technology that is developed for higher education purposes is teaching technology, in the sense that it reflects the "hydraulic model" in which learning is equated with the transfer of information from teacher to student (Neal, 1998). There are many examples of such subject or logistical oriented teaching technology in web-courses and CD-ROM based learning tools.

The focus of this kind of teaching, obviously becomes the teacher performance, i.e. the teacher's ability to present curriculum in a structured and entertaining way. Ironically, most of the discussion on higher education teaching and learning advocates other approaches than the hydraulic model, but that dos not seems to effect the educational technology developers. The paradox is, that by developing teaching technology that favors the hydraulic model, teaching is forced into using corresponding teaching methods, and the learning process becomes a transfer of information.

As the example with the slide shows it is essential to develop and use educational technology that supports the chosen type of teaching. If the wanted outcome of teaching is not simply to transfer information to the students, but, as much of the discussion on teaching and learning in higher education reflects, to enable students to work methodically with problems, to apply and reflect critically on the foundation and relevance of theories, to take responsibility for their own learning process and develop personal and interpersonal competence, then, the focus of technological development must facilitate those learning processes. That is, to develop and use technological tools that are made on behalf of the student, not the teacher and facilitate the types of teaching needed for reaching the above learning objectives: Learning technology instead of teaching technology.

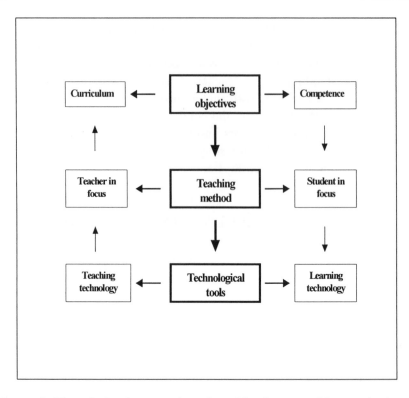

Figure 2: The relation between learning objectives, teaching methods and the use of ICT.

The left side of figure 2 illustrates the consequences of using educational technology developed according to the hydraulic model where teachers are forced into curriculum oriented types of teaching. On the right side of figure 2, learning objectives influences the chosen type of teaching and educational technology is then developed to support and improve those teaching types. Instead of letting the technology direct the teaching and the related outcome, it is necessary to turn it around and direct the technological development according to the teaching types which enable the students' to gain competencies instead of information (curriculum).

4. TYPES OF TEACHING

If we want the students to gain competencies, some criteria for the type of teaching can be stated. The students' ability to take responsibility for their own learning process points in the direction of highly participation-directed instead of teacher-directed types of teaching. The ability to apply theories to issues and problems, to reflect critically on the foundation and relevance of those theories and the ability to work methodically with problems, points in direction of problem-based instead of subject-based (or curriculum-based) types of teaching.

If different types of teaching are placed in relation to those two dimensions, participation directed/teacher directed and subject based/problem-based, we get a picture like figure 3.

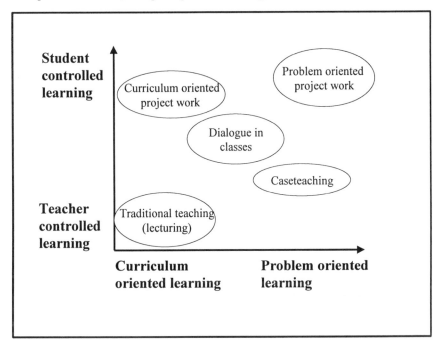

Figure 3: Teaching types related to control and content.

In figure 3 some common types of teaching are presented according to who is in control of the learning process and the degree to which the teaching is directed by curriculum. In the lower left corner is the traditional lecture, where the teacher presents a subject to the listening crowd who is supposedly prepared for receiving the message. Both the teacher and curriculum direct this type of teaching. Moving to the upper right corner of figure 3, where problems and participants directs the teaching, relevant types of teaching are dialogue based teaching, case teaching and project work. Those teaching types are more oriented towards interdisciplinary and collaborative learning than towards the transfer of information from teacher to student.

Thus, the relevant types of teaching are then to focus more on dialogue-based teaching, Case teaching and project-based teaching, than on lecturing.

5.   THE NEED FOR NEW TOOLS TO SUPPORT THOSE TYPES OF TEACHING

But as teaching is being more managed by the students than by teachers and more directed by problems than by curriculum, there is a growing demand for interdisciplinary and methodological tools to support the students ability to formulate and work efficiently with problems independently.

The risk exists that by expanding problem-oriented teaching without introducing any additional tools, the teaching turns into a kind of laissez faire approach. The students hold all the responsibilities for their own learning and as problems opposed to curriculum direct the teaching, the learning turns into a "trial and error" process. If lucky, the good student's do actually learn something, but it will probably be a tough road to wisdom. And the less intelligent or less enthusiastic students are left without much help.

One reason for this is that the roles of the teacher shifts from I know the stuff you need to know to a role of supervisor and discussion facilitator. The teachers are confronted with subjects far from their own area of research and are supposed to guide on a more methodological and interdisciplinary level. But they face difficulties with the task of passing on their own experience in doing research.

5.1   Teachers as project supervisors

When functioning as a project supervisor one of the key tasks is to serve as an "eye opener" (Tofteskov, 1996). The goal is to make students aware of the many possible ways to analyze a problem and the effects those choices have on the resulting solutions. Doing that, the supervisor is tempted to tell what or how to do and thereby take back control of the process; or doing the opposite, lean back and let the students make the mistakes they have to do to learn the good workmanship of formulating and investigating problems. The laissez faire approach. Neither is, of course, the answer to being a project supervisor, but often that is the way it is actually done. The results are that the learning objectives stated have a hard time being realized. If the supervisor really should function as an "eye opener", the main activity for the supervisor would be to ask questions and thereby getting the students to reflect on their own way of doing things. The students can ask questions as well, but not as much concerning the exact content of the project, as of the investigation process, the problems in collecting and analyzing data, methodological issues and how to choose and apply theories.

5.2 Teachers as discussion facilitators

Likewise in case-teaching, and other dialogue-based types of teaching as well, the teacher is confronted with new demands. First of all it takes a lot of time and is a discipline in it self to write a good case (Leenders, Erskine & Maufette-Leenders, 1998). At CBS, Case-writing workshops are arranged once a year, but the experience so far is, that the teachers afterwards have problems allocating time to this activity (partly because there is no reward-system for this kind of work).

Another problem is the case-method itself (as practiced in the North American tradition). It bears the risk of using tailor-made cases, which are better suited as examples than as problem-oriented teaching. If the subject for example is organizational development, the information in the case all most only concerns organizational matters. It seldom includes enough information to experience the task of collecting and screening data. And even if the case includes that much information, it would still be a linear presentation of an event, a history, which had to be read in its entire length.

The tailoring of cases also means that the ability to choose an appropriate theory according to an actual problem, reflect critically on the foundation and relevance of that theory and apply the theory to the problem are problematic qualifications to acquire by case-teaching.

In table 1 some of the learning advantages and disadvantages concerning lecturing, case-teaching and project-based teaching are listed.

Table 1. Types of teaching.

Type of teaching	Learning advantages	Learning advantages
Lectures	• Fundamental understanding • Structure & overview • Exemplification • Inspiration • Communication of Theory	• Inefficient for analysis training • Deactivating students • Inefficient for the learning of skills • Inefficient for the use of theory
Project-based teaching	• Problem-oriented • Activating • Facilitates analysis • Methodological oriented	• Hard to manage for supervisors • Time consuming for students • Risk of lack of Theory • Risk of slow learning process
Case-teaching	• Problem-oriented • Activating • Facilitates analysis • Facilitates decision making • The use of Theories	• Time consuming and difficult to write good cases • Linear presentation • Risk for tailor-made cases (subject-oriented, non-methodological)

6.   ICT TOOLS TO SUPPORT PROJECT-BASED TEACHING AND CASE TEACHING

The challenges in developing educational technology then, are to develop tools that improve, support and comprehend for the weaknesses primarily in project-based teaching and case teaching. The technological developments are then directly focused on reaching some learning objectives, and the main drivers for the use and development of educational technology are needs from the students' point of view, not either from the teacher's viewpoint or from the technology itself. Some examples of these kind of technological tools, developed at CBS, are described here.

6.1   Example of ICT tools to support project-based teaching

Relating to project-based teaching the Teaching & Learning Advisory Unit at Copenhagen Business School in 1997 decided to develop additional tools to introduce general social science work and research methods to the students. The idea is to develop an interactive "project guide", which can support the students' work in the different phases of a social science project. At this point, an interactive tool to help students formulate a thesis statement has been developed. A tool for the use of theory in projects and a tool about written communication are currently being developed. Other topics under consideration are tools for working in-groups and collection and analysis of empirical data.

The thesis statement guide developed so far, called Scribo (meaning "I write" in Latin), helps the students define the precise subject and formulate a concrete problem. Scribo asks all the questions that a good supervisor would ask; however, it is the students themselves who must formulate their hypotheses. The program stimulates thoughts and ideas about the project subject and helps the student overcome "writers block". The program is useful in the following situations: 1) as a checklist for identifying and formulating the problem, 2) for focusing the subject, 3) if a group of students have different suggestions and want to discuss around a common structure, and 4) as preparation for a meeting with the supervisor. The interactive program basically consists of four parts. The most important part is the interactive questionnaire, with examples and explanations. It has an overview of all the questions, which at the same time illustrates the working process. Besides this the program consists of a lexicon with explanations of all Scribo subjects, an introduction section and help.

Tools such as this do not replace a real life human supervisor but help on the critical tasks of interdisciplinary and methodological supervision. Learning with such tools is less based on the trial and error process than before and the students have better chances to gain the intended knowledge of the process.

6.2   Example of ICT tools to support case teaching

The disadvantages to "traditional" case teaching were on one hand that it is time consuming and difficult to write good cases and on the other hand the case method itself. This line of reasoning made the Teaching and Learning advisory Unit at CBS initiate the development of a new kind of case, the Multimedia Case Material (MCM). An MCM is an extensive collection of authentic data about an enterprise, structured concerning the origin and relevance of data, but not focused on a specific subject as a traditional case. The MCM is not produced on the basis of related questions and data are not edited from a targeted, discipline perspective. On the contrary, data are as unedited as possible and although data are structured to some extent, it is not in a linear way.

The students are placed in a very real life situation, where problems have to be identified before they can be analyzed and solutions discussed. They have to decide which methodology and theories are relevant to a given problem. It is up to the each teacher how and for which purpose she wants to use the MCM. It can be used for learning purposes such as analytical skills, use of theory, problem identification, decision making or methodological thinking. The same enterprise can be viewed from very different perspectives and subject areas.

7.   CONCLUSION

The critical task in developing and using educational technology has in this paper been discussed as the task of matching learning objectives with types of teaching, and afterwards identifying the needs for ICT tools to improve those teaching types. The focus of the development and use of ICT tools will then be the student learning process, instead of the teaching process, which are the focus of much of the current developments.

This shift in technological development strategy is not simple. Most of the educational technology developed today is developed within the software industry or in technical units in universities. As mentioned, those technical oriented development units seem to be familiar with only the teaching technology approach, the hydraulic model. This has to be changed if we want educational tools in line with much of the debate on higher education teaching and learning. Then, the teaching and learning competencies have to be the core input, and the main area of concern, in the development process. For that to happen, organizational changes have to take place in Universities and Business Schools, and our focus has to be changed from technological possibilities to learning possibilities.

REFERENCES

Erskine, J.A., Leenders, M.R., & Mauffette-Leenders, L.A. (1998). *Teaching with cases.* *London.* Ontario: Ivey Publising.

Gandz, J. (1997). The death of teaching: The rebirth of education. *Ivey Business Quarterly,* (Autumn), 11–13.

Neal, E. (1998). Using Technology in Teaching: We need to Exercise Healthy Skepticism. *Chronicle of Higher education.* (June 19), B4-5.

Owston, R.D. (1997). The World Wide Web: A Technology to Enhance Teaching and Learning? *Educational Researcher, Vol. 26,* No.2, 27–33.

Ramsden, P. (1998). Managing the Effective University. *Higher Education Research and Development, Vol. 17,* No. 3, 347–370.

Ravitch, D. (1998). *The great technology mania.* Forbes, New York, (March 23), 134–140.

Tofteskov, J. (1996). Projektvejledning–og organisering af projektarbejde. København: Samfundslitteratur.

Learning by Sharing: a Model for Life-Long Learning

Thomas J.P. Thijssen[1], Rik Maes[2] & Fons T.J. Vernooij[3]
[1]Anton Dreesmann Institute for Infopreneurship, Amsterdam, The Netherlands, [2]Department of Information Management, University of Amsterdam, the Netherlands, [3]Graduate School of Teaching, University of Amsterdam, the Netherlands.

1.   INTRODUCTION

The university as an institution is at a decisive moment in its history. It is confronted with numerous outside challenges: the demand as well as the supply of education is globalizing, the coming generation of students differs significantly from preceding ones, the need for life-long education is replacing the classical learning period between ages 18 and 23, and new technologies call for new learning models. If concepts like "learning organization" and "learning society" are valid, then the university should be a pioneer in this field.

However, despite the changes of the past 30 years, the (European) university system has not been altered fundamentally. Learning still precedes working. Professors teach students the outcomes of their research, or they teach what they have read before. Students attend lectures, read books and articles, and take exams. Most of the time, learning processes at the university still take place in the splendid isolation of the ivory tower.

One of the most disturbing aspects of universities is that learning continues to be viewed as a *passive process*. The teacher is perceived as the unquestioned dispenser of objective knowledge, and students as the uncritical receivers. Students can complete their study by sheer absorption and accumulation of knowledge. The actual learning process follows a predetermined route, that is, a fixed curriculum, even though universities tend to emphasize self-guidance on the part of students in carrying out

189

T.A. Johannessen, A. Pedersen and K. Petersen (eds.),
Educational Innovation in Economics and Business VI, 189–198.

learning tasks. The teacher's role is restricted to designing the curriculum, prescribing the learning path to be followed, and giving students feedback on the extent to which they have acquired the learning content. Moreover, most students work their way toward graduation in solitude.

In the past 20 years the Department of Information Management of the University of Amsterdam has experimented with alternative learning models, most of them incorporated in a successful postgraduate course in Information Management. The lessons learned from this ongoing experience have now been fully adopted by the Anton Dreesmann Institute for Infopreneurship. In this institute both entrepreneurship and ICT-based learning are at the core of all activities.

Past experience and new explanations both make clear that the traditional learning model must be replaced by a multi-dimensional learning model. The traditional model is basically one-dimensional (from teacher to student) and sequential (learning precedes working). At the Anton Dreesmann Institute this model has been replaced by the "Learning by Sharing" model. This article outlines the new learning model.

2.   LEARNING BY SHARING: AN ECLECTIC LEARNING MODEL

Solutions for the problems mentioned in section 1 can actually be found in existing learning models. These models are the collaborative, the constructivist, and the cognitive (information-processing) models of learning (Leidner & Jarvenpaa, 1995). The solutions they provide are incorporated and further extended in the Learning by Sharing model.

Firstly, drawn from the collaborative approach, the basic premise of the Learning by Sharing model is that "Learning emerges through the shared understanding of more than one learner" (Leidner & Jarvenpaa, 1995, p. 270). It is argued that learning should not be a solitary process: "Knowledge is created as it is shared, and the more it is shared, the more is learned" (Leidner & Jarvenpaa, 1995, p. 268).

Secondly, drawn from the constructivist approach, the Learning by Sharing model is learner-centered and not teacher-centered. For the student this means that the notion of self-guided study is complemented with a self-guided educational program (Kaldeway, Haenen, Wils & Westhoff, 1998). This extends the constructivist belief that "Individuals learn better when they discover things themselves and when they control the pace of learning". In the new model, therefore, students design their own curriculum. They create an individual learning route according to their interests, abilities and learning style.

The teacher in this *education-à-la-carte* plays the role of coach, and presents the student with various opportunities and possibilities for designing a personal curriculum. The teacher coordinates the entire learning process and gives feedback when and where needed. Ideally, the teaching style will match the learning style of the student (Kaldeway et al., 1998, p. 274). The learner-centered approach transforms the passive attitude of the student into an active attitude. The student constructs his of her own knowledge structure.

Thirdly, drawn from the cognitive approach is the importance of the monitoring process. Teachers need to help students develop their abilities to direct their own learning process. An essential feature of the Learning by Sharing model is its emphasis on the meta-level of the learning process, that is, the meta-cognitive level. This entails the need to reflect on the learning process, for both teacher and student. The teacher is in a process of *learning to educate* and the student is in a process of *learning to learn*. For the teacher, this means constantly reflecting on the teaching approach and improving it where possible. For the student it means ongoing self-evaluation of the course of the self-guided learning process. As noted by Kaldeway et al. (1998) this self-evaluation includes assessing whether or not the intended learning goals have been met.

In order to introduce real-life experience and hence to establish a learning community, the Learning by Sharing model introduces a third party into the learning process: business individuals. By bringing in business individuals, the learning process changes drastically. In contrast to the traditional student-teacher relationship, the business individuals introduce a real-time and real-life link to everyday practice. Business individuals, students, and teachers learn by interacting in three ways.

3. LEARNING BY SHARING: A MODEL OF COLLABORATION

The Learning by Sharing model incorporates the collaboration of three parties in real-life learning: the outside world as represented by *business individuals*, universities as represented by *teachers/researchers*, and the young generation as represented by *students*. These three parties interact in various ways, as shown in Figure 1. Their interactions are shown along the three sides of the learning triangle: learning by experimenting, learning by investigating and learning through practice. These will be dealt with in turn.

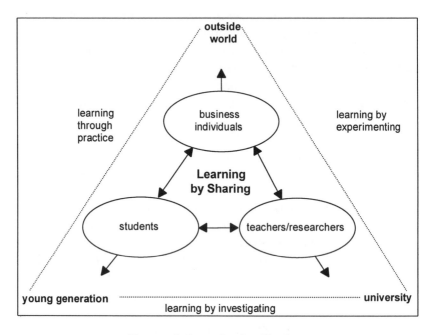

Figure 1: Learning by Sharing.

3.1 Learning by experimenting: more interaction between teachers/researchers and business individuals

The key to enhancing the social character of academic learning is the collaboration of universities with communities of practitioners. Many universities already maintain such partnerships, but don't take full advantage of the possibilities. To achieve this, we advocate not only intensification of these partnerships, but also redefinition. Traditionally these relationships are dominated by the stereotypical notion of the practitioner as "... the passive (and theoretically ignorant) recipient of the expertise of academics" (Argyris & Schön, 1996, p. 34), and of the academic as "... the theoretically well grounded scientist, lacking considerable insight into the real world".

In the Learning by Sharing model, the notion of *learning by experimenting* is important: teachers/researchers and business individuals work together in research projects. Researchers behave as practitioners and practitioners behave as researchers. This results in a sustainable information exchange between the parties involved. To this end, teachers/researchers in business economics should engage in dialogue not only with others in the academic community but also with business individuals actually working in the field. Such dialogue can develop into practical collaboration, both in research and in teaching, on specific topics of mutual interest.

As far as research is concerned, the direct link between the two communities enables researchers to identify areas in which to conduct truly relevant and innovative research. This ensures the production of useful knowledge, that is, knowledge useful for practitioners (Argyris & Schön, 1996, p. 43). The notion of *researchers as practitioners* refers to the empirical testing of a theory, after which it can be adjusted according to (business) practice. In this way, applied research becomes research that matters, research where results are immediately applicable.

On the other hand, the notion of *practitioners as researchers* refers to practitioners putting theories to everyday use (Argyris & Schön, 1996, p. 50). They can adjust their by incorporating insights form new theories. Nothing is more practical than a good theory.

For the research community, the combination of new theories and practical topics ensures that the contributions made by the collaboration of researchers and business individuals (joint applied research) are not only grounded in theory but also relevant to business practice. At the same time, participation in research activities enables practitioners to significantly enhance their operating abilities (operational excellence), and to keep abreast of state-of-the-art developments in academic disciplines. Partnerships between academics and practitioners on key issues in business practice are therefore mutually beneficial.

As far as teaching is concerned, a second exchange is possible. Business individuals can also be called in as teachers in educational programs: *practitioners as teachers*. For students this provides an opportunity to learn from the first-hand experience of business individuals. When interacting with students, the visiting teachers are called upon to reflect on their business practices, because students question particular cases from the perspective of the theories they have studied.

A final aspect of "learning by experimenting" is that researchers are called in as advisers in a business environment: *researchers as consultants*. In this role the researcher reflects upon business practices from a theoretical point of view.

3.2   Learning by investigating: more interaction between students and teachers/researchers

Universities today face two major educational problems. Firstly, since the 1950s research has outgrown teaching in importance (Leggon, 1997, pp. 221-243). The amount of time needed to introduce new research topics into current curricula results in an curriculum being continuously outdated.

Secondly, the traditional perspective in which the student is considered a "knowledge consumer" and the teacher a "knowledge provider" results in impersonal student-teacher relationships and a one-way flow of knowledge. To cope with these educational problems, new ways should be found to integrate research and educational activities.

To tackle the problem of outdated curricula, teachers and students should collaborate in research projects. In the Learning by Sharing model this collaboration is an important notion: *learning by investigating*. Students formulate their educational needs and look for teachers to do research with. Teachers serve as coaches and facilitate the self-guided education of students.

This collaborate research solves as well the problem of a one-way flow of knowledge. Students can influence future research by pointing out the topics that interest them and participate in this research. They may publish their findings and should explain what they have discovered, leading to the notion of students as teachers. Teachers receive direct response from their students on the curriculum which may encourage teachers to change their teaching method. In the research, teachers may find new teaching material, leading to the notion of teachers as students.

3.3   Learning through practice: more interaction between students and business individuals

In the relationships between university students and business individuals, we notice a gap between learning and working, between theorizing about practice and putting theory into practice. This is why we advocate learning through practice to bridge the gap on the way to life-long learning (cf. Roobeek & Mandersloot, 1998). One common attempt to solve this problem is through internships or traineeships.

Traditionally, internships are intended to diminish the gap between learning and working. But there are some problems. The first is that a common objective between students and business individuals is often missing (cf. Ghoshal & Bartlett, 1997). The second is that most internships lack academic challenge because students are exploited as cheap labor. The third is that the duration of internships varies tremendously from several weeks to an entire year (Ontwerp Hoop 1998, 1997). This makes it difficult to organize supervision of students in their work situation. The fourth problem is that the quality of guidance by both the university and by business individuals often falls short.

In the Learning by Sharing model, *learning through practice* is an important notion. It bridges the learning-to-working gap. By intensifying interactions between students and business individuals, the traditional boundaries are blurred. Students and business individuals interact in an earlier stage of the study with high frequency. During their entire academic career, students should participate in projects with various business individuals. This leads to the notion of *students as practitioners*. For example, students might work one day a week in a business environment and build up relevant working experience.

At the same time, business individuals are confronted with fundamental questions students pose about traditions of the companies they are working with. Business individuals are forced to think about the logic of their behavior in the context of new practices emerging from information and communication technology. This results in the notion of practitioners as students.

The benefits of theorizing about practice and putting theory into practice are shown in Table 1 (adapted from Roobeek & Mandersloot, 1998). The student is a *learning worker* and the business individual is a *working learner*. Simultaneously, the student and the business individual learn how to assess the benefits of combining theory and practice. As just one example, both become aware of the occurrence of confusing homonyms and synonyms, like costs, expenses and expenditures, in textbooks and in the business environment (Vernooij, 2000). The student can reflect on his own body of knowledge and learn from this reflection. At the same time, the business individual benefits from the immediate employability of the working student.

Learning through practice enables students to carry out research projects in practical situations. For example, research questions for graduation projects might be derived from problems encountered in the business environment. These problems are tackled by students and business individuals can apply the findings of the students. This way the business individuals possibly gain from the enhancement of their businesses by the application of new knowledge, derived from the student projects.

At the same time, both students and business individuals are expanding their network of relationships. Students are exposed to business individuals from several organizations. Business individuals get acquainted with students from different universities.

In summary, for students, "learning through practice is" a basis for life-long learning, and for business individuals, it is part of life-long learning.

The building of the curriculum on "learning through practice" has repercussions for the university. Firstly, the university must serve as an intermediary between students and business individuals. Secondly, the university must ensure the educational value of the learning-through-practice relationships. Thirdly, the university must offer guidance to students in developing relevant ways of thinking and practicing.

Table 1: Learning through practice.

Students:	Business individuals:
theorizing about practice	putting theory into practice
Learn and work	Work and learn
Relevant practical situations for theories (work experience)	Relevant theories for practice
Immediate chance to reflect on acquired knowledge	Immediate employability of student
Do practical research projects	Gain from research findings
Networking (learning to know various business individuals and organizations)	Networking (learning to know various students and universities)
Basis for life-long learning	Part of life-long learning

4.   THE ROLE OF ICT IN LEARNING BY SHARING

Information and communication technology enables business individuals, teachers/researchers and students to share their learning with each other, wherever and whenever they want. ICT not only facilitates communication, collaboration and coordination among participants, it also facilitates access to educational resources and support of specific learning processes (OECD, 1997, pp. 121-122).

Communication tools, like e-mail and ICQ, offer the functionalities needed to support the exchange of information between the parties involved, regardless of temporal and spatial obstacles. These technologies enable intensification of the three-way communication between business individuals, teachers and students. They offer possibilities for a dialogue between researchers and business individuals, for a two-way flow of knowledge between researchers and students, and for a more intense interaction between students and business individuals.

Collaboration tools, like groupware and websites, facilitate experimenting, investigating and practicing together. For example, a group decision room can support the decision-making process of formulating joint projects of business individuals, researchers and students.

Coordination tools, like agent technologies and tracking technologies, are necessary to enable participants to learn in parallel. Activities carried out and results achieved by various participants must be aligned with each other. Agent technologies facilitate the matching of various participants based on the maximization of each individual's needs and the needs of the entire group. Tracking technologies, on the other hand, are useful for keeping track of each individual's performance. They also give suggestions for adjustments.

As far as *access to educational resources* is concerned, ICT overcomes many temporal and spatial constraints. For example, participants can enroll in any digital course any time, anywhere. And, participants have easy access to worldwide information resources, such as databases, newsgroups, websites and virtual communities. For example, members of the academic community can gain access both to an enormous range of academic communities worldwide, and to various global business communities. In other words, yesterday's knowledge is widely available, ready to be transformed into tomorrow's knowledge.

Support of specific learning processes can be facilitated by ICT in many ways. Firstly, ICT facilitates the creation of a common knowledge base for participants, including frequently asked questions. Secondly, ICT enables immediate feedback on activities carried out by participants, facilitating real-time parallel learning. Thirdly, based on their individual needs and the tracking history of their performance, intelligent applications could be designed to give suggestions for a student's next step in the learning process. For example, based on student interests, agent technologies could advise a student to enroll in certain courses, or to apply for participation in research projects with certain business individuals and researchers.

Fourthly, ICT supports education-à-la-carte, because individual education is too expensive in the university system. ICT stimulates the individual discovery process, whereas the teacher/researcher (or the technology) serves as a coach. For example, computer-based training programs enable students to follow their own path to acquire the knowledge they have chosen, and hypermedia let users search educational material in a way that suits their own logic.

Finally, ICT makes multi-perspective education possible. For example, virtual reality enables a participant to analyze a problem from the perspective of a producer, a merchant, a civil servant and a client. In this way, ICT can be useful for customizing education according to different learning styles. It has the potential to facilitate in an intelligent way the structuring of information to match the student's individual way of processing information. It aids the process of self-guided discovery.

As a last remark on this topic, students, as opposed to teachers, are more likely to be early adopters of emerging technologies. Teachers can use their students' knowledge to learn about the capabilities of new technologies in order to enhance their educational program. These new insights could lead teachers to change the way they teach.

5.   CONCLUSIONS

In this article, an integrative learning model, Learning by Sharing, is described as a model for life-long learning. Its main improvements on existing learning models are the systematic introduction of the external world into the learning process and the reciprocal nature of the interactions involved: business   individuals   with   students,   students   with teachers/researchers, and teachers/researchers with business individuals. All learn from the shared learning experiences.

The Learning by Sharing model, as outlined, is under full implementation at the University of Amsterdam. To facilitate contact between participants, meetings and informal gatherings are held to bring students, teachers and business individuals together. These gatherings result in many new ideas, out of which several useful projects have already been developed. The use of the Learning by Sharing model increases the speed and depth of learning considerably, and the interaction satisfies the educational needs of all three parties involved.

REFERENCES

Argyris, C., & Schön, D.A. (1996). *Organizational Learning II: Theory, Method, and Practice.* Reading, MA: Addison-Wesley.

Ghoshal, S., & Bartlett, C.A. (1997). *The Individualized Corporation: A Fundamentally New Approach to Management.* New York: HarperBusiness.

Kaldeway, J., Haenen, J., Wils, S., & Westhoff, G. (1998). *Leren leren in didactisch perspectief.* Groningen: Wolters-Noordhoff.

Leggon, C.B. (1997). The Scientist as Academic. In Daedalus. Proceedings of the American Academy of Arts and Sciences, *Journal of the American Academy of Arts and Sciences.*

Leidner, D.E., & Jarvenpaa, S.L. (1995). The Use of Information Technology to Enhance Management School Education: A Theoretical View. *MIS Quarterly,* (September), 265-291, Sept.

OECD (1997). ICT as a Tool for Lifelong Learning. In OECD (1997). *Information Technology Outlook.*

Ontwerp HOOP 1998 (1997). Ontwerp-Hoger Onderwijs en Onderzoek Plan 1998, Ministerie van Onderwijs, Cultuur en Wetenschappen, directie Voorlichting, 16-09-1997

Roobeek, A.J.M., & Mandersloot, E.H.U. (1998). *Lerend Werken Werkend Leren: een kennisnetwerk voor duale leertrajecten.* Amsterdam: Van Gennep.

Vermunt, J.D.H.M.(1992). *Leerstijlen en sturen van leerprocessen in het hoger onderwijs: Naar procesgerichte instructie in zelfstandig denken.* Lisse: Swets & Zeitlinger.

Vernooij, F.A.T.J. (2000). Tracking down the knowledge structure of students. In L. Borghans, R. Milter, J.E. Stinson, & W.H. Gijselaers, (Eds.), *Educational Innovation in Economics and Business V.* Dordrecht, London, Boston: Kluwer Academic Publishers.

PART III

CURRICULUM DESIGN AND CONTENT

Student-Focused Learning: the Goal of Learning to Learn

Thomas Neil[1], Ben Martz[2] & Alessandro Biscaccianti[3]
[1]Clark Atlanta University, Atlanta, USA, [2]University of Colorado, Colorado Springs, USA,
[3]Groupe ESC, Dijon, France

1.   INTRODUCTION

Problem-Based Learning, Activity Learning or Learning Centered Education are evolutionary interpretations of contextual-based learning, the outcome of the progressive education movement of the early 1900's and its primary proponent John Dewey. For example, Learning Centered Education has been offered as one response to the criticisms by Porter and McKibbin (1988) of business school curricula. Differences between "skills obtained" by graduating seniors and those skills sought by recruiters have been documented and exist as a real area of concern (Newman, 1994).

In direct contrast to the traditional "smokestacks" university teaching methodology, Learning Centered Education (LCE) "places learning and learners at the core of the educational process" (Bilimoria & Wheeler, 1995). The goal of LCE is to establish a learning partnership wherein the teacher identifies what needs to be learned and students accept the responsibility of identifying the means by which their learning occurs. In the LCE partnership, the teacher facilitates and the student participates. (In the learning partnership we will present, students identify what needs to be learned within the context of a presented issue, as one principle of Student-Focused learning)

In essence, contextual-based learning is a tautology, since all learning is contextual. When a student walks into a classroom and sits down, she/he has entered a "learning context". The same can be said for the context of the

T.A. Johannessen, A. Pedersen and K. Petersen (eds.),
Educational Innovation in Economics and Business VI, 201–213.

hallway, the lunchroom, the video game, the after-school job, or the internship. All of these contexts provide learning opportunities along a continuum from incidental and informal to formal and planned, yet these contexts vary in efficiency and effectiveness. The incidental, informal learning of the hallway, lunchroom or especially the video game involves all of the student's senses in a 'real' context. Learning in a "real" informal, context is relatively easy, you don't have to take notes, read a text, get ready for an exam, or worry about a grade. And, perhaps most significantly, the learner is choosing to be in the 'real' context. In a "real" context, self-learning occurs effortlessly, at least it seems that way. On the other hand, meta learning, understanding relationships in a 'real' context is effortful. Why? Understanding meta-relationships requires the individual to be aware of and reduce the influence of self-reference. Thus, a key role for the educator/coach/mentor is to expand a learner's self-understanding by challenging existing paradigms.

Contrast the "real" context to the planned contextual learning of the typical classroom. Rows and columns of desks face the front where the knowledge provider resides. Lesson plans, information transmitted in textbooks, on the black/green-board, with overheads or projected by PowerPoint, assessment of retention by T/F, multiple-choice, and essay tests or, to the extent applicable, standardized problems, e.g. an accounting case. In relatively static environments, where accumulated knowledge can be tested through trial and error with minimal negative consequences, passive learning may have its place. However, in dynamic, complex environments with significant levels of uncertainty, the learning of knowledge can not be driven by a static learning process. The utility of "real" context learning, although understood since the earliest use of the apprenticeship, has had difficulty in being accepted and translated as a viable modality and process in 20th century education.

This paper is the result of a serendipitous meeting of the three authors in SessionV.2 "Innovative Learning Methods" (EDINEB, 1999). We discovered, as each of us presented, that we were operating from similar principles and conceptualization of the learning process. The uniqueness of the presentations was in demonstrating, inadvertently, the ability to apply these principles and conceptualizations differentially. The paper discusses the existing formal learning context, research on student and teacher variables contributing to understanding learning effectiveness, and the principles of "Student-Focused Learning". The paper continues with the application of the S-FL principles in a course on Human Systems – Organizational Behavior.

2. THE FORMAL LEARNING CONTEXT: THE SYSTEM - THE TEACHER - THE STUDENT - THE CONSUMER

The evolution of the modern institution of higher learning has approximated the smokestack industry's manufacturing process with similar, unfortunate consequences:

1. Functional separation of the knowledge disciplines, which discourages intellectual integration and knowledge sharing.
2. Aggregation of students (raw material) which permits assembly line efficiency but delimits each student's uniqueness.
3. A compartmentalized Learning (production) process which is efficient for the system but requires the student (customer) to integrate the various knowledge's components.
4. Preference for easily scored quantitative measures of outcome which reinforces linear learning.
5. The stability of repetitiveness and control rather than the uncertainty of creativity and innovation.
6. The ability to facilitate individual learning is subjugated to technical, domain-focused expertise.

2.1 The system

Just as smokestack industries, because of their strategic and operating paradigms, had difficulty effectively responding to changes in their environment, institutions of higher education have created their own paradox. The overt control and the covert affects of the traditional educational institution constrain the student/learner, faculty/instructor, and the consumer, those who hire graduates. Yost and Keifer (1998) suggest "In traditional programs, there is a tendency to rely on institutional learning, a focus on theory and the basic truths of management. This approach has been labeled "just in case", students are expected to absorb knowledge "just in case" they ever need it." Thus, the business-consumer hires an individual whose GPA reflects an ability to absorb knowledge and regurgitate it in response to straight forward, structured assessment. Unfortunately, most businesses do not exist in static, placid environments where rote knowledge is applicable.

Within the Silo University, each faculty acts as a stand-alone production station and, therefore, does not consult with other faculty regarding instructional activities, workload demands, or assessment schedules. One, among many, unintended consequence is students must learn to respond to four or five different management styles, sets of expectations and task requirements varying over the course of each year or semester. This consequence subverts learning effectiveness.

2.2   The teacher

Traditionally, teacher development in Western cultures has made a clear distinction between those teaching at the elementary level and those teaching in higher education. The elementary school teacher is exposed to a broad array of disciplines while being taught "how to teach" and the "psychology of the learner". At the elementary level, the goal of teaching focuses on the development of the whole child not just the intellect.

At the university level, the professor is the product of a specific discipline (finance, economics, English). He/she acquires his/her teaching model serendipitously, through modeling, observation and shaping, and association with research-oriented faculty rather than with master teachers.

The goal of university teaching is the shaping of the intellect, the acquisition of knowledge, with student maturation a by-product of time. The preferred teaching modality is lecturing on domain specific knowledge, with the student responsible for knowledge acquisition. Two other teaching modalities, (1) teaching as facilitating a student's independent learning through an understanding of the student's perspective, and (2) teaching as a transmission of knowledge while facilitating the student's independent learning, are in use but receive significantly less support among faculty. In addition to a preferred teaching modality, faculties use different motivational styles in an attempt to control the transfer of knowledge. These motivating styles exist on a continuum from highly controlling; the faculty directs all components, to highly autonomy supportive, the faculty encourages student exploration and creativity.

2.3   The student

Prior to entering the formal educational process, children emulate sponges in their openness to experiencing. We marvel at their inquisitiveness, creativity, and capacity to learn quickly. However, once the formal process of acculturation and education begins the wellspring of learning is dammed and channeled into acceptable activities and experiences. Despite our extensive knowledge and understanding of the learning process, the commitment to mass education has dominated all academic levels with unforeseen but predictable consequences.

As sentient beings, we are endowed with the ability to learn both mindlessly and mindfully. To protect our selves (physical, intellectual, emotional, and spiritual), we are efficient adapters. In the early years of formal education, the child learns to sublimate her/his natural inquisitiveness and creativity or bear the consequences of deviancy. The child gradually learns without having to think about it. By the time the student enters the domain of higher education, she/he has been shaped into a sensitized receptacle, classifiable on her/his ability to efficiently absorb and effectively retransmit bounded domain specific knowledge. Interestingly, faculty and administration will often bemoan the lack of students' creativity and willingness to accept challenges.

2.4   The consumer

Historically, those who hire business graduates have exhibited benign neglect, accepting the preparation and proffered competencies as a truism. Business education was a no-brainer; the business recruited the highest grade point average in a discipline (e.g. finance) since the student was merely moving from one apparently closed system to another.

As the uncertainty of environmental futures became a reality, corporations have increasingly invested vast amounts of time and money into newly graduated college seniors. By all definitions then, a major concern for universities, students and corporations is whether students are being prepared with the skills and knowledge to succeed in today's dynamic workforce. Various criticisms regarding business school curricula have been raised. One real area of concern centers around the differences between "skills obtained" by graduating seniors and those skills sought by recruiters. Trauth *et al* (1993) studied the priorities of educators and practitioners in the Information Systems field. In their analysis, they identified a "curriculum gap." Articles over the past several years have focused on skills sought out by hiring managers or recruiters. Publications such as Forbes, Computerworld or Business Week provide some insight to the skills sought by corporations though various types of surveys. However, truly integrative approaches by schools to include this type of feedback appear to be less than optimal.

3.   RESEARCH BASE

An extensive research base, focusing on the primary components of the learning process, is available for analysis. Of particular interest is the research on student and teacher factors.

Student Variable – Achievement goal theory has emerged as a major direction in understanding motivation as it applies to the learning process.

This theory focuses on how students think about themselves, their tasks, and their performance in an achievement oriented setting. Achievement goal motivation distinguishes between two orientations: the goal to develop learning, task or mastery, and the goal to demonstrate ability performance, ego, or ability. Individuals who seek to increase their understanding and skill are more likely to seek challenges and measure progress in self-referential terms. Individuals who are ability-oriented seek favorable judgments of competence or avoid unfavorable judgments. These individuals tend to not accept challenging situations but prefer situations believed to be within their competence range.

The volition process, as part of the self-regulatory mechanisms that mobilize one's attention and efforts toward a goal, is increasingly seen as an essential element in sustaining knowledge acquisition. Volition includes the thoughts and/or behaviors that are directed toward maintaining one's intention to attain a specific goal in the face of both internal and external distractions. A student's level of volition is especially critical in maintaining necessary performance levels when course tasks span a significant amount of time and/or the goal is long-term.

Teacher Variable – The influence of the teacher on the learning process can be separated into personal characteristics and level of competence. The teacher's motivating style has been found to affect students' development and academic outcome. Teachers' motivational style exists on a continuum from teacher controlling to autonomy supportive. Controlling-oriented teachers set their own agendas and then use directives and extrinsic motivators to encourage the student to follow the agenda. Autonomy-oriented teachers encourage students to pursue self-determined agendas and then they support the students' initiatives and intrinsic motivation. Students with autonomy-supportive teachers, as compared to control-oriented teachers, report greater perceived academic outcomes (Ryan & Grolnick, 1986), a preference for optimal challenge (Pittman, Emery, & Boggiano, 1982), and higher academic achievement (Boggiano, Flink, Shields, Seelbach, & Barrett, 1993), among other outcomes.

The concern with teacher effectiveness has been an on-again off-again affair influenced by sociopolitical and economic forces as well as national concerns during periods of perceived threat, e.g. the emphasis on science when Russia's Sputnik won the race to the heavens. Most recently, the 'globalization affect' has raised the specter of inadequate instruction within America's Higher Education. The teacher's effectiveness appears to account for approximately 22% of the variance.

Studies appear to indicate three interrelated dimensions of effective teaching. First, the teacher who genuinely respects students and treats them as equals is regarded positively. Second, organization and presentation skills provide the framework and the element of arousal necessary for focusing the learning. The third factor, ability to challenge students, is characterized in part by setting high, but realistic goals for students.

4. PRINCIPLES OF STUDENT-FOCUSED LEARNING

The principles of Student-Focused Learning have their roots in the literature on Contextual Learning, Problem Based Learning, and Learning Centered Education and the research cited earlier. Chickering and Gamson (1987) identify seven "principles" for introducing student focused learning into undergraduate education. In 1996, the American Association of Higher Education (AAHE, 1996) added five more principles and moved further in their classification scheme to divide all twelve into three groupings based around quality: organizational culture, curriculum and instruction. Bilimoria and Wheeler's (1995) review of Learning Centered Education highlights six "correlated components."

1. Re-conceptualizing education as driven by learning.
2. Provide opportunities for self-directed learning.
3. Reshape authority in the classroom.
4. Adopt a relational learning approach.
5. Pay attention to context.
6. Foster life-long learning.

Our principles originate from the components and focus on the student, the instructor, and the learning process. In regard to the student, we believe:

1. Each individual wants to learn (but is often reluctant to accept responsibility).
2. each individual has the ability to guide her/his own learning.
3. Each individual brings unique experiences and perceptions to the learning encounter.
4. Each individual has a preferred mode for learning.
5. Each individual will challenge self if placed in a non-threatening but challenging environment.

In regard to the instructor-facilitator, we believe:

1. Each individual needs to be able to step outside her/his ego.
2. Each individual needs to able to translate and articulate tacit knowledge.
3. Each individual must understand the conditions necessary for providing an effective learning experience.
4. Each individual must be committed to providing a quality learning experience to each student.

5. Each individual must exhibit superior interpersonal communication skills.
6. Each individual must be sensitive to the diversity among the students.
    In regard to the learning process, we believe:
1. Learning is more than an intellectual exercise.
2. Learning is an emotional experience, it can be enjoyable.
3. Learning occurs at the juncture of the intellect and emotions.
4. Learning occurs when the student's existing learning paradigms are challenged.
5. Learning is facilitated in a non-threatening environment.
6. Learning requires complementary feedback.
7. Learning is an exchange process amongst three main stakeholders: the students, the instructors, the consumers/professionals (those who hire the graduates).
8. Learning is a collaborative effort among all principal stakeholders.
9. Learning, to be a systematic process, involves instructors and professionals in conjoint, continuous analysis, feedback and ongoing refinement of the guiding principles and their enactment.

5. THE APPLICATION OF STUDENT-FOCUSED LEARNING

Each of the authors, based on unique experiences, evolved a philosophy and principles of instruction and learning that has remarkable similarities. The application of our combined philosophies and principles, Student-Focused Learning, is demonstrated in a course, Human Systems – Organizational Behavior.

5.1 Student-focused learning and a human systems course

"Tell me what I need to do to get an A in this class."

With those words, the reverie regarding my ability as an instructor in the CAU/MBA program was disrupted. Based on my experiences as a student in a flagship institution, I had disavowed the straight lecture approach opting for an interactive medium involving cases, situations, and projects. I presented students with Socratic questions encouraging thinking rather than puppet responses. I was considered a "good" instructor. Yet, this statement suggested, at least for this student, the approach I was using was still more teaching than learning oriented. Thus began my continuing exploration for a learning process that would enhance the efficacy of learning. One approach I developed was "Learning through Confusion". Learning through Confusion is designed to challenge the student's paradigm regarding the process of acquiring knowledge within the traditional, formal educational system. In this traditional realm, the student assumes the role of a vassal at the feet of a learned master, scribbling furiously on parchment the precious words, and then, on command, spouting them back in an acceptable form.

5.2   The course

Courses for MBA programs seem to be designed using the principle of generalized knowledge supported by a concentration, a specific knowledge domain. The well-rounded MBA "should be acquainted with" economics, finance, accounting, marketing, management, production, and strategy, the traditional functional and processes areas of a business. An analysis of a typical syllabus reveals an identification of the required text, a short description of the course objectives, grading policy, assignments, class attendance, and material to be covered, usually referenced to the text, on specific dates. A comprehensive course plan including instructional objectives, learning modalities, learning exercises and assessment process (not when an exam is scheduled) is seldom prepared or available. Furthermore, a comprehensive learning plan integrating all the MBA courses is rarely available. Thus, in the traditional MBA program, knowledge is presented as parts of a salad, which the student must assemble. To produce, what: a Caesar salad, a Cobb, a Waldorf, or just a mess of Greens?

The course's learning objectives are:

1. To facilitate understanding of an organization as a goal oriented system composed of five inter-related sub-systems.
2. To facilitate understanding of complex human systems through the use of context based vignettes based on actual interpersonal issues.
3. To facilitate understanding of the group decision-making process.
4. To facilitate the ability to work effectively in team-based projects.
5. To approximate the interpersonal conditions found in typical organizations.
6. To challenge each student's learning paradigm.
7. The accomplishment of these learning objectives occurs through the use of minimal structure (e.g. instructions, goal definition, and instructor directed processes) and the manipulation of context.

The course is divided into two modules: 1) Design of a human system and 2) Application of the human system principles through case analysis. The Learning through Confusion approach is most visible in its impact during the first module. The class, as a whole, must design a business system, e.g. a restaurant, consulting firm. The students are assigned, at random, to one of the five subsystems, production, maintenance, boundary-support, adaptive and management, which constitute any human system. The student is provided with the purpose and dynamic goal for each subsystem. The designed business must incorporate specific concepts such as productivity, quality, diversity, entrepreneurship, and knowledge management. A time frame for drafts and final product is provided. The students must establish the processes by which they will interact to produce the final product. The students determine the format for the product, the description of how the business functions. The instructor provides information about the functioning of human systems on a developmental basis and outside readings. The students are required to develop supporting evidence for their decisions.

The goal of the case analysis module is for the student to be able to: determine the primary issue, the decision point, identify the essential bits of information supporting the decision point, and describe the most effective resolution based on the essential information. The format for case analysis includes establishing a timeline, identification of the essential information, identification of the perceptions of the key players, a description of the resolution, and the rationale for the selected resolution. The cases selected for analysis are short, 2-3 pages. Each case is selected on the basis of appearing to have an obvious answer while actually being complex.

6.   STAGING CONFUSION

Given a choice, the individual will avoid uncertainty not of her/his choosing. Given no choice, the individual will resolve the uncertainty by applying the set of beliefs she/he is comfortable with not the one that most closely approximates the uncertainty. At the core of any individual's belief set is the premise that certainty can be made from uncertainty, e.g. "Meaning is inherent in uncertainty if only we can discover it". The resolution of uncertainty using a belief set occurs either mindlessly or mindfully (Langer, 1989). Mindless resolution generates two types of knowledge, conditioned and shaped. Conditioned Knowledge provides the "shouldas" and "oughtas" for morale application. Shaped Knowledge provides domain specific information for specific, functional application. Mindful resolution generates complex knowing, which provides the individual with the potential for bridging to other complex knowing. Learning, to the extent it is considered mindful, requires the engagement of not only the intellect but also the emotions.

The goal of Learning through Confusion is to challenge the student's mindless response to knowledge acquisition through the presentation of uncertainty that cannot be directly avoided. First, a goal with specifics as to content is provided. But, the student must determine the configuration as well as the process to piece it together. The student is involved in constructing a puzzle with X parts that performs Y functions. The puzzle can have any shape and be put together by any process. The apparent lack of structure generates requests for more definitive goals, definitions and what should be included in the design of the project. The instructor, using reflective inquiry, guides student self-discovery. Gradually, the students begin to accept responsibility for establishing their own criteria.

Second, the MBA student is required to learn within a teamwork format, which necessitates time management and collaboration but also tends to elicit social loafing. Social loafing begins to appear as a problem as the deadline for the first draft approaches. Individuals from teams will request consultation with the instructor regarding handling the social loafer. The requests permit the introduction of a class discussion on social loafing, its causes and resolution. Time management arises as the demands of the other core courses increase. Traditional courses have weekly assignments and scheduled tests, which dominated the student's perceptual field. The short-term demands of the traditional course result in a time management process best-labeled as "What is needed this week?" Short-term oriented team members affect the student, who is attempting to manage her/his time both short and long-term. When the orientations clash, a class discussion focused on melding individual and group needs is held. The need for collaborative efforts among the five teams usually occurs after the first draft is critiqued. At that point, I might comment, "How does your production process fit into boundary-support's distribution process?"

Third, compartmentalized thinking is elicited through labeling. Project teams are labeled according to the five subsystems; production, maintenance, boundary-support, adaptive, and management. This labeling, in-conjunction with minimal structure tends to generate sub-optimization. The management team attempts to control and coordinate all activities, since these are two of management's functions. However, an individual in another group often takes on management's third function, the resolution of conflict. The other teams tend to resist management's attempt at control because they see themselves as knowing more about their functioning than anyone else. The teams gradually see a need to establish a coordinating entity. Yet, they tend to share information reluctantly.

7.   FINDINGS FROM STUDENT'S COMMENTS

Assessment of the course and process occurs at two points, end-of-term and after the summer internship.

- In assessing my experience as it pertains to working with the group, I can think of just one word to describe it "Confusing". First, we had to find out exactly what roll we played in the entire business and then be able to relate it to the other subsystems. The complexity of the project made the process of understanding long. Third, working with a group of people inevitably results in roadblocks. Yet, I learned a lot about the inner workings of a system.
- My understanding of human systems was sharply enhanced by the interaction within my group.
- I found that the group consisted more of workers than creative people. Value added process is lost among 6 people when only one is coming up with ideas and the rest are following orders.
- This was a very challenging project due to the need to coordinate.
- This project showed me how difficult it may be to work in corporate America because of the different personalities that must be blended together. I now see that I need to find a way to do more even when competent people surround me.
- During the first weeks of the project, I thought it was really stupid. I now understand the method in your madness.
- The experience was phenomenal – in every sense of the word.
- I have a greater of individual effort when you struggle in a team.

REFERENCES

AAHE (1996). What Research Says About Improving Undergraduate Education, compiled by Peter Ewell, American Association of Higher Education Bulletin, April, Vol 5.

Boggiano, A.K., Flink, C., Shields, A., Seelbach, A., & Barrett, M. (1993). Use of techniques promoting students' self-determination: Effects of students' analytic problem-solving skills, *Motivation and Emotion, 17*, 319-336.

Bilimoria, D., & Wheeler, J.V. (1995). Learning-Centered Education: A guide to Resources and Implementation, *Journal of Management Education, Vol 19*, No. 3, 409-428.

Chickering, A.W., & Gamson, Z.F. (1987). 7 Principles for Good Practice in Undergraduate Education. *The Wingspread Journal*, (June).

EDINEB, 1999, Bergen, Norway

Gardner, P.D., Nixon, D.C., & Motschenbacker, G. (1992). Starting Salary Outcomes of Cooperative Education Graduates, *The Journal of Cooperative Education, 27* (3), 16.

Langer, E.J. (1989). *Mindfulness.* Addison-Wesley, Massachusetts.

Pittman, T.S., Emery, J., & Boggiano, A.K. (1982). Intrinsic and Extrinsic Motivational Orientation: Reward Induced Changes in Preference for Complexity, *Journal of Personality and Social Psychology, 42*, 789-797.

Porter, L.W. & McKibbin, L.W (1988). *Management Education: Drift or Thrust into the 21st Century?* New York: McGraw-Hill.

Ryan, R.M., & Grolnick, W.S. (1986). Origins and Pawns in the Classroom: Self-report and Projective Assessment of Individual Differences in Children's Perceptions, *Journal of Personality and Social Psychology, 50*, 550-558.

Yost, E.B. & Keifer, J.L. (1998). Application of Problem-Based Learning Pedagogy to Management Education. In R.G. Milter, J.E. Stinson, & W.H. Gijselaers, (Eds.), *Educational Innovation in Economics and Business III* (pp. 283-299). Dordrecht, London, Boston: Kluwer Academic Publishers.

Trauth, E.M., Farwell, D.W., & Lee, D. The IS Expectation Gap: Industry Expectations Versus Academic Preparation. *MIS Quarterly*, (September), 293-307.

Enterprise Development: Strategic Collaboration for Economics and Business

Jerry Courvisanos
School of Economics University of Tasmania,Launceston, Australia

1. STATE OF PLAY

An uncomfortable tension exists between economics and business within universities, both at the teaching and the research levels. At the teaching level, there is the challenge of business courses in accounting, management, marketing and international business that are strongly attracting students while enrolments in traditional economics degrees are declining.[1] Lawson (1997) identifies the lack of "realism" in the study of economics as the source of this decline, where students are voting with their feet to more "relevant" courses in business. The irrelevancy of economics is based on both the abstract nature of the economic models taught and the perceived less vocational orientation of practical skill formation compared to business courses. The issue generally gets raised only in the context of business course coordinators demanding "more relevant and less abstract" economics material in the compulsory "economics for business" unit in their business-based degrees. EDINEB provides the appropriate forum to discuss this unease link between economics and business. The link tends to be ignored, with the focus staying firmly within each sector, except in terms of what basic economics is needed in business degrees.

At the research level, economics is dominated by a static *a priorist* model in which analysis is conducted on the basis of the deductive approach (Jones, 1994). This entails setting up an optimal allocation solution and challenging

---

[1] See for example in Australia, Lewis and Norris (1996). Lawson (1997) refers to similar evidence appearing in the U.K. and North America.

T.A. Johannessen, A. Pedersen and K. Petersen (eds.),
Educational Innovation in Economics and Business VI, 215–234.

agents to alter their decisions so that they conform to the economic rational predictions in the model. The approach is completely at odds with the imperative of business management research to understand and develop effective practical skills in administering and planning firm operations. This entails the use of an inductive approach based on benchmarking and establishing quality standards for agents of firms to use as guidelines for decision-making.[2]

Placing the above tensions within the context of rapid structural change in capitalist economies provides the opportunity for resolution of the dilemma. Fostered by the shift in "techno-economic paradigm" from mass manufacturing production to digital (IT) information technology (Freeman & Perez, 1988; Tapscott, 1996), business is experiencing fundamental change in processes and economic activity has greater cyclical volatility.[3] these elements are not central to current mainstream commerce-based university research and education. Expressions of this dissatisfaction from leading heterodox writers in economics and business management throughout the 1990s has led to a set of new analytical frameworks at the frontiers of research (and corresponding new degree courses) within each sector. Appreciating these new perspectives and their points of intersection allows for a powerful productive collaboration between economics and business in terms of enterprise development for both new courses and in research. Such collaboration can bring to an end the uneasy economics-business tension.

2.   RATIONALE FOR ENTERPRISE DEVELOPMENT

Enterprise development in this paper refers to the development of business activities by individuals and teams (either as owner-managers or as employees at any level) who see change as opportunities to create wealth in society by a process of problem-avoidance. This requires entrepreneurial skills that involve holistic perspective, dynamic (change) process and

---

[2] Legge and Hindle (1997, xi) describe management "…as a purposive activity…to preserve the *status quo* against forces that may tend to disrupt it." This highlights the wide chasm between *status quo* management and *a priorist* economics.

[3] Courvisanos (1996) examines this intensification of business cycle activity from its source in the increased volatility of business fixed investment spending by firms. Increased uncertainty in the new IT-based paradigm, together with reduced government support, makes investment cycles more susceptible to over-shooting and under-spending. Exacerbated cyclical volatility has been evident recently both in terms of recessions (OECD in the early 1990s, Asian "tigers" in 1997-98) and booms (Asian "tigers" in mid-1990s, USA and Australia in the late 1990s).

handling uncertainty. A course in enterprise development needs to be placed within the context of innovation occurring globally through the expanding information knowledge economy.

From the business management perspective, Drucker (1980) argues that problem-solving skills have dominated in the reactive mode. This orients firms to finding solutions when real problems occur. There needs to be an improvement in problem-avoidance skills in the area of anticipating and identifying opportunities. Barker (1992) applies Drucker's perspective on problem-based skilling to the new information economy, in which the uncertainties of the future demand anticipation of opportunities through innovation. Mintzberg (1994) takes this one step further by setting out formal planning procedures to turn innovation strategies into executable plans. Shift to this new business paradigm in the anticipative mode is required to match the techno-economic paradigm shift.

Set up by the Australian Federal Government, the Industry Task Force on Leadership and Management Skills chaired by David Karpin made their first recommendation as the development of an enterprising culture within formal education and training, specifying the need to "(e)xpose students...to the value of enterprising and entrepreneurial behavior" (Karpin, 1995, p. xxiii). This is the essence of enterprise development, i.e. creative business applications within an economic environment of structural change that offers opportunities for such applications. The report goes on to relate evidence that current business courses pay "scant attention" to these aspects, while... entrepreneurial skills are not seen as a critical component of management education." (1995, p. 34) Evidence is collated that shows entrepreneurial skills are low in Australia and yet they can be taught (1995, pp. 111-14). A research report to Karpin shows that this requires a "whole-of-business" view with problem-based learning that is project centered involving teams and work placements (Clegg et al., 1995, p. 1324).

Entrepreneurship is the term usually associated with "the creative application of change" (Legge & Hindle, 1997, p. xii). Although valid within its own business management terms, for the purpose of this collaboration with economics, the term is limited in two ways. First, the term has historically come out of small business studies programs and tends to relate to the creation of new ventures.[4] This precludes the study of entrepreneurial ventures and project developments within large corporations (sometimes called "intrapreneurship"). Second, the term lacks a precise research base

---

[4] *The American Journal of Small Business* changed its name to *Entrepreneurship Theory and Practice* in 1988, yet the editor clearly noted that there "...will not be a drastic change in our mission." (Bagby, 1988). Karpin (1995, xxiii) reports on the need to "[p]rovide units in entrepreneurship and small business formation and management in vocational and professional courses."

from which to conduct inquiries. Entrepreneurship textbooks (e.g. Dollinger, 1999; Hisrich & Peters, 1998) have a segment in Chapter 1 showing the vast and divergent ways that the term has been defined over the years, with the "small business" version having been appropriated by journals and "do-it-yourself" management writers. Further, Binks and Vale (1990, 2) argue that the "accumulation of empirical evidence which refers to entrepreneurship has been generated in an ad hoc manner as a consequence of a general absence of a systematic approach to the subject." Bygrave and Hofer (1991) explain how theorizing about entrepreneurship has been stifled by these limitations.

From the economics perspective, the orthodox static equilibrium analysis that dominates all major dualistic microeconomics-macroeconomics textbooks has no way of incorporating innovation and the entrepreneurial function. "[I]t is almost irrelevant to consider entrepreneurs in the context of neo-classical analysis, since their operations refer to the adjustment processes which are assumed to be instantaneous for the purpose of analytical clarity." (Binks & Vale, 1990, p. 13) Two broad resolutions of this dilemma have emerged within the economics discipline.

One is based on remaining firmly within the priorist model and assuming that an entrepreneur is engaged by "the firm" as its agent to take the innovation from its concept stage through to a fully functioning business enterprise. This involves establishing an "organizational architecture" with appropriate decision right assignment that combines microeconomic rational reward and performance evaluation systems (Brickley et al., 1997).[5] The major objective of this principal-agent theory approach is to ensure that the entrepreneur sets up appropriate economic rational "signals" within the organisation, resulting in maximum value added from the innovation. Deviations from this "optimal solution" are seen as evidence of breakdown in principal (p)-agent (a) relations between either "the firm" (p) and its entrepreneur (a), or the entrepreneur (p) and the "nexus of contracts" involving employees, suppliers, customers and creditors (a). This approach takes an inherent dynamic process and places it within the static algorithm of neoclassical economics that assumes "…there is a perfect but unobservable reality underlying temporal phenomena." (Legge & Hindle, 1997, p. 560) The explanatory power of this a priori theory is limited by the inability for research to show that such optimal contracting is most beneficial to the entrepreneurial process of innovation. "[I]f underlying reality is perfect, then it cannot change." (Legge & Hindle, 1997, p. 560)

---

[5] Shapiro and Varian (1999) is an excellent business management application of this approach to the information economy.

The other resolution from economics is to adopt "variant approaches, particularly in areas where conventional tools simply fail." (Arrow, 1994, p. x)[6] Nightingale (1996, p. 44) calls this the struggle out of orthodoxy. Two remarkable personal accounts of such "struggle" come from the Prefaces of two recent books. One is by Arthur (1994), a mathematical economist who applies the innovation technology concepts of lock-in and path-dependence to the economics of increasing returns which produce "unwelcome implications" in tracking mathematical equilibrium solutions. Prior to Arthur's work, these increasing return results were treated as pathological specimens interfering in the natural workings of the economy. Instead, there is a self-organizing evolving "complexity" system that emerges out of chaos and changes over time in concert with the sequential planning of many institutions.[7]

Snooks (1998) outlines in his preface how, as an economic historian he also has struggled out of the orthodoxy of neoclassical economics, as well as the tendency of economic historians to limit themselves to interpreting historical episodes. Examining the historical account of technological paradigm shifts, Snooks identifies the unfolding of dynamic strategies in a competitive environment that explains the processes of innovation, business cycles and structural change. "A dominant dynamic strategy will be pursued until it has been economically exhausted, which will occur when the marginal cost of investment in this strategy equals its marginal revenue. This leads not to collapse but to stagnation." (Snooks, 1998, p. 253)

From these two diverse disciplines within economics emerges a strategic self-organizing system that evolves over time and unites the two elements of Adam Smith; that of the invisible hand and the specialization innovation strategy which in consort lead to monopoly power. Evolutionary economics draws these elements together into a systemic approach to map and monitor innovation and the entrepreneurial process so that the guidelines for private and public decision-making can be identified, encouraged and supported (see

---

[6] Kenneth Arrow is the Nobel laureate economist who in 1954 refined the neoclassical process to show that every competitive general equilibrium is a social optimum (Arrow-Debreu Model). Arrow (1994) provides a "Foreword" to Arthur (1994), concluding with the following: "Arthur's views are indeed more nuanced; they show how the same mechanisms can lead to inefficiency under suitable initial conditions or random fluctuations, and so they provide a necessary corrective to some overly optimistic current tendencies in thought."

[7] "Arthur is one of those economists whom other economists regard as dangerously radical, while practical managers and marketers come upon his work and express surprise that anyone should put so much effort into proving the blindingly obvious (see, for example, Dickson, 1995)." (Legge and Hindle, 1997, 566) This is another example of the chasm existing between economics and business.

especially Dosi et al., 1988).[8] Shift to this new economic paradigm is required to match the techno-economic paradigm shift and complement the shift to the anticipative mode in business management paradigm.

Returning to the definition of enterprise development, this term provides a neutral meeting space between economics and business. Such a space is not on the intellectual territory of the other and allows for collaboration without giving ground in an analytical sense. This space is where the evolutionary system approach to economics augments standard neoclassical economics and intersects with the anticipative "whole-of-business" management approach that is augmented with inductive-based entrepreneurship studies. Within this space, intellectual efforts in one aspect will feed through to the other, informing both the economics and business disciplines. In this process of collaboration the intellectual paradigm shifts should speed up. Kirchhoff (1991, p. 109) provides an example of how this can happen: "Entrepreneurship research continues in many different disciplines so that it gradually increases the pressure for a paradigm shift within economics." The inverse can also occur, where strategic-based economics research produces a rigorous and coherent approach to entrepreneurship that would put pressure on business management to be more anticipative.

3.   COLLABORATION

Crucial to the delivery of a degree in enterprise development is a group of academics that understand and are sympathetic to the rationale outlined in the previous section. A holistic perspective is needed both in teaching across the different units and within the units where team teaching is required. This perspective must extend to the nature of the research being conducted and the ability to translate such research into meaningful conclusions to team members who are experts in other fields. Gradually this should lead to collaborative inter-disciplinary research that feeds the forces of paradigm shift.

In this collaborative process, three elements predominate:

---

[8] Austrian economics is an alternative innovation-based dynamic system of analysis (see especially Kirzner, 1973, 1985). Chaos is organised through competition to extract supernormal profits and move on to other "disequilibriums" in the economy. Any attempts to provide order and strategic private or public pathways through this dynamic process are doomed to fail from this approach. Legge and Hindle (1997, 561) argue that this approach is "...used to justify every form of speculation and market manipulation, and provides a theoretical fig leaf for the use of the term 'entrepreneur' to describe the financial manipulators of the 1980s."

1. instability that comes from uncertainty in real historical time with respect to innovation and technology;
2. complexity of self-organizing economic systems that produce mutation, selection and adoption of technologies at different diffusion rates;
3. evolutionary structural change that has feedback and interaction for the innovation process as industries grow, mature and then decline.

The innovation-based evolutionary systems approach to economics provides the framework around which the three elements operate (Hofer & Polt, 1998, pp. 7-11). Enterprise development needs to take these elements out of economics and apply them to all commerce disciplines, identifying how these elements can be used to analyze relevant issues in each discipline. These elements provide a unity of purpose in the degree structure and in the focus of learning whatever distinct skills are specified in each unit.

The Launceston campus of the University of Tasmania is where this enterprise development degree has emerged. The commerce staff is small and share common facilities and secretarial support. This is an excellent base for collaboration. In large university campuses staff from different commerce disciplines rarely meet in social, administrative and academic discourse-type formats (seminars or informal morning breaks). This lack of contact makes any collaborative process more difficult as academics are usually obsessed with their own activities. The Launceston staff came together to identify their own competitive strengths. Consensus of the staff was that the small staff numbers provided limited depth in any one area of commercial studies. However, the need for each staff member to teach a wide group of subjects and for staff to communicate regularly with each other provided Launceston with its one competitive strength; its ability to collaborate relatively easily.

At Launceston there are academics in the areas of economics, accounting, business law, marketing, management, information systems. All these areas arose out of the need to service highly specific traditionally focused business degrees (e.g. accounting, human resource management). The rationale above establishes the need to move out of these traditional static-oriented boxes of expertise and embrace enterprise development with its three dynamic systems elements and collaborative synergies of competitive advantage.

One final aspect to collaboration is with the business community. When designing a curriculum and its content, the three innovation-based economics elements above need to be related to the skill requirements of the entrepreneurial business function. To achieve this objective faculty staff contacted those parts of the business community that appreciate the nature of innovation and its development requirements within the business environment. In respect to this degree, the faculty met with senior operatives from:

- regional business development board (Business North),
- business development centers and IT incubation centers,
- enterprise development workshops run by State chamber of commerce,
- IT-focus business network (Tasmanian Community Network),
- work-based learning (school-industry partnership) board,
- technology park-based businesses,
- secondary college and vocational tertiary enterprise educators,
- business consultants and business training providers,
- Department of State Development.

In a "focus group" approach, faculty staff asked these operatives if there was a need for an innovation-based enterprise development degree. The perception from the group was that current discipline-specific undergraduate commerce degrees and general management-based MBA programs do not fill the enterprise development gap. The former relates to specific skill-based careers, while the latter are for senior management generalist skills training. Neither route offers advancement of skill needs from those currently taught at basic levels within a haphazard plethora of short courses, skill-based school-to-work programs, workshops, seminars, on-the-job, and "learning-by-doing". The enterprise development degree's point of departure was seen by the focus group as the type of learning occurring in these skills formation formats.

The focus groups identified the following as being required in this degree:
- innovation-based business approach (both in small and large firms),
- competitive strengths and strategic implementation,
- business logistics in changing environment,
- project management and finance,
- problem-based learning,
- anticipating problems and opportunities,
- work placement in innovative firms,
- flexible delivery mode with modular course structure,
- multiple entry points, in particular from non-traditional sources currently not seen as university-based entry pathways (enterprise education delivery operators),
- multiple exit points, where such exits allow due recognition of work completed.

Overall what emerged was a unanimous agreement that a holistic business enterprise development degree was indeed required. Its framework would need to relate to the three elements specified above within a cohesive focused understanding of enterprise development. The focus comes from all the discipline-based staff at the faculty and input from skilled personnel based in the above listed business organizations. The next section shows how these aspects have been incorporated into the enterprise development degree.

4. OUTLINE OF ENTERPRISE DEVELOPMENT DEGREE

Table 1 below sketches the course structure of the proposed Bachelor of Business Administration (Enterprise Development). The units within the Bachelor of Business Administration (Ent Dev) are shown on the table in a 12.5% grid, with seven units comprising one year of full time study. One first year unit is *Foundations of Enterprise Development*. This is the "flagship" unit of the course and is a full year (25% weighting) program that establishes the basic principles and fundamental issues in the strategically focused area of developing new enterprises or redesigning extant enterprises. Appendix 1 sets out the curriculum details for the Foundations of *Enterprise Development* unit.

The BBA (Ent Dev) degree consists of 16 specified core units and seven elective units. The specified core units are delivered from four of the schools within the faculty as follows: Accounting and Finance (3) Economics (5) Information Systems (2) and Management (5). The remaining core unit is Data Handling and Statistics 1 from the School of Mathematics and Physics, consistent with the same servicing of this quantitative unit in the other BBA programs based in Launceston. Table 1 identifies four units with asterisks (*), indicating new units created specifically for this course. Three of these units are enterprise development content specific, the final unit is a business placement activity program.

Crucial to this degree is the "whole-of business" strategic focus in the context of rapid structural change. This needs to be introduced to students from day one of their degree course, and followed throughout this degree program. These specific enterprise development units allow this to be realized. In Year 1, the *Foundations of Enterprise Development* unit allows fundamental problems and principles to be introduced on the nature of strategic development in new and redesigned organizations, and in specific development projects.

In Year 2, the information systems and the finance perspective to this strategic focus are developed in the two specific units *Business Logistics* and *Project Financing*. In Year 3, two recently introduced economics units in the Bachelor of Commerce Business Economics major will be used for exactly the same purpose but from the economics perspective.

Table 1: Bachelor of Business Administration (Enterprise Development): Degree Structure.

Year 1	Year 2	Year 3
BFA103 Accounting & Financial Decision Making S1	BMA201 Organizational Behavior S1	BEA326 Entrepreneurship and Innovation S1
BSA101 Business Information Systems S1	BEA110 Economics For Business S1	BMA308 Electronic Marketing S1
BMA101 Introduction to Management S1 or S2	BSA2XX * Business Logistics S1	BEA3XX * Field Operation S2
BEA 1XX* Foundations of Enterprise DevelopmentS1 and S2	BFA2XX* Project Financing S2	BEA302 Economics, Management and Organization S2
BEA 1XX* Foundations of Enterprise DevelopmentS1 and S2	BFA141 Commercial Transactions S2	BMA302 Strategic Management S2
KMA153 Data Handling & Statistics 1 S2	Elective	Elective
BMA251 Principles of Marketing S2	Elective	Elective
Elective	Elective	Elective

* = New units

Finally, the *Field Operation* unit aims to be the capstone unit, where skills developed throughout the course are brought together in an activity-based unit. Each student is placed in a business organization to contribute to a specific project or activity that requires enterprise development skills, either in helping to design or implement some new/redesigned aspect of the business. The students must commit a three week block (five days a week) in July before the start of Semester Two, followed by one day a week for the remaining 13 academic weeks. Assessment will be based on an activity *pro-forma* completed by a senior member of the organization in which the student has worked plus a report from an academic staff member who is appointed as the student's supervisor for the period. All Launceston staff will be involved in supervising students in their business placements through this unit. See curriculum details of the *Field Operation* unit in Appendix 2.

To successfully market this degree it is crucial to offer a complementary first-year only award of Diploma in Enterprise Development. Graduates from the Diploma can articulate into the second year of the BBA (Ent Dev). This will allow students to enroll in the Diploma for the first year, without intimidating them with a three-year commitment. The Diploma is offered in a full-fee paying format through Unitas Consulting (commercial arm of the university) with the contact hours fitting in with work commitments: residential schools, evening blocks, summer "sandwich" semesters. The faculty will also provide certificates for students who wish to exit from the BBA (Ent Dev) after first year or second year, or who want to complete the specific core units within the following modules: economics - five BEA units, management - five BMA units, commerce - six BFA/BSA/KMA units.

Problem-based learning approach with flexible teaching modes is the focus in this degree. The four new units created for this degree will strongly reflect this focus, as will some of the other units closely identify with the objectives of this degree. Specifically, the approach involves students in problem-anticipation workshops, identifying opportunities, screening projects, case study assessments, developing financial feasibility plans, managing portfolio of activities in actual business environment, devising business plans, incubation activities using IT (information technology) support, reporting on strategic business experiences, and including the participation of successful entrepreneurs.

Assessment will reflect flexible pedagogy. This consists of a combination of persuasive writing projects, group workshop presentations, executive reports, practical problem-anticipation exercises, oral presentation, IT-based practicals, developing business plans, activity-based assessment (e.g. forming companies, stock market operations) and examinations.

Figure 1 shows the variety of entry points into the degree. Many of these entry points do not exist for standard commerce and economics degrees. TAFE (Tertiary and Further Education) vocational diplomas and matriculation are standard entry points. Where this degree is concentrating its admission of students is through the other entry points, notably from diplomas and certificates that relate to enterprise education. The Tasmanian Enterprise Workshop (TEW) is conducted by the Tasmanian Chamber of Commerce involving group work in preparation of a detailed business plan based around accounting, finance, management and marketing principles and its presentation to senior business people in the State. Successful completion leads to the Diploma in Entrepreneurial Management (DEM) under the auspices of The Enterprise Development Institute of Australia. Through Unitas Consulting will come the Diploma of Enterprise Development graduates and other more specific vocational diplomas like the Diploma in Call Centre Management. At a lower certificate level there is enterprise education and an interview process will assess their ability and motivation for entering the BBA (Ent Dev). Finally, direct marketing of the degree to the business organizations listed above that were involved in the initial conceptualization of this program will aim to have the operatives encouraging their employees to enroll (and pay their fees). Such people will be able to enter the program on the bases of relevant prior business experience.

5.   FUTURE ROLE FOR ENTERPRISE DEVELOPMENT

A University of Tasmania student in the economics unit *Economics, Management and Organization* completed a case study on the demand for business graduates at the end of 1998. This study identified many broad "whole-of-business" recent graduate job descriptions in the national based newspaper *The Australian*, where a commerce degree is asked for but no specialization is specified. Structural change has meant that there are now many opportunities for graduates who have generalist skills in business within the context of a continually changing entrepreneurial environment.

Discussions with the business community in Tasmania, and particularly in the north of the State, have indicated the need for such an enterprise development approach to business education. A recent survey by Business North of responses from 279 businesses revealed that factors impeding business growth were broad-based. Asked to nominate their most serious business skill impediment, the survey showed the lack of the following factors: financial management (18%), business planning skills (18%), government policy and practice information (19%), product marketing and promotion including e-commerce (13%), job readiness skills for the workforce (12%). Thus, there is a need for a generalist undergraduate degree to cover all such aspects from the "whole-of-business" perspective. The business skill market identified above needs to be serviced by an undergraduate enterprise development degree. This proposal is unique in Australia (as at mid-1999) and differs markedly with programs in the USA and UK. The latter programs are based around the concept of entrepreneurship and they have become an important part of business education in those countries over the last decade in the form identified by Vesper and McMullan (1988). This form has weaknesses discussed earlier and rarely provides the explicit economic perspective that has been the focus of this paper and the enterprise development degree proposal.

BBA (Ent Dev) degree is a flexible problem-anticipation and interactive learning program with many opportunities to apply and demonstrate these skills in virtual and actual business environments. This approach enables the degree to attract target groups that have not previously considered university education as relevant. Support from the Karpin Report for this strategy is set out in the following quote, which makes a clear distinction between "enterprise education" and standard MBA courses:

> The Task Force concludes that the primary focus of enterprise education should be on those in the education system, particularly the young and, in the case of entrepreneur education, on potential workers and managers rather than existing SME [small-to-medium sized enterprise] managers. (Karpin, 1995, p. 114)[9]

Karpin's view adds to the argument that there is a strong future role for enterprise development as a distinct collaborative effort that stands in contrast to management-based entrepreneurship courses and degrees.

6.   IMPLICATIONS FOR BUSINESS AND ECONOMICS

The major limitation of the degree structure outlined in this paper is that the majority of subjects offered are "borrowed" from other courses in the faculty, with only five semester-based subjects out of 24 developed specifically for this degree program. This is due to severe resource constraints and the "university politics" of needing to frame this degree within an established BBA shell. This limitation implies that the enterprise development degree structure outlined above is only a small step in the direction that the rationale argued for at the beginning of this paper. However, it is a crucial step, since it places on the academic register "enterprise development" as an approved area of research and learning. Only future success will overcome the two stated constraints.

Future success in collaboration between economics and business in the area of enterprise development should also have wider implications. First, by building a strong collaborative vehicle for the two broad disciplines of

---

[9] In support of the Karpin quote on the role of enterprise education: the Tasmanian Enterprise Workshop (TEW) has over 350 alumni as potential students, while the Launceston Secondary College's new enterprise education course has increased from an introductory pilot group of 20 in 1998 to 250 in 1999. Many participants in both these courses have indicated to their teachers that they would like to continue further study in enterprise development, but with no current option available for a more rigorous and analytical extension of strategic innovation developments.

economics (including economic history, applied economic policy, history of economic thought, econometrics, industrial relations) and business (including accounting, management, marketing, international business, information systems). Second, by creating a synthesis between the two disciplines, which should result in a unique evolutionary and anticipative mode of analysis. Third, by responding positively to the structural changes in capitalism and the demands of "new age" business for analytical skills and creative (or divergent) thinking.[10] Fourth, by attracting a non-traditional source of young people to university education through different multi-faceted entry points and career pathways in enterprise education which currently are very limited or non-existent. Fifth, by endowing both broad disciplines with what each requires most of, relevance in economics and analytical specificity in business.

Finally, collaboration between economics and business allows the unfolding of a distinct research agenda. From a major dissenting economist writing back in 1943, Michal Kalecki, there is a standout entrepreneurship quote that should generate inquiry. This quote challenges the (still) dominant orthodox economics position on the efficient capital market. It also questions the orthodox entrepreneurship position on the central role of "entrepreneurial ability": Many economists assume, at least in their abstract theories, a state of business democracy where anybody endowed with entrepreneurial ability can obtain capital for starting a business venture. This picture of the activities of the 'pure' entrepreneur is, to put it mildly, unrealistic. The most important prerequisite for becoming an entrepreneur is the ownership of capital. (Kalecki, 1971, 109, italics in the original)

Given the extreme difficulty pioneer innovators have to finance new venture creations and the financial "deep pockets" of large corporations for research and development (Legge & Hindle, 1997, p. 507), the Kalecki quote deserves significant research inquiry using the collaborative strengths of both the economics and business disciplines. Kalecki's work identifies investment in productive capacity as the driver of economic growth and the determinant of business cycle activity. The entrepeneurial function is significant if it leads to business fixed investment, and this means a need to explain how innovation is financed. The resolution of these issues within an economy determines the structure of capitalism and the public policy role of government as a strategic partner in the flowering of competitive advantage.[11]

---

[10] Vesper and McMullan (1988, 10) argue that entrepreneurship needs the major element of "exercise in 'divergent thinking', a mode of thought suppressed in most traditional business courses."

[11] See Kannegiesser (1996, 120-39) for a detailed account of the role of economics in the entrepreneurial process from a public policy perspective.

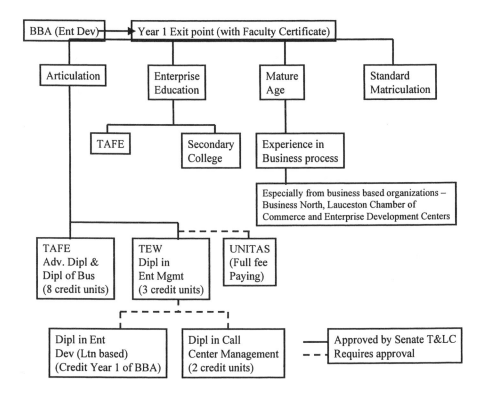

Figure 1: Entry Points into BBA (Ent Dev)

7.   ACKNOWLEDGMENT

The author acknowledges the support of the Faculty of Commerce & Law at the University of Tasmania in the development of the Enterprise Development degree and presentation of this paper at Bergen. All the staff of the Faculty at the Launceston campus have contributed with help and advice on this degree proposal's evolution. Particular thanks go to Prof. Peter Dowling, Hilary Haugstetter, Harvey Griggs and Maxine McKibben. All facts and views expressed in this paper are the author's alone.

APPENDIX 1:

Foundations of Enterprise Development: Brief Unit Outline
This is the "flagship" unit for this degree. It introduces and begins to apply key strategic-based principles to issues that arise in enterprise development. The unit provides a solid foundation for the elements that distinguish entrepreneurial activity from status quo delivery of business service. The most common issues influencing an individual business are examined in this unit: market pressures, changing economic circumstances, role of information technology, compliance requirements, and management strategies (planning, human resource management). Problem-avoidance learning techniques are applied based on obtaining information, understanding models, anticipating problems and opportunities, and researching specific case studies. Strategies and their implementation are examined in the context of the economic institutions in operation. In this context, the Australian experience is compared to international best practice throughout all topics in this unit.

Unit Objectives

On successful completion of this unit, a student will have:
a   knowledge of key enterprise development principles and an understanding of how these principles apply to developing new enterprises and/or redesigning extant enterprise;
b   capability to critically assess the nature, role and outcomes of strategic actions as they apply to competitive advantage, innovation, planning, leadership and decision-making;
c   ability to apply enterprise development principles to specific problem areas and different business environments, especially in Australia vis-à-vis international best practice;
d   understanding of key structural elements in the business economy which affect enterprise (especially information technology, rapidly changing environment, stronger stakeholder interest).

Content

The unit is introduced in the first week under the topic heading:
Enterprise development in a rapidly changing economic environment.
    The following topics will be examined in two week problem-solving blocks:
    1.   Operations of business in the current economic, political and social environment.
    2.   Strategy and competitive advantage: basis of enterprise development principles.
    3.   Innovation: result of enterprise development application.
    4.   Entrepreneurship: creative application of evolution and change.
    5.   Organizational forms conducive to change: entrepreneurs and intrapreneurs.
    6.   Strategic management and planning in a change environment.
    7.   Project management and financing: stakeholders and borrowing options.
    8.   Human resource management and teamwork: understanding people at work.
    9.   Leadership role and effective decision making: understanding decision role.
    10. Information technology applications: business logistics.
    11. Compliance requirements, ecological sustainability and strategic positioning.
    12. Globalization and localization options in enterprise development.

The unit concludes with a one week debriefing on:
Enterprise development and the future.

Guest experts in specific areas will be invited to initiate some of these above content block topics.

Assessment
Continuous Assessment (50%):

Oral presentation of group workshop deliberations	10%
Tutorial problem-avoidance assignments (2 x 10% @)	20%
Case study report assessing one of the unit blocks	20%
Final Examination (3 hours)	50%

APPENDIX 2:

Field Operation: Brief Unit Outline
This is the capstone unit in the degree and provides an opportunity for students to apply the conceptual, technical and personal skills gained during the course in a "real-time" environment. Each student is placed in a business organization to contribute to a specific project or activity that requires enterprise development skills, either in helping to design or implement some new/redesigned aspect of the business. A student may be "placed" in her/his own business activity (either as owner or employee) with someone responsible for reporting on the activities involved.

Unit Objectives

On successful completion of this unit, a student will have:
a. experience of applying enterprise development skills in an actual business situation;
b. understanding and appreciation of the difficulties and support that accompanies any attempts to change the business environment within an organization;
c. contributed to using acquired skills through this whole course into a 'real-time' environment and appreciated aspects needed to improve on such contributions. Recognized elements in a business that are/are not conducive to change and development.

Content

Business placement for the whole of Semester 2.
The program consists of:
a. One introductory session where all students gather to understand the rules of this business placement. To be held prior to the placement starts.
b. Placement Phase 1: Three week block (five days a week) in July before the start of Semester Two. This establishes the specific project activity and provides a period of sustained activity.
c. Placement Phase 2: One day a week for 13 academic weeks of Semester Two. This enables students to follow-up and fine-tune the project activity. The longer period allows some assessment of the project's action, success and influence on the organization.

d. Full day session where all students gather to present short project (assessable) reports on the success, failure and frustration's of each of their project activities to their fellow students and all the invited staff.

Staff Involvement

A coordinator is appointed to establish business links and establish work placements for students; to make the business placements and set up supervision both from within the business and with the Faculty; to organize and chair both the introductory session and the final full day session; to submit graded results for this unit.

Launceston staff across all schools will be appointed as Supervisors for students in this unit. The Supervisor is responsible for visiting the student at her/his work placement; discussing progress and problems in the activity with the student and senior management in the organization; reading and assessing weekly student activity diary; assessing final student report and submitting final mark to the coordinator.

Assessment

Grading of this unit will be based on:
(i) Activity pro-forma - completed by a senior member of the organization in which the student has been placed. This form provides information on the type of activity, nature of student's contribution, role of other staff in this activity, student's regular project involvement and the state of the project/activity at time of writing.
(ii) Weekly student activity diary - completed by the student each week identifying activity involved in that week and some brief assessment of project involvement which isolates breakthroughs and problems. The diary must be submitted in a weekly basis to the student's supervisor.
(iii) Project report - completed by the student for presentation at the final day session which sets out:
- Brief overview of the activity;
- Success and failure during the activity;
- Final assessment of their own contribution in the work placement;
- Future work required (if needed).
Assessment weighting
- Activity pro-forma   30%
- Weekly student activity diary   40%
- Project report   30%

REFERENCES

Arthur, W.B. (1994). *Increasing Returns and Path Dependence in the Economy*. Ann Arbor: The University of Michigan Press.

Arrow, K.J. *Foreword*. In W.B. Arthur (1994), pp. vii-x.

Bagby, D.R. (1998). Editorial: The winds of change. *Entrepreneurship Theory and Practice, 13* (1), (Fall), 5-6

Barker, J.A. (1992). *Paradigms: The Business of Discovering the Future*. New York: Harper Business.

Binks, M., & Vale, P. (1990). *Entrepreneurship and Economic Change*. London: McGraw-Hill.

Brickley, J.A., Smith, C.W., Jr., & Zimmerman, J.L. (1997). *Managerial Economics and Organizational Architecture*. Chicago: Irwin.

Bygrave, W.D., & Hofer, C.W. (1991). Theorizing about entrepreneurship. *Entrepreneurship Theory and Practice, 16* (2), (Winter), 13-22.

Clegg, S., Dwyer, L., Gray, J., Kemp, S., Marceau, J., & O'Mara, E. (1995). Embryonic industries: Leadership and management needs. In *Industry Task Force on Leadership and Management Skills, Enterprising nation: Research report, Volume 2*. Canberra: Commonwealth of Australia, 1289-1347.

Courvisanos, J. (1996). *Investment Cycles in Capitalist Economies: A Kaleckian Behavioural Contribution*. Cheltenham: Edward Elgar.

Dickson, P. (1995). Review of 'Increasing returns and path dependence in the economy'. *Journal of Marketing, 59* (3), (July), 97-9.

Dollinger, M.J. (1999). *Entrepreneurship: Strategies and Resources*. (2nd. ed.). New Jersey: Prentice Hall.

Dosi, G., Freeman, C., Nelson, R., Silverberg, G., & Soete, L. (Eds.). (1988). *Technical Change and Economic. Theory*. London: Pinter.

Drucker, P.F. (1980). *Managing in Turbulent Times*. New York: Harper & Row.

Freeman, C., & Perez, C. (1988). *Structural Crises of Adjustment: Business Cycles and Investment Behaviour*. In Dosi et al. (Eds.), pp. 38-66.

Hisrich, R.D., & Peters, M.P. (1998). *Entrepreneurship*. (4th. ed.). Boston: Irwin McGraw-Hill.

Hofer, R., & Polt, W. (1998). Evolutionary Innovation Theory and Innovation Policy: An Overview. In Bryant, K., & Wells, A. (Eds.), *A New Paradigm? Innovation-based Evolutionary Systems* (pp. 5-16). Canberra: Department of Industry, Science and Resources, Commonwealth of Australia.

Jones, E. (1994). The Long Tyranny of a priorism in Economic Thought. *History of Economics Review, 22,* (Summer), 24-69.

Kalecki, M. (1971). *Selected Essays on the Dynamics of the Capitalist Economy, 1933-1970*. Cambridge, UK: Cambridge University Press.

Kannegiesser, H. (1996). *Ever the Clever Country? Innovation and Enterprise in Australia*. Sydney: McGraw-Hill.

Karpin, D. (1995). *Enterprising nation: Report of the Industry Task Force on Leadership and Management Skills*. Canberra: Commonwealth of Australia.

Kirchhoff, B.A. (1991). Entrepreneurship's Contribution to Economics. *Entrepreneurship Theory and Practice, 16* (2), (Winter), 93-112.

Kirzner, I.M. (1973). *Competition and Entrepreneurship*. Cambridge, Mass.: Harvard University Press.

Kirzner, I.M. (1985). *Discovery and the Capitalist Process*. Chicago: University of Chicago Press.

Lawson, T. (1997). Money Modellers Miss the Point. *The Times Higher Education Supplement*, (24 January), p. 16.

Legge, J., & Hindle, K. (1997). *Entrepreneurship: How innovators create the future*. South Melbourne: Macmillan.

Lewis, P., & Norris, K. *Recent Changes in Economics Enrolments*. Paper presented at the Economic Society of Australia 25th Conference of Economists. Canberra: Australian National University, 22-26 September.

Mintzberg, H. (1994). *The Rise and Fall of Strategic Planning: Reconceiving Roles for Planning, Plans, Planners*. New York: The Free Press.

Nightingale, J. (1996). Evolutionary Processes and Revolutionary Change in Firms and
    Markets: An Economist's Perspective. In P.E. Earl, (Eds.), *Management, Marketing, and
    the Competitive Process* (pp. 8-46). Cheltenham: Edward Elgar.
Shapiro, C., & Varian, H.R. (1999). *Information Rules: A Strategic Guide to the Network
    Economy*. Boston: Harvard Business School Press.
Snooks, G.D. (1998). *Longrun Dynamics: A General Economic and Political Theory*.
    London: Macmillan.
Tapscott, D. (1996). *The digital economy*. New York: McGraw-Hill.
Vesper, K.H., & McMullan, W.E. (1996). Entrepreneurship: Today courses, tomorrow
    degrees? *Entrepreneurship Theory and Practice, 13* (1), (Fall), 7-13.

Teaching Introductory OB as Propaedeutic

Bogdan Costea & Norman Crump
Lancaster University, Bailrigg, Lancaster, UK

1.   INTRODUCTION

> Motto: "The world is at least as complex as the most complex thought of
> the world that we are capable of thinking." (Henrich, p. 99)

The main theme of this study is that from both intellectual and pedagogical viewpoints course design at introductory undergraduate level is a more profound occasion to think about the domain of organizational behavior (OB) than customarily assumed. Here we discuss the process of re-designing a course for first year undergraduates in the Department of Behavior in Organizations at Lancaster University.

We will explore this experience by focusing on three areas of reflection. First, we explore some of our deeper assumptions about what first year students are in the partnership of academic learning. Secondly, we investigate our implicit views about the horizon of our disciplinary area (OB), views discernible from the structure and content of dominant teaching materials. Thirdly, we discuss our understanding of introductory level learning processes and their purpose in the field of OB and we introduce a new course design framework.

Overall, the paper offers a general commentary upon differing conceptual views of OB and their pedagogical implications at introductory level. This seems important because undergraduate introductory course design engages academics with their own conceptual horizon in a unique fashion stemming

T.A. Johannessen, A. Pedersen and K. Petersen (eds.),
Educational Innovation in Economics and Business VI, 235–249.
© 2002 *Kluwer Academic Publishers. Printed in the Netherlands.*

mostly from the multidisciplinary and multi-paradigmatic nature of the field of OB.

2.   FIRST YEAR STUDENTS AND COURSE DESIGN

The first part focuses on our assumptions about first year students as partners in academic learning. These assumptions are central in shaping introductory material in complex social science fields.

We contrast two relatively familiar positions: one which considers the teacher-student relationship as characterized by divergent agendas, the other which places teachers and students on the same side of the study process. Introductory pedagogy in social sciences faces a major dilemma in this respect: should we reduce complexity entirely and consider first year students limited in their capacity to face the field? Or should we treat them as young adults for whom academic education is an opportunity to take a new step on the path to independent thinking?

Another way to ask these questions is whether we should apply the golden rule "from simple to complex", hence reduce complexity to a bare minimum of constructs, or should we structure introduction as an open but safe inquiry into that irreducible complexity itself?

Our view of students often is a turning point. The dominant position appears to be favoring a reductionist version of introductory pedagogy. This can be easily gauged from textbooks. The approach seems to assume inherent restrictions in the intellectual "baggage" of young students. Authors and academic teachers appear to see school leavers as virtually lacking any experience of *formal* organizations, and understanding of academic study. Things are made harder in most universities by increasing class sizes . Yet we found that these features are not necessarily sufficient for a decision to avoid some of the more difficult issues emerging in the study of management and organizations.

What is more interesting is that making the curriculum appear simple and coherent, universities enforce the limited initial expectations students have. Contemporary culture plays a serious role in shaping their expectations of management education. The latter finds itself playing a core part in relation to contemporary business corporations (see Thrift's analysis, 1997). As a result of this centrality, young generations expect business schools to offer functional skills which might guarantee them a place in the "globalized" corporate world. And in most cases these expectations appear to be met by curricula which render the complexity of human practices very simple, using models which transform every aspect into a functional or structural problem to which there are quasi-technical solutions. This pedagogical mode of relating to first year students has, however, a somewhat perverse effect in the wider cultural context. It is compounded by the fact that a large majority of students are concerned less with the security and authority of academic knowledge claims than they are with finding simple answers to questions about how business "works". Such answers, students feel, would enable them to contribute to business itself, to contriving better ways of accommodating to it, or finding their way around it. Their cognitive interests tend toward "incorporating", "soaking up" an expected repertory of significant skills which might warrant successful progress in employment.

Agendas thus converge and form an alliance which reinforces the assumption that introductory courses have to be very simple.

The approach we take relies on the opposite view of students' potential. We found that first year students are indeed inexperienced but not unable to grasp complex social science thought. Students intuitively appreciate that social practices of managing and organizing are not unchanging and immutable, that they are not independent of history or culture. They acknowledge the high diversity of human experiences. They have a psychological readiness for embracing historical variety and dynamism as the main dimensions of the reality of practice despite the paucity of historical knowledge in contemporary culture. What they require are historical narratives which inspire understanding of the general field of study. It can be argued that the degree to which we are obliged to restrict course content, due to students' limited experience, is less problematic than we usually assume. In order to place them in a position to understand aspects of general modern management and organizations, the process of study itself must be opened to multiple conceptual narratives. We engage students precisely with the multidisciplinary of OB as part of the main purpose of introductory study.

3. CONCEPTUALISATIONS OF THE OB DOMAIN

Our second area of consideration regards the way we understand the intellectual nature of the OB field itself and what possible contributions it might make to students' learning.

The view which dominates mainstream OB teaching material can be described as functional-structuralist and essentially a-historical. In contrast, we adopt a perspective which aims to be precisely the opposite: phenomenological rather than functional, historical rather than a-historical.

Under the pressure of industry and students, but also under the pressure of other business disciplines, OB teaching has aspired for the last four decades to achieve instrumental legitimacy and relevance alongside other business disciplines. OB is one of the three pillars of the business and management curriculum together with quantitative techniques and economic discourses.

Yet, in contrast with the latter, OB presents intrinsic complications in its theoretical constitution. Its domain is vast and highly imprecise in nature. Dealing with the "immaterial", the "soft" or "human" side of business life, OB phenomena do not lend themselves to true mathematization or scientific modeling. OB is, moreover, multidisciplinary. Ideas, models, theories are drawn from different social sciences: sociology, anthropology, psychology, psychoanalysis, ethno methodology, economics, history, etc. It must thus be emphasized that OB is not in itself a discipline. It is a domain of research which leads in a different intellectual direction than the more unitary bodies of knowledge like accounting, finance, statistics, or economics.

So "behavioral sciences" appear to offer less instrumentally relevant knowledge. There is some difficulty clarifying how OB enables optimization of resource allocation, or increased organizational performance. However, there is a permanent expectation that it will clarify the "human side" of organizations on the basis of general causal models which will inherently be of practical utility. However, the extent to which behavioral science can deliver is felt as intensely problematic. In an attempt to cope with this uncertainty, the *Financial Times Mastering Management* series was pointing out in 1997 that:

> "Organizational behavior is one of the most complex, but perhaps least understood academic elements of the modern general management, but since it concerns the behavior of people within organizations it is also one of the most central... its concern with individual and group patterns of behavior makes it an essential element in dealing with the complex behavioral issues thrown up in the modern business world."

This passage gives an image of the core tension in mainstream OB approaches: on the one hand, OB deals with a mysterious, ungraspable phenomenal field which does not lend itself to theoretical closure; on the other hand, it is precisely the pragmatic concern with mastery over this field which is central to OB, "the understanding, prediction and control of human behavior" (Mullins, p. 14).

What teaching strategy would legitimize this aspiration and resolve this tension? Any answer must be based upon some way of thematizing the domain. This involves drawing "lines", boundaries around the field of OB, defining themes within it, and choosing possible theoretical standpoints to illustrate each theme. This process is a key premise of any pedagogical discourse.

Mainstream OB has traditionally defined its intellectual strategy along lines of functional and structural simplification of reality. It hoped to move intellectually closer to other functional areas. Economics, accounting and other disciplines in the business curriculum draw on unitary discourses operating both in knowledge production and teaching. Their introductory courses usually consist of a process of learning a specific "language" and becoming proficient at using it through application to different examples. The pedagogical process is analogous to natural science disciplines. The philosophical justification is that economics, for example, is a different form of knowing than mere perceptual or common sense knowing. Scientific theories of economy "explain" perceptual phenomena with respect to "imperceptibles" that "lie behind" the common-sensical surface of everyday occurrences. Such "imperceptibles" are economic aggregates like inflation, capital investment, GDP, exchange rates, the 'Dow Jones Index' and so on. Their existence is postulated by theory and 'detected' indirectly through the use of models applied to data collected according to the needs of each model. Sometimes these "imperceptibles" are principles which appear paradoxical to intuitive thinking but are consistent with the logic of the discipline. In this sense, the work of such a discipline is a work of science as we know it from the philosophy of natural *sciences*. It is a search for transcendental, universal elements in the phenomenal.

Mainstream OB aspired from early days to such a mode of teaching. Yet it lacked one element: a set of universally recognizable 'facts' to be modeled. Its phenomena are *human practices*. The notion of "work practice" does not summon up any demarcated content – whereas "markets", "prices", "exchange rates" do. There is a certain intuitive understanding presenting itself, but there is hardly any direct way of rendering practices into 'objects' of scientific study. The category of "practice" remains immaterial and un-mathematical in its ontological character. Nonetheless, OB is concerned precisely with human practices.

Dominant OB introductory teaching discourses by-pass the fundamental questioning of the nature of practice by constructing and postulating a set of foundational "objects" which constitute all practices. The majority of textbooks and syllabi formalize "individuals" and "collectives" as unquestionable realities of the realm of OB.

The first step when it comes to teaching introductory-level undergraduates is not an exposition of the phenomenal field of inquiry ("practices") but the construction of a hierarchy of abstractions. Examples abound: below we will briefly discuss Mullin's view (Mullins, 1999); but equally illustrative is for example "PESTLE – A field map of the organizational behavior terrain" guiding the structure of Huczynski and Buchanan's edition of 2001. From such pyramids of theory, learning is supposed to proceed deductively downwards, through closed models, toward "real occurrences". The approach is usually defended by recourse to students' lack of experience of *formal* organizations. Teaching through questioning the nature of the object of study (as in all social sciences) is deemed unworkable.

But this view points to a more profound intellectual tendency in the field of OB. Introductory material postulates without questioning in a meaningful way the *a priori* possibility of systematic, general and even positive knowledge of the "real essence" of human behavior. The subject can then be taught as scientific knowledge about a set of *foundational objects* which re-constitute 'objective reality' in the student's mind. Such knowledge is relevant to further deductive thinking. The initial "lack of experience of formal organizations" has thus also been by-passed.

The *foundational objects* of "OB reality" tend to be organized in a hierarchy of phenomenal fragments. Of uppermost generality are usually categories such as *individual, group, organization,* and *environment* (see, for example, Mullins; Luthans; or Buchanan & Huczynski); they are followed by "composites" – e.g. *"process of management", "organizational processes and the execution of work", "organizational context", "behavior of people", "improved organizational performance and effectiveness"* (Mullins, p. 15). Eventually, the image of a tripartite "system" develops which can then be circumscribed by academic disciplines. The *human individual* falls within the domain of *psychology*, social interactions are the object of *sociology*, and *"culture"* is the domain of *anthropology*. The design of a course about humans in organizations unfolds as a process of abstracting from the unitary domain of practice separate "objects" for the gaze of scientific disciplines. The claim which logically follows is that each discipline contributes some form of determination of these objects through models which are the student's tools for understanding, predicting and controlling the field.

The process of teaching and learning proceeds from "models" to "phenomena". Thinking too becomes unidirectional: it can only be engaged on a vector pointing from the *rational* to the *real*. Placing pedagogy on this track we run the risk of 'freezing' the life-world of practice in static models, of relinquishing the historical and cultural dynamics of management and organizations.

The general intention here is to raise some of the consequences of scientific theorizing processes in OB teaching. This discussion is obviously limited. Yet the question remains fundamental: how do such theoretical objects or artifacts reduce the complexity management and organizational processes to representations allowing scientific generalizations?

One possible answer is that this theoretical choice is made not because teaching requires simplicity at any price. Simplicity is not an *a priori* pedagogical imperative for any discipline at academic level. Moreover, simplicity does not imply reductionism. Rather what occurs in mainstream OB is due to the epistemological imperative of a hypothetico-deductive approach to knowledge. In this sense the dominant approach to teaching OB can be described as reductionist in functionalist and structuralist terms. History shows that indeed OB found *objectivist theories* fundamentally appealing. Behaviorism, functionalism, structuralism (Litterer), systems theory [the socio-technical systems of the Tavistock school of thought (Emery & Murray), or Forrester's systems modeling (Forrester)], or universal explanations of motivation offered by management theorists (e.g. Herzberg's, or McGregor's), likewise the appeal of Maslow's hierarchy of needs – are all the bases upon which the core of human being can be invested with a stable set of general characteristics.

Teaching OB becomes a process of reducing the complexity of human experience at work rather than engaging with it. The human actor is *ab initio* drained of existential reality. The individual's involvement is reduced to analytical units derived from functionalist and structuralist sociologies and psychologies. This remains his only place in models of behavior. Logically, analyzing organizations does not take any longer into account the *subjective* element of actors' consciousness, intentions, and agency. The entire analysis can be narrowed down to the *objective*, structural and functional conditioning of action. Patterns of human behavior become universal features of social existence and organization; hence they can be seen as transcending specific historical situations. At a stroke, references to the historical and cultural contexts of social phenomena are also removed. The human is represented as a constant set of elementary units which manifests itself in a determined number of combinations.

This approach is seductive: it makes complicated things simple, facile. But in doing so, it also generates a form of intellectual injustice. The infinite variety of managerial and organizational practices becomes reified into a small number of disciplinary areas. The pedagogical effect is of import: the fields of theory and practice remain concealed rather than being adequately introduced. The ability to think about them cannot thus be developed. If introductions do not fulfill their purpose of beginning a process of reuniting theory and practice on a higher plane, then how will the ability to act reflectively be arrived at later on?

The divorce between the perceived world of everyday practice and management theory is a problem we aim to address through a phenomenological and historical reframing of OB thinking.

We try to find a language which reveals that "practice" is the "real thing", that reality does not hide beneath phenomena (Heidegger, *Being*, p. 51). We aim to overcome the deep dualism between appearance and essence which dominates Western metaphysics.

Our aspiration is to establish with students that OB is not a technical set of concepts about universal "human objects", leading to models which can be "learned" like any other tool, technology or technique. We suggest that such models, tools, or techniques do not represent in any meaningful way what it is *to be* a manager, that they only deepen the split between theory and practical reality.

We propose that concrete practices are the real world, that there is no split between the appearances of management and the supposed essence of management. The matter for the study of management and organizations becomes the examination of phenomena as they present themselves in the life-world, a world in "constant motion," in which people relate to each other and to object-contents not as univocal 'realities' but through particular thematic options for their affection and action. The *life-world* is "a total sphere of affection and such that the affecting objects are now thematic, now unthematic" (Husserl, p. 109). In this world people "function together, in the manifold ways of considering, together, objects pre given to us in common, thinking together, valuing, planning, acting together" (Husserl, p. 109).

We emphasize that human practices are not mere superficial illusions, they are – in Husserlian terms – "the things themselves" of management and organizations as they reveal themselves to us (Heidegger, *Being*, pp. 49-50). Consequently, we develop a perspective which allows engagement with the endless historical and contextual diversity of human practice. We aim to help students move the object of inquiry in OB beyond mechanical disciplinary knowledges, and situate thinking in the wider traditions of the humanities.

In other words, the first question of course design is aimed at achieving a clearer understanding of what we, as academics, constitute as the sources of knowledge to be drawn upon in teaching. What is the sense of "organizational behavior" for us? How can we help students make sense of the human ability to make sense – as the grounding for studying management, organizations and people? If the human is not a straightforward stable cognitive "subject," if the world is not made of straightforward "objects," then what is the stance we take regarding the nature of these occurrences?

Answering these questions enables us to re-think our intellectual and pedagogical foundations. First, we realized that we have to problematise the entire "space" of relationships between traditional *subjects* and *objects*, and show that it is variable in historical and cultural contexts. Secondly, the variability of human practices has epistemological consequences: objectivist models have some heuristic possibilities for teaching, but nothing more. After they exhaust their "representative ness", practice remains unexplained in its ontological essence. In other words, the more we "*scientifically explain*" the more unexplained the nature of management and organizations is left. This requires a break of the epistemological deadlock between theory and practice in favour of the latter.

To do this we rely on the traditions of historical and existential phenomenology. Both allow us to "return" to phenomena, and to assume a more open attitude to that which cannot be scientifically known.

This option helps us recover with students the sense of academic questioning: what is the *phenomenon* that escapes objective modeling? What is "human work practice"? Instead of asking how do we fix or optimize behavior, we return to the question of the nature of the object of inquiry itself: what is it that management and organizing processes are about?

We aim to convey that they are not simple objects, that perhaps they are not "objects" at all. Rather we suggest that they are part of the *life-world*, ontologically different than "natural objects". Practices are idiographic, non-measurable, non-experimental, as opposed to material, physical objects of natural science which are nomothetic, in apparently constant relations of magnitude, measurable and thus susceptible to experimentation.

Although business management might think it is concerned solely with finding solutions to "resource allocation problems," teaching *management* cannot circumvent the ontological core of practice. At the core lies, assembled, the entire human being with its "human action and concern, works and suffering, living in common in the world-horizon in their particular social interrelations and knowing themselves to be such." (Husserl, p. 146) The *human* is the very subject of human knowing about management and organizations. Academics and students of management must understand that they carry out a form of "knowing" as part of humanity, not outside it. A coherent theoretical interest in human practices seemed conceivable to us only if directed at the historical and cultural character of the life-world in which these take place: a world "constantly in flowing particularity" (Husserl, p. 145), a world in which managerial practice is endlessly variable, each "instant" is unique in its texture and rhythm because each involves unique human beings whose very subjectivities are in some sense "pre giving the world" in which practice takes place. This conception of human beings is captured by Merleau-Ponty's image:

> "I am not the outcome or the meeting-point of numerous causal agencies which determine my bodily or psychological make-up. I cannot conceive myself as nothing but a bit of the world, a mere object of biological, psychological or sociological investigation. I cannot shut myself up within the realm of science." (Merleau-Ponty, viii-ix)

The design of an introductory OB course develops thus a new path which aims to convey a sense of thinking about the *entire* human as domain for reflection. Pedagogically, we found ourselves trying to find ways of bringing to life the "intelligibility correlative with our everyday background practices" (Dreyfus, p. 10).

If the diversity of practices is irreducible to a *scientistic* discourse then it can only reveal itself through thinking about *phenomena* themselves. We have to bring them to the fore through illustrations of the historical variability of management and organizational practices, ideologies, and theoretical frameworks.

4.   AN ALTERNATIVE TO COURSE DESIGN

We take the view that OB studies complex and historically variable phenomena. This challenges us to think about a course design that offers an introduction to this complexity, rather than circumventing or retreating from it.

This new design offers students the opportunity to "map" historically the domain of study. We present *human beings* as the "raw material" of management: complex, multi-faceted, individual and collective at the same time, often ambiguous, often counter-intuitive, certainly changeable, and, finally, un-knowable.

To achieve this, we changed the sources of teaching material. Instead of operating with abstract objects (models), we focus on concrete contexts of practice and on systems of ideas dedicated to their historical study. We use work from various disciplines and paradigms offering ways of thinking about human practices. We place students before a rich "map" of this complex terrain. On this map it is possible to situate OB, sociology, anthropology, psychology, philosophy, and their representatives as assisting the process of "thinking about" the human subject, and its practices. It offers a new image of the domain for reflection. What we are gives is guidance to what "thinking about" management and organization might entail. We do not give a rigid answer to what management and organizations are, but an introduction to ways of thinking about them.

This creates a broader perspective of these processes emphasizing their historical and cultural foundations. It also creates a space were students can explore views from different disciplines without blurring their paradigmatic boundaries. Sociology remains sociology, psychology remains psychology, and so on.

The design of the course attempts to give life to a process of learning similar to what Blackler calls "knowing":

> "The term "knowing" as we use it here is intended to avoid the imagery which is so often associated with the term "knowledge" (often assumed

to refer to a timeless, uncontroversial body of fact) and "learning" (which can be taken to refer merely to the passive absorption of such knowledge)." (Blackler et al, 1998, p. 207).

Given the arguments outlined above, one could say that the "object" of the course is to enable the development of 'knowing' students.

The course is organized around three themes: (i) thinking about capitalism and modern society as contexts of management and organizations; (ii) thinking about management ideas and organizational practices in the 20th century; (iii) thinking about conceptions of the human self.

In this way, we create a context for learning about management and organizations as social processes in historical contexts. The course contextualises historically systems of thought regarding each aspect. It moves toward the *present* seen as outcome of trends of socio-historical and cultural development, rather than a mere set of contingent economic circumstances.

The first theme explores the historical context of *modern capitalism* and its specific modes of organizing. We work with ideas from classical sociology through the works of Weber, Marx and Durkheim. As social theorists, they operated on wide canvas and commented on the historical foundations of modernity. Their thought offers the basis for discussing the boundaries of capitalism as social order, and of managerialism as one of its phenomena. Working with such ideas also allows us to introduce sociology as a mode of thinking about human practices.

We discuss *management* in the twentieth century through the work of Barley and Kunda who build up a historical analysis of changes in dominant management discourses from the 1850s to the present. Waves of ideology have succeeded each other moving within a dualism of "normative and rational rhetorics" of control. Barley and Kunda tie these historical trends to "cultural antinomies fundamental to Western industrialized societies: the opposition between mechanistic and organic solidarity and between communalism and individualism." This allows a link back to the first theme and helps contextualise management in wider social spaces. We focus on three systems of ideas and practice of management: F.W. Taylor and *Scientific Management*, Jay Forrester and *Systems Rationalism*, and the *"cultural turn"* of the '80s. From a pedagogical standpoint, students are made aware of the recursive nature of much managerial discourse.

The final theme introduces ideas about the nature of *the human self*. In some ways it is the most difficult part, but also one which relies on something which we all have in common: being human. We explore how certain disciplinary practices have produced a particular view of the human subject. We investigate three areas: *experimental psychology, psychoanalysis* and *existence philosophy*.

What does this lead to in pedagogical terms? What does "thinking" mean in this context? The ideas we introduce are complex. Yet the link between them and concrete contexts of practice, together with the historical grounding of the material allow first year students to engage and feel comfortable with the notion that management and organizations are complex, non–mechanical realities. Complex ideas help study in the way maps help journeys across mountains and moors. Maps are better than books of photographs; complex ideas are better than simplistic notions. The ability to find one's way in theoretical and practical complexity calls for complexity in thinking. Perhaps success in the academic study of management and organizations relies upon the early introduction to thinking, reading and writing about complicated issues in social and human dynamics.

The course aims to help students develop their critical-analytic *thinking* by studying certain management ideas and practices in themselves, but also by going beyond and beneath: attempting to grasp the implicit articulation of the world of experience contained in these systems of ideas.

Thinking also requires a *dialogical* space in which different conceptual frameworks are allowed to develop in historical contrast with each other. Thinking in this context calls to be done in front of and with students.

Team work became almost unavoidable as the basis of conveying the value of conceptual variety. A distinctive feature in the classroom itself has been "team teaching" which establishes a continuous experience of dialogue and debate. It is an effective way of conveying the nature of managerial theories and practices: that they can be developed from a multitude of perspectives. Team teaching conveys the pluralist essence of human experience as crucial in comprehending the diverse possibilities of thinking about management and organizations. The presence of two people with distinctive perspectives makes the introduction of difficult material easier: students receive two interpretations complementing and challenging each other.

We designed assessment along the same lines. Its aim is to support the development of critical, historical and interpretative (hermeneutic) thinking, as well as reading and writing. Each element of coursework is different and each outcome represents an *"apprentice piece"*, a personal manifestation through the learning process. Each piece should be a fully fledged process of analysis. The difference is one of scope: some pieces are smaller, but of the same essence.

They follow the developmental logic of the course. Instead of asking reductive questions calling for repetitive answers, students are stimulated to "bite off a bit more than they can chew" and yet remain safely in control of the task. For example, we ask questions such as "What would the emergence and dominance of supermarket chains represent in Max Weber's view of Western capitalism?"; or "Taking Émile Durkheim's line of analysis, what do you think are some of the transformations brought about by mobile telecommunications technology to our communities?"; or "How would Karl Marx think about home working and teleworking in terms of alienation and commodification?". Similar tasks articulate assessment for the other themes.

Such challenges are beneficial for students; they mark a gradual change in the nature of thoughtful endeavors from school to university. Each enters academic work without facing an artificial standard. The challenge is to engage in a process of learning based on the individual's capacity to work with her/his own thoughts in a more open reflective space.

5.   CONCLUDING REMARKS

We aimed in this study to raise several issues. Overall, we think that designing introductory courses in OB should be a distinctive occasion for academics.

The reasons are more profound than they might seem. As opposed to more advanced courses, introductory ones are faced with a more intricate intellectual and pedagogical agenda arising from the encounter between first-year students and the irreducibly complex OB domain. To meet credibly this agenda, our own views must undergo a thorough examination in the first place.

Secondly, by comparing two contrasting intellectual perspectives on the nature of OB, the paper shows that designing an introductory course calls for a *propaedeutic* in the width, breadth and depth of studies in the social sciences and humanities. Our attempt to develop such pedagogy is characterized by a mapping of the field with examples of main theoretical and historical occurrences, rather than by teaching technicalities of each possible domain.

Our third comment follows logically the second. From a pedagogical standpoint, the process underlying such a course cannot be one of preliminary instruction in the use of a *specialist disciplinary language*. On the contrary, it ought to focus on commencing the development of students' own abilities to engage with the many "languages" and modes of inquiry available through personal critical thought and interpretation, development which would be continued throughout their academic studies and beyond.

Our main contention is, essentially, that an "*Introduction to OB*" would not achieve the goals of allowing students closer to both practices and theories *unless* it is a propaedeutic. The direction of learning should not be confined to a mere transmission-accumulation of so-called specialist content. This view places the course in direct opposition to the dominant business school approaches to OB in which social processes appear as versions of functional 'problems' (occurring in the present and awaiting to be solved by that superior agent, the "manager"). We aim to re-situate work, organizations and management in the historical context of human practices as part of the *life-world*.

A correlate aim is to overcome students' expectation that managerial work consists of straightforward interventions to optimize production processes (a pseudo-heroic role cultivated by images of corporations seen as Arcadias recovered from jungle darkness by enlightened executives, etc.). For us, the purpose of introduction is quite different: to develop students' capacity to doubt, but to be articulate about their thought processes and arguments, to engage in reflection about perpetually dynamic relations in which the subject-object horizon is fundamentally unstable, to construct and write personal views on both theoretical ideas and social practices.

For us, studying OB is not a vocational pursuit. As part of university education, it is oriented toward the acquisition of knowledge. Yet, an introductory course, as any beginning, must also have something to do with "un-knowledge". It should convey to students that being comfortable with mystery, undergoing some sort of intellectual initiation into new modes of thinking, and taking time to engage in contemplation of ideas are all legitimate modes for being a student and part of the academic study experience.

Viewed in this way, the benefits for students are long-term, learning outcomes cannot be judged in isolation from the students' general academic experience, nor can they be analyzed through short-term, punctual criteria.

The paths opened by this design are far from simple and straightforward. In their unfolding, imperfections are discovered, and better ideas reveal themselves. The dynamic character of the approach puts it by definition on a spiral of development from year to year. Better ways of approaching certain subjects present themselves, new ways of using the potential of the students emerge. The learning experience is open to variety from intake to intake. The most important conclusion for us is that the approach to introduction must equally be a continuous process of self-reflection based on intellectual openness and self-criticality.

REFERENCES

Financial Times Mastering Management. Introduction to Module 6, Organisational
      Behaviour. FT Pitman Publishing, 1997.

Barley, S., & Kunda, G. (1992). Design and devotion: surges of rational and normative ideologies of control in managerial discourse. *Administrative Science Quarterly 37,* 363-399

Blackler, F., Norman, C., & Seoinadh, M. (1998). In G. von Krogh, J. Roos, & D. Kleine, (Eds.), *Knowing in Firms.* London: Sage.

Buchanan, D., & Huczynski, A. (1997). *Organizational behaviour: an introductory text.* (3rd. ed.). Englewood Cliffs, N.J.: Prentice Hall.

Dreyfus, H. (1991). *Being-in-the-world*: a commentary on Heidegger's "Being and Time". Division I. Cambridge, Mass: MIT Press.

Forrester, J.W. (1968). *Principles of systems: text and workbook.* (2nd. ed.). Wright-Allen.

Heidegger, M. (1962). *Being and Time.* New York: Harper & Row.

Husserl, E. (1970). *The Crisis of European Sciences and Transcendental Phenomenology.* Evanston, Ill.: Northwestern U.P.

Litterer, J.A. (1980). *Organisations: Structure and Behaviour.* (3rd. ed.). New York: Wiley.

Luthans, F. (1992). *Organisational Behaviour.* (6th. ed.). McGraw-Hill.

Mullins, L. (1999). *Management and Organisational Behaviour.* (5th. ed.).London: FT Pitman Publishing.

Porter, L.W., & McKibbin, L.E. (1998). *Management education and development: drift or thrust into the 21st century?* McGraw-Hill.

Thrift, N. (1997). The Rise of Soft Capitalism. *Cultural Values 1,* 21–57

Trist, E., & Murray, H. (Eds.). (1990-1997). *The social engagement of social science: a Tavistock anthology.* London: Free Association Books.

Is the Fragmentation of Strategic Management Theory a Handicap for Business?

Adam J. Koch[1] & Graham Hubbard[2]

[1]*School of Business, Swinburne University of Technology, Hawthorn, Australia*, [2]*Monash Mount Eliza School of Business, Mount Eliza, Australia*

1.   INTRODUCTION

Commonly regarded as the most complex of all business disciplines, strategic management is an inherently integrative activity in an organization. Many authors (Barney, 1997; David, 1997; Mintzberg, 1996; Miller & Dess, 1996; Pearce & Robinson, 1997; Schon, 1993) point, among others, to strategic management's double reliance on analysis and intuition. The operating principles of these two forms of intellectual activity being very dissimilar, their parallel implementation in strategic management processes must strengthen the perception of their complexity.

Whilst the logic of strategic management is clearly integrative, its theory has developed in a very fragmented fashion. Little effort has been expended to build a unified framework, spanning all management cultures and contexts. Economic theories (Rumelt, Schendel & Teece, 1991; Williamson, 1975), agency theory (Jensen & Meckling, 1976; Fama, 1980), design school theory (Andrews, 1971; Porter, 1980), behavioural theory (Cyert & March, 1992; Weick, 1969), resource, based theory (Wernerfelt, 1984; Prahalad & Hamel, 1990), game theory (Dixit & Nalebuff, 1991), institutional theory (Nelson & Winter, 1982) and learning theory (Senge, 1990) represent the main theoretical lenses through which strategic management has been viewed.

T.A. Johannessen, A. Pedersen and K. Petersen (eds.),
Educational Innovation in Economics and Business VI, 251–271.
© 2002 *Kluwer Academic Publishers. Printed in the Netherlands.*

In his recent work, Mintzberg (1994) presents ten contemporary schools of thought on strategy formation and ten corresponding views of the strategic planning process he has identified (see Table 1).[1]

Table 1: Schools of thought on strategy formation.

School	View of Process
Prescriptive	
Design	Conceptual
Planning	Formal
Positioning	Analytical
Descriptive	
Cognitive	Mental
Entrepreneurial	Visionary
Learning	Emergent
Political	Power
Cultural	Ideological
Environmental	Passive
Configurational	Episodic

(based on: Mintzberg 1994, p. 3).

Mintzberg schools can be classified in various ways. To begin with, three of them are prescriptive, and the remainder are descriptive.[2] Further, all these schools implicitly, or explicitly, refer to either a stage in the life of an organization (*entrepreneurial, environmental, configurational*), an approach to the strategic planning process (*design, positioning, planning*), or an aspect of the strategic planning process (*cognitive, learning, political, cultural*). Further, the last seven in Table 1 represent the subjective/personal approach to planning whilst the first three are closer to the rational/analytical end of the spectrum.

One should mention here other recent proposals regarding classification of schools of thought in strategic management. McKiernan's classification (1996) comprised of *planning and practice school, learning school[3], positioning school* and *resource-based school* underscores the principle of separation between the content- and process-focused schools. A recent attempt by Rajagopalan and Spreitzer (1996) to produce synergies for the theory of strategic change by proposing an integrative framework that would

---

[1] Strategic management takes in strategic planning as its crucial component.

[2] 'Hard-edged', or quantitative, prescriptive thinking, can be traced back to management scientists and operation research, while the 'softer end' descriptive thinking is representative of the human relations movement (Bowman and Asch, 1987). Descriptive thinking is more representative of sociological and socio-psychological disciplines, which provide a more comprehensive perspective on the firm, encompassing the subjective elements of context as well.

[3] Incidentally, McKiernan learning school is subdivided into five branches: *the natural selection view, the incremental view, the cultural view, the political view* and *the visionary view,* which increases the total number of distinct views as proposed by this classification to eight.

use *rational, learning and cognitive lenses* deserves a brief mention here, as well.

It has been noticed that those who operate exclusively within the confines of their particular schools of thought, or individual mindsets, often end up getting to know more and more about less and less. These dangers were appreciated already by Marshall (1961) who warned:

'Specialists who never look beyond their own domain are apt to see things out of true proportion; ... they work away at the details of old problems which have lost much of their significance and have been supplanted by new questions rising out of new points of view.'

Each of the existing schools of thought on strategy formation, and we will from now on be focusing in this paper on those identified by Mintzberg, applies its specific perspectives and forms of analysis. The prescriptive schools concentrate on high-level quantitative "facts"; the descriptive ones - on personal and group-based subjective perceptions. All schools show the tendency, to a varying degree, to ignore other possible perspectives and the corresponding tools of inquiry. This is clearly seen in journal debates between protagonists of different schools.[4] In this paper, we examine some practical implications of these partial approaches.

Not much seems to be known about the relative popularity in business practice of each of these schools of thought and any possible correlation between certain business context characteristics and the following of individual schools of thought on strategy formation. Neither is much known about their actual and relative capacity to improve the quality of an organization's strategic decisions.

Further, we do not know much about joint deployment of the elements of reasoning typical of different schools by business organizations in their decision-making. If they are deployed jointly, does their deployment follow sequential, or concurrent, pattern? Should the cases of joint deployment of more than one of these schools be studied from an interpersonal, or an intra-personal, perspective? Complete and reliable answers to all these, and similar, questions are yet to be found.

In this paper we focus on the practical implications of the fragmentation of strategic management theory when applied to business situations. We will show that different solutions can be proposed to the same problem by each of the schools and then ask how strategic management might find a way to seek out better solutions through a more integrated approach. Finally, we

---

[4] For instance, see the debate between Mintzberg (1990, 1991) and Ansoff (1991), and between Ghoshal and Moran (1996) and Williamson (1996).

will propose adoption of three basic dimensions by the strategic management analysis to further improve its overall quality.

2.   A COMPANY WITH A STRATEGIC PROBLEM

To show the possible practical consequences of the multiplicity of partial theoretical perspectives for the strategic management process, we shall refer here to a hypothetical Organization X that struggles with certain strategic management problem. Organization X manufactures and sells consumer durables. **It has been hamstrung over a period of time by its inability to swiftly adapt its strategies and stocks of resources to its rapidly transforming external environment.**

The industry of which the organization is a part is in the midst of a period of dramatic technological change, which has just created new, very attractive business opportunities. Organization X has been an industry leader, but is losing this position. Its financial, market and operating performance is declining. Its management has been in the industry for a long period with little turnover and its operating and technological capabilities are no longer at the industry forefront.

The described situation calls for a very deep revision of corporate strategies and re-evaluation of underlying capabilities and gaps. As a result of these sweeping changes, capabilities and competitive advantages defined in the past will need to be re-evaluated, some traditional competitive advantages will need to be strengthened and new ones established so that Organization X can compete successfully in the future.

3.   ONE PATIENT, MANY MEDICOS

What should Organization X do? The awareness of available perspectives from which one can investigate the causes of an organization's unsatisfactory strategic management performance is of tremendous significance. As such, it will directly influence the choice(s) of remedies. These choice(s) will also be affected by a host of interrelated factors including the character of the business environment, relevant management perceptions, the existing business strategy, organizational culture and values, competitive strategies, current performance levels, relevant past management decisions (and their outcomes) and personal predispositions of managers.

Personal predispositions of managers to address the strategic situation are likely to be influenced by an organization's corporate culture, power balance and current management system. These predispositions will also be often affected by their particular professional and educational experiences (Papadakis, Lioukas & Chambers, 1998) and their perceptions of the external and internal environment (Glaister & Thwaites, 1993; Piercy & Giles, 1990; Prince, 1992). A major component of everyone's educational experience is the conditioning to particular perspectives from which to look at various categories of strategic management problems. Readers may want to pause here and imagine differences in strategies likely to be recommended in the situation by students and protagonists of, say, Mintzberg, Porter, or Hamel and Prahalad.

Let us assume for the sake of this discussion that no strategic management participant in Organization X uses more than one perspective in his, or her, analysis. Let us also assume that each of the schools of thought is represented in this strategic management process by at least one person. These two assumptions will help us demonstrate some practical implications for the Organization X of the current fragmentation of contemporary strategic management theory.

Table 2 below suggests what could be possible diagnoses and remedies for this ailing organization, that could be put forward by adherents of each of the ten Mintzberg schools of thought.

3.1 Design school

With their focus on the conceptual and organizational design aspects of the strategic management/planning process (Mintzberg, 1990), adherents of the design school are likely to suggest that redesigning the organizational structure can cure the problem. The issues discussed will include inappropriate division/demarcation of strategic planning and operational roles and responsibilities, centralization/ decentralization of strategic planning and modifying corporate governance forms.

The remedial action is likely to be carried out by top managers only. The changes will be assumed to be capable of effecting desirable behavior modification. Those proposing this course of action may at the same time hope to "buy" extra time for the effects of such a redesign to present themselves. This would be tantamount to an extended period of freedom from the post-change scrutiny and evaluation.

3.2 Planning school

A largely mechanistic approach is to be expected from the planning school. Since well designed and executed strategic planning is believed to be a main success factor, those subscribing to this school are likely to see the solution of the problem in introducing or redesigning the strategic planning system. A more formalized, more "rational" system, which may be based on a modified view of the strategic planning/management process, would be a very likely suggestion to be expected from an adherent of this school. The likelihood of an organization adopting this point of view will often depend on managers' qualifications and on their conditioning by the relevant management practice (Papadakis *et al.*, 1998).

The course of remedial action will be decided by top managers and will involve those whose planning responsibilities are to be significantly modified.

3.3   Positioning school

The marketing analysis dominated thinking of the positioning school may produce a view that it is targeting wrong market segments, which is at the very core of the organization's deficient market response capacity. In other words, it may be suggested that the organization has chosen "wrong" market segments for itself, competing in such segments for which it is ill equipped to compete successfully. The argument of poor strategic match may be based e.g. on the experienced intensity of change inside the relevant market segment(s) and on the definition of critical competencies and capabilities required of competitors there. A repositioning suggestion may be received by some within the Organization X as a break-up with its tradition and thus cause opposition from these quarters.

The course of remedial action suggested here is far more likely to be adopted by companies whose management culture has a very strong marketing thinking component.

3.4   Cognitive school

Rarely, a necessary improvement in making sense of the external and internal environment changes can occur without changing the mindsets of the company's senior management. If the current incumbents have shown strong resistance to attempts to modify their thinking, an organization may resort to transfusion of "new blood" from outside. Bringing charismatic managers from different experiential backgrounds may be a very effective course of action, particularly in the medium and long term. Staff receptiveness to new ideas and management ways, as well as their ability to master these promptly, are going to be also very important. A series of seminars, workshops and other complementary forms of training, will be required to introduce employees to the logic of another school of thought in strategic management, to gain their wide acceptance thereof, and to develop the necessary level of related skills.

Changing cognitive patterns and modifying related performance standards may be much easier and swifter a process with some employees who represent certain psychological profile(s) and superior intellectual capacity. Should others lag behind them in this regard, communication incoherencies are bound to develop causing a worse than anticipated company performance.

3.5 Entrepreneurial school

Companies that have long been managed in a non-participative fashion may be quite willing to implement recipes offered by this school if a major change in their environment has occurred and caused a considerable deterioration of their performance.

An established inward focus, scarcity of new ideas, incremental approach and complacency with organization's market position and performance would often encourage this school's adherents to suggest an injection of entrepreneurialism through bringing in more dynamic management possessed of wider vision. It would assume that new management could swiftly change the old, non-entrepreneurial culture. Implementation of this recipe may be hampered by the availability of suitably experienced and skilled people.

A strong perception of transitory windows of opportunity open to companies capable of
- embracing the opportunity swiftly and
- creating new competitive strengths in non-traditional areas, may encourage reliance on the entrepreneurial thinking and the associated modes of operation.

3.6 Learning school

An incremental improvement philosophy pervades this school's thinking. It quite readily admits it does not know what the outcomes are going to be of adopting some of its recipes. If they are consistent, both externally and internally, the company will move in the right direction and in so doing become gradually cognizant of some of the success factors and principles unknown at the outset (Milliken & Lant, 1991). The effectiveness of recipes based on this thinking would largely depend on
- the richness of individual reflection generated within the company,
- the commonality of reflection sharing between the employees, and on
- the absence of institutional obstacles to implementing change based on learning.

A solid overall grasp of the good management principles and roles of individual management subsystems' makes it easier for the company to improve its various internal processes. The downside of recipes offered by this school may be the amount of time required for the new experience based reflection to translate into new, more adequate business management system. Hence, this may not be a viable option for a company that has to achieve the necessary performance improvement very quickly.

3.7   Political school

Essentially, solutions to two categories of strategic management problems are offered by adherents of this school:
- a power stalemate and
- an ill match, or an outright conflict, between the perceived strategic interests of the dominant power group's and the course of remedial action proposed by outsiders.

Changing the balance of power, either through bringing in "new blood" or by causing some desirable allegiance shift, would normally be advocated in such a case. Alternatively, some effort may be worth putting into changing the above-mentioned perceptions of conflict if it holds good promise of success. Always, we would have to assume that the dominant power group indeed has the right solutions, is committed to change, and would know how to implement the proposed solutions.

3.8   Cultural school

An ill match between the current organizational culture and values it underscores, and the strategic objectives currently considered most appropriate for the organization, may encourage the organization to implement some advice coming from the cultural school. Following a proper definition of the required attributes of new organizational culture as well as associated values, relevant gaps will be established. This will usually lead to a combination of retrenchment and training of the other staff to ensure sufficient level of understanding and support for the new culture and values.

Recipes of this school may work particularly well with companies operating in mature markets, particularly if these prescriptions lead to a better coordination and utilization of the company resources. These recipes may also reduce conflict and encourage cooperation.

3.9 Environmental school

Companies that have never availed themselves enough information on their external environment are likely to be inwardly focused, have very incomplete and out-of-date view of the situation as well as interpret and predict market situations poorly. Bringing more external perspectives to bear on the decisions and abandoning narrow industry blinkers will be the likely two suggestions coming from adherents of this school. Staff open-mindedness and ability to procure sufficient new information are essential in the successful implementation of this strategy.

For an environmental school's recipe to effect a swift company performance improvement, hiring a number of suitably experienced and skilled outsiders might be required. Their task would be to implement best practice in market information procurement and analysis to make it possible for the company to enhance and intensify its strategic decision-making.

3.10 Configurational school

To suggest the best moment for an internal change to commence, this school relies on a systematic examination and anticipation of the external environment trends.[5] Choosing that moment is vital for the success of any strategy, since the process should commence when the anticipated market dynamics and time requirements of the undertaken internal change fit each other well enough.

Bringing about a more accommodating attitude to change as well as increasing staff motivation levels will often be regarded as pre-conditions of any success when implementing the recipes devised by adherents of this school. Achieving this can be facilitated through appropriate management training aimed at strengthening the management internal locus of control and at validating and sharing their perceptions. Due to the need to effect the change quickly so as to utilize the above-mentioned fit between the external and internal environment, high levels of the change efficacy may be required here.

---

[5] This would suggest that the company must be able to anticipate future situation accurately enough (which would require appropriate information gathering, scenario building and forecasting capacity), and understand its various resource requirements when adjusting the company to the anticipated state of its external environment.

4.   SINGLE OR MULTIPLE PERSPECTIVE?

As the remedies proposed by various schools are likely to differ widely, the chances for Organization X reaching an internal consensus as to the choice of remedies, and to implement these swiftly and efficiently, seem poor.

It is clear that each of the schools of strategic management thinking can be of assistance when diagnosing certain situations and systems and developing and implementing strategy to eliminate certain organization weaknesses. Each school has a capacity to help find some causes of unsatisfactory strategic management performance, eliminate obstacles found responsible for the deficiencies or help improve strategic management performance through a valid analysis of relationships between external and internal environment components capable of influencing this performance. However, no one school can certainly offer the whole answer to all strategic management problems.

In this light, an integrated, or holistic, approach seems a more valid option for strategy theory and practice. The discussion of implications of single and multiple strategic management perspectives may focus on three following questions of very considerable practical significance. The first is: **Could following any one of these schools of thinking prove a sufficiently valid basis for a complete diagnosis and choice of remedial actions with respect to at least some categories of strategic management enhancement tasks?**

Now, if management challenges an organization's managers encounter over a period of time are of similar nature and the competitive environment does not put a great deal of pressure on their organization, following just one school of thought may still prove enough in some cases to create a 'sufficiently valid basis for a complete diagnosis and choice of remedial actions'. However, due to the limitations of our understanding of influences on strategic management outcomes, no organization can be really certain that remedies arrived at through taking one particular outlook on the situation will be able to eliminate all major causes of its strategic problems, many of whom can be expected to have multiple, multi-level roots. Bearing this in mind we propose the following:

Proposition 1: In some relatively simple strategic management situations following in analysis a single school of strategic management thought may be sufficient to produce a valid and complete diagnosis and identify most appropriate remedial actions.

Surely, a search should continue for the rules with which to define situations that could rely on a particular school of thought for strategic enhancement solutions. The second question we formulate here is: **How could one tell in any strategic management situations which of the perspectives should be adopted as more promising, or more suitable?**

This question is about decision rule(s) with which to select perspective(s) more suitable to the particular strategic management context and management enhancement goals. We propose that these rules apply to such situations where a consensus has been reached between independent analysts representing various strategic planning schools of thought as to the most significant strategic management performance gaps in need of addressing by the organization. These rules would link certain categories of strategic management situations and associated performance gaps with the most suitable school of thought with which to remedy them. Each such rule would be based on a systematic, in-depth analysis of a large number of strategic management processes.

We suggest the following:

> *Proposition 2*: With respect to such situations where a consensus has been reached between independent analysts representing different schools of thought with regard to the most significant strategic management performance gaps there, appropriate rules may be applied which link certain categories of strategic management performance gaps with the most suitable school(s) of thought to use in each such situation.

The third, and last question concerning the perspective selection rules that we ask here is: **In what strategic management situations would using multiple perspectives be likely to produce superior analytical and implementation results in strategic management?**

It is clear that ignoring *a priori* any perspective or approach or systematically neglecting any analytical tools can often produce an incomplete picture of the strategic management situation and hence - its less than reliable diagnosis. A multiple perspective approach will always produce a more valid and reliable picture of the strategic management decision context. Yet, much of the contemporary business practice runs against this recommendation since a multiple perspective approach is a great deal more time-consuming and costly. Managers often choose what they regard as more convenient or follow the analytical format, which has been most popular with their organization (Isenberg 1984; Mintzberg 1996a; Schon 1993).

As the requirement to use all ten available perspectives in every strategic management situation analysis would prove unrealistic and extravagant in a vast majority of cases, there arises an obvious need for appropriate rules to be developed to decide which perspectives should be pursued in any defined context. This cannot be achieved without a further refinement of the conceptual framework of strategic management enhancement. In pursuit of this aim, three criteria for enhancing strategic management decision-making are proposed here: *effectiveness, efficiency* and *responsiveness*. The definition of strategic management effectiveness could be based on the notion of sustained business performance:

> *Definition:* An organization's strategic management has been effective when the organization has demonstrated a superior capacity to ensure a good dynamic match between its own and accessible current and future resources and market opportunities or, alternatively, when it has shown a sustained capacity to produce successful competitive strategies.

Efficiency in strategic management enhancement is defined in this paper in comparative terms:

> Superior *efficiency* in strategic management demonstrates itself through resource requirements used in achieving objectives having been smaller than either anticipated by the organization itself, or required by its competitors in a similar situation.

Finally, we define responsiveness in this paper as:

> The organization's capacity to receive and make sense of signals from its environment and subsequently to rapidly modify its strategic intent and means of achieving its strategic objectives accordingly.

Thus, we propose that the overall quality of an organization's strategic management and of its individual strategies be assessed along these three dimensions that jointly represent a comprehensive and valid assessment framework.

It is in the context of this last proposition that one more pertinent observation should be made: whilst the multiple perspectives option requires more time and other resources to run, and as such is less efficient than any of the single perspective alternatives, it may influence the effectiveness and/or responsiveness aspects favorably.

For this reason we propose that the superiority, neutrality or inferiority of the multiple perspective option versus the single perspective option may only be ascertained on a case-to-case basis. This leads to the third, and last, proposition of this paper:

> Proposition 3: The superiority of the multiple perspective option in strategic management can only be ascertained on a case-to-case basis.

5.   HOW COULD ONE BETTER INTEGRATE STRATEGIC MANAGEMENT?

One of our crucial arguments in this paper has been that no strategic analysis should be *a priori* exclusive of any perspective. We suggest that it ought to be as inclusive of alternative perspectives as possible, always considering the feasibility and advantages of such an approach in particular circumstances.

How can this be achieved, though? How could one effectively involve more than one perspective in an analysis? Resource and responsiveness-related implications of such a major modification to the conduct of strategic management are certain to engender more than a fair degree of reservation amongst many managers. A few further questions are likely to be asked on such occasions: By how much could the company's profits grow in the long term, if at all, as a result of such a modification? What would be a justifiable level of the extra expenditure of cost and time to have it implemented and preserved?

5.1   Two unworkable options

Let us consider two opposing options faced by an organization that wants to apply a multiple perspective approach to solving its strategic management problems. One option would be to get one, or a selected few, persons to use all ten perspectives in an effort to generate ten diagnoses and then integrate ten sets of remedial actions aimed at enhancing company strategic management performance. The other – to ask ten individuals to simultaneously do the same from the point of view of one school assigned to that person.

Implementing either of these two approaches is likely to encounter massive difficulties with a vast majority of organizations. In the first case, they will be caused mostly by the cognitive and other psychological barriers on the part of involved individuals, as well as by the amount of time required from these individuals. In the second case, most companies will find it difficult to find ten suitably experienced, and trusted, individuals well versed with one school of thought each and get them to spend a considerable amount of time on the exercise which they may be weakly motivated to participate in. We therefore suggest that neither of these two opposing approaches appears generally workable.

A variant of the latter approach, though, of involving several people with differing preferable perspectives at various stages of analysis appears more realistic and could be applied in cases where organizations are not under extreme time pressure to bring about a substantial strategic management enhancement. However, would involving insiders and outsiders in such an analysis always be a superior option to using the services of just one of these two categories?

5.2   Dimensions of enhanced analysis

As already pointed out, the conflict between effectiveness- and efficiency-based arguments seems very likely there. Yet, unless organizations are inclusive rather than exclusive of various strategic management perspectives, the viability of their strategies may be severely jeopardized. The circumstances under which a decision to involve most, if not all, perspectives and possible perceptions would be appropriate would require a separate examination.

A second aspect of this discussion relates to the dependence of individual perceptions on perspectives represented by individuals. The currently prevalent strategic management approach is clearly one where the focus in diagnosing is laid on gathering and examining "objective" facts about the external and internal organization environment. Rarely is a systematic exploration of different individual perceptions of those facts done from a variety of possible perspectives (Anderson & Paine, 1975; Glaister & Thwaites, 1993; Ireland et al., 1987; Prince, 1992; Starbuck & Miliken, 1988).

Multi-outlook strategic management analysis is likely to produce a superior understanding of business situations and a better quality of strategic decisions.

A possible three-dimensional framework of integrated strategic management diagnosis[6] is presented in Figure 1. In Figure 1, the **X**-axis represents the "objective" components of the strategic management analysis, often referred to as the "facts and figures".

The **Y**-axis introduces perceptions of all individuals involved in the analysis, and the subsequent decision making process. It points at the importance of perceptions in the strategic management process and their dependence on emotional, cognitive and behavioral attitudes and predispositions of individuals and the circumstances of the context in which these individuals have operated, or are anticipated to operate. Y value depends on the number of sufficiently different perceptions involved in the strategic management process.

---

[6] Strategic management diagnosis depends on all involved perceptions (Barnes 1984, Ireland *et al.* 1987) and perspectives.

The **Z**-axis represents perspectives from which the strategic management situation is analyzed. The **Z** value would then denote the number of perspectives from which the strategic management analysis is conducted.

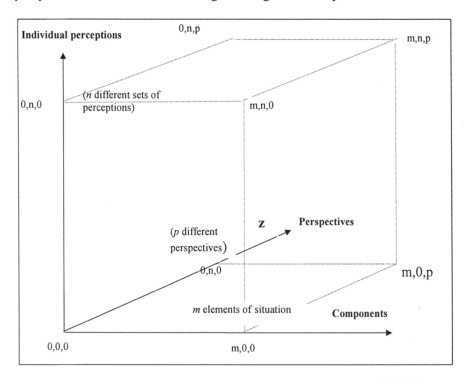

Figure 1: Three dimensions of the strategic management diagnosis.

The space taken up by the cuboid, whose faces connect all eight points on the **X**, **Y**, and **Z** axes supposed to characterize the strategic management situation (Figure 1) would then include the entire class of possible interpretations of elements of a given strategic management situation. In general, this proposed conceptual development could be used to represent and compare the complexity of strategic management analysis involving various perspectives and perceptions.

If one considers the currently prevalent strategic management practice, of the three diagnosis dimensions represented in Figure 1, only with respect of the **X** axis which represents business situation components could one reasonably expect many companies to aim for a (near) full coverage of their strategic management analysis.

Involving various schools of thought when diagnosing strategic management problems, represented by the Z-axis would be a very rare instance in business practice (Bourgeois, 1996; David, 1995; Miller & Dess,

1996; Mintzberg, 1996; Schon, 1993; Thompson & Strickland, 1998). Most likely, only one or two out of ten schools of thought discussed by Mintzberg would be followed in each individual case.

The degree to which various perceptions of the external and internal environment phenomena, as represented by **Y** axis, are involved in the strategic management analysis, would depend mostly on how participative is the strategic management process developed by the organization.

5.3   Role of effective communication

A third important aspect of relevance is that of the effective *communication* of all perspectives and perceptions in the strategic decision making process (Lewis, 1987; Stohl, 1995; Wofford *et al.*, 1977). Without an established pattern of wide strategic management participation, many employee/stakeholder perceptions may be systematically ignored or distorted. As shown before, for all valid perspectives to be properly considered, each of them would need to have at least one champion. This would imply, again, the need for a wide employee/stakeholder participation in such a modified process.

We suggest that the bottom-up-followed-by-top-down sequence of the strategic decision-making is likely to increase the effectiveness of related communication, as it would reduce the likelihood of the top management perspectives and perceptions represented by higher management echelons dominating the analysis (Janis & Mann, 1979). Involving all management functions in this process would have a similar beneficial effect.

Corporate cultures that stimulate employee reflection-in-action and promote reflection-sharing often have a communication effectiveness advantage (Schon, 1993). They involve a wider array of perceptions and perspectives in the strategic decision-making process and stimulate the relevant reflection (Mintzberg, 1996). The extent of this advantage may be attenuated by the efficiency and responsiveness considerations.

Certain decision criteria applied in the strategic management enhancement process may require more specific knowledge and skill (e.g. marketing, or entrepreneurial) to be brought to bear on this process. If so, they may encourage a more effective communication to make better use of such knowledge. A wide array of individual perceptions and perspectives would be revealed in the same process.

Communication and perception affect, to a varying extent, views of various components of the internal and external environment held by individuals and thus also the strategic decisions. Figure 2 below shows all major areas affected by these processes.

An integrated theory of strategic management theory must concern itself with all aspects of communication occurring between all major groups of insiders and outsiders to the company. It also needs to consider that communication in strategic management is influenced by a number of broad categories of factors external or internal to the organization (Goldhaber, 1977; Greenbaum, 1974; Lewis, 1987; Stohl, 1995).

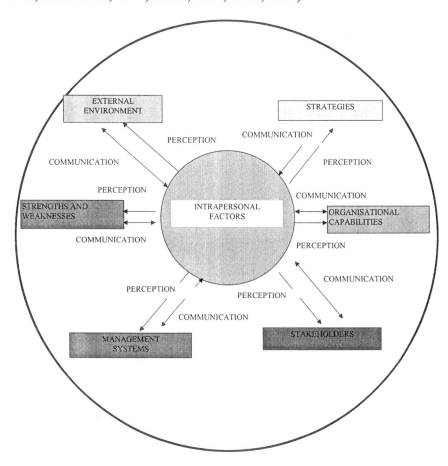

Figure 2: Perception and communication in strategic management.

6.   CONCLUSION

Each of the existing schools of thought on strategy formation uses its own specific perspectives and forms of analysis. As shown in the course of this discussion, adherents of each school are likely to
- differ greatly in the strategic management remedies they propose, and
- to neglect, to a varying degree, other possible perspectives and the corresponding tools of inquiry.

We have shown that the practical implications of this fragmentation of strategic management theory are quite considerable.

The choice of remedies in any strategic management endeavor largely depends on the awareness of, and familiarity with, available perspectives from which one can investigate the causes of an organization's unsatisfactory strategic management performance. On the other hand, these choices are affected also by a host of interrelated factors including the character of the business environment, relevant management perceptions, the existing business strategy, organizational culture and values, competitive strategies, current performance levels, relevant past management decisions (and their outcomes) and personal predispositions of managers.

As shown in this paper, the existing schools of thought are likely to differ greatly in the strategic management remedies they propose. This gives rise to a number of questions of considerable practical significance. They concern capacity of individual schools of thought to provide a sufficiently valid basis for a complete diagnosis and choice of remedial actions, the rules to be used in selecting perspectives suitable for a given category of strategic management enhancement situations, and the categories of situations with regard to which the multiple perspective approach is likely to prove superior.

We propose that strategic management performance be evaluated against the three criteria of **effectiveness, efficiency** and **responsiveness**. Our analysis of the implications of the multiple versus single perspective approach to strategic management analysis leads us to three relevant rule propositions. To increase the validity of the strategic management analysis and to improve the quality of strategic decisions three dimensions of the strategic management diagnosis are proposed (**components, individual perceptions** and **perspectives**).

We further propose that there are other application issues of general significance for strategic management outcomes:
- definition of rules by which to decide whether involving more than one perspective or school's view would be appropriate and beneficial in a particular case,
- ways of effectively involving different individual perceptions and perspectives, and

- effective organization-wide communication of strategic management information.

Our general conclusion is that a more integrated framework is more likely to produce better strategic management decisions. However, organizations must at all times exercise their best judgment in every decision-making situation to choose ways of implementing the proposed integrated approach which would consider their industry contexts, resource limitations and strategic objectives.

REFERENCES

Anderson, C.R., & Paine, F.T. (1975). Managerial perceptions and strategic behavior. *Academy of Management Journal 18*, 811-823.

Andrews, K., (1971). The Concept of Corporate Strategy. Homewood, Il., Irwin.

Ansoff, I. (1991). Critique of Henry Mintzberg's Design School. *Strategic Management Journal, 12*, 449-461.

Barnes, J.H. (1984). Cognitive Biases and their Impact on Strategic Planning. *Strategic Management Journal, 5*, 129-137.

Barney, J.B. (1997). *Gaining and Sustaining Competitive Advantage*. Reading, Mass., Addison Wesley.

Bourgeois, L.J., III, (1996). *Strategic Management: From Concept to Implementation*. Fort Worth, The Dryden Press.

Bowman, C., & Asch, D. (1987). *Strategic Management*. London: Macmillan Education.

Cyert, R., & March, J. (1992). *A Behavioural Theory of the Firm*, (2nd. ed.). Englewood Cliffs: Prentice Hall.

David, F. (1995). *Strategic Management*. Englewood Cliffs, NJ: Prentice Hall.

Doktor, R.H., & Bloom, D.M. (1977). *Selective Lateralisation of Cognitive Style Related to Occupation as Determined by EEG Alpha Assymetry*. Psychophysiology pp. 385-7).

Dixit, A., & Nalebuff, B. (1991). *Thinking Strategically*. New York: Norton.

Fama, E., (1980). Agency Problems and the Theory of the Firm. *Journal of Political Economy, 288-307.*

Ghoshal, S., & Moran, P. (1996). Bad for Practice: A Critique of the Transaction Cost Theory. *Academy of Management Review, 21*, 13-47.

Glaister, K., & Thwaites, D. (1993). Managerial Perception and Organizational Strategy. *Journal of General Management, 13* (4), 15-33.

Goldhaber, G.M. (1979). *Organizational Communication* (2nd. ed.). Dubuque, IA.: W.C.Brown Company.

Greenbaum, H.H. (1974). The Audit of Organizational Communication. *Academy of Management Journal, 17*, 739-754.

Ireland, R.D., Hitt, M.A., Bettis, R.A., De Porras, D. (1987). Auld, Strategy Formulation Processes: Differences in Perceptions of Strength and Weaknesses Indicators and Environmental Uncertainty by Managerial Level. *Strategic Management Journal, 8*, 469-485.

Isenberg, D.J. (1984). How Senior Managers Think. *Harvard Business Review 6*(84), 80-90.

Janis, I.L., & Mann, L. (1979). *Decision Making*. New York, Free Press.

Jensen, M., Meckling, W. (1976). Theory of the Firm: Managerial Behavior, Agency Costs and Ownership Structure, *Journal of Financial Economics, 3*, (October), 305-360.

Lewis, P.V. (1987). *Organizational Communication: The Essence of Effective Management* (3rd ed.). New York: John Wiley & Sons.

McKiernan, P. (ed.). (1996). *Historical Evolution of Strategic Management*. Dartmouth Publ..

Mc Kinsey, and Associates. (1996). *Marketers' Metamorphosis*. New York.

Marshall, A. (1961). *Principles of Economics*. London: Macmillan.

Miller, A., & Dess, G.G. (1996). *Strategic Management*. (2nd. ed.). New York: McGraw Hill.

Milliken, F.J., & Lant, J.T. (1991). The effect of an organization's recent performance history on strategic persistence and change: The role of managerial interpretations. In J. Dutton, A. Huff, & P. Shrivastava, (Eds.), *In Advances in Strategic Management*. Greenwich: CT JAI Press.

Mintzberg, H. (1990). The Design School: Reconsidering the Basic Premises of Strategic Management. *Strategic Management Journal, 11*, 171-195.

Mintzberg, H. (1991). Learning 1, Planning 0: A Reply to Igor Ansoff. *Strategic Management Journal, 12*, 463-466.

Mintzberg, H. (1994). *The Rise and Fall of Strategic Planning*. Prentice Hall International (UK) Ltd..

Mintzberg, H. (1996). Five Ps for Strategy. In The Strategy Process, Concepts, Contexts, Cases, (3rd. ed.). Mintzberg, H., & Quinn, J.B. (Eds.). New Jersey: Prentice Hall Inc..

Mintzberg, H. (1996a). The Manager's Job. In The Strategy Process, Concepts, Contexts, Cases, (3rd. ed.). Mintzberg, H., & Quinn, J.B. (Eds.). New Jersey: Prentice Hall Inc..

Nelson, R., Winter, S., (1982). *An Evolutionary Theory of Economic Change*. Cambridge, MA.: Harvard University Press.

Papadakis, W., Lioukas, S., & Chambers, D. (1998). Strategic Decision-making Processes: The Role of Management and Context. *Strategic Management Journal, 19*, 115-147.

Pearce, J.A. II, Robinson, R.B., Jr. (1997). *Strategic Management. Formulation, Implementation, and Control*. (6th. ed.). Chicago: Irwin.

Piercy, N., & Giles, W. (1990). The Logic of Being Illogical in Strategic Marketing Planning. *The Journal of Services Marketing, 4* (3), 27-37.

Porter, M.E. (1980). *Competitive Strategy: Techniques for Analyzing Industries and Competitors*. New York: Free Press.

Prahalad, C.K., & Hamel, G., (1990). The Core Competence of the Corporation. Harvard Business Review, (May-June), 79-91.

Prince, M.W. (1992). Implications of perception and strategy for engineers in construction management, *Construction Management and Economics, 10*, 93-105.

Rajagopalan, N., & Spreitzer, G.M. (1996). Toward a Theory of Strategic Change: A Multi-Lens Perspective and Integrative Framework. *Academy of Management Review, 22* (1), 48-79.

Rumelt, R.P., Schendel, D., & Teece, D.J. (1991). Strategic Management and Economics, *Strategic Management Journal, 12*, 5-29.

Senge, P.M. (1990). *The Fifth Discipline*. Harper & Row.

Schon, D.A. (1993). *The Reflective Practitioner - How Professionals Think in Action*. New York, Basic Books.

Starbuck, W.H., & Milliken, F.J. (1988). Executives' perceptual filters: what they notice and how they make sense. In Hambrick, D. (Eds.). *The Executive Effect: Concepts and Methods for Studying Top Managers*. Greenwich: CT, JAI Press.

Stohl, C. (1995). *Organizational Communication: Connectedness in Action*. Thousand Oaks, Cal.: Sage Publications.

Thompson, A., & Strickland, III A.J. (1998). *Strategic Management: Concepts and Cases.* Boston, Mass.: Irwin/Mc Graw Hill.

Weick, K. (1969). *The Social Psychology of Organizations.* Reading: MA, Addison-Wesley.

Wernerfelt, B. (1984). A Resource-based View of the Firm. *Strategic Management Journal, 5,* 171-180.

Williamson, O.E. (1975). *Markets and Hierarchies: Analysis and Antitrust Implications.* New York: The Free Press.

Williamson, O.E. (1996). Economic Organization: The Case for Candor. *Academy of Management Review, 21,* 48-57.

Wofford, J., Gerloff, E., & Cummins, R.C. (1977). *Organizational Communication: The Keystone to Managerial Effectiveness.* Tokyo: Mc Graw Hill.

Trainer, Mentor, Educator: What Role for the Business Faculty in the 21st Century

S.D. Malik[1] & Ken Morse[2]
*[1]New Paradigms Consulting Group, Pittsford, NY, USA, [2]Waikato Management School,
University of Waikato, Hamilton, New Zealand*

1.   A SHORT HISTORY

From earliest documentation, business operations have traditionally been regarded as skills that ware passed from one trade member to another. A good example of this was Charles Dickens' 1843 description of Ebenezer Scrooge's training under Mr. Fezziwig. As is evident in Dickens' text, teaching a business trade typically took the form of an apprenticeship. A young man/woman would become apprenticed to a journeyman/woman or master of a trade or skill for a set period of time. During that period, the apprentice would learn the skills of the trade through close observation, intense coaching and repetitive practice. Once the apprentice satisfied the master's requirements, the apprentice assumed the mantle of journeyman and was considered to be an expert in the skill s/he had just been taught. The journeyman status also allowed the student to take on apprentices of his/her own, thereby spreading the skills to carefully selected newcomers. In this educational capacity, the journeyman served as a trainer and mentor to the apprentice. Teaching emphasis was on the acquisition and perfection of the skill or trade being taught. Mentoring was geared toward establishing the new journeymen in a career of their own.

The idea of educating students in fundamentals of business skills was introduced to the academic world through institutions that focused on teaching technical skills. These technical or vocational schools trained students about the content and the process of developing technical skills. The

T.A. Johannessen, A. Pedersen and K. Petersen (eds.),
Educational Innovation in Economics and Business VI, 273–282.

educational aspect of these programs was primarily centered on the mastery of specific skill domains, and students who successfully completed requirements of these programs were thought to be qualified for a position in that trade. European and Asian educational systems still maintain these technical institutions, and students may choose the university system for a typical liberal arts education or a technical institution to be trained for a skilled profession. In fact, these educational systems maintain a distinction between tertiary educational institutions like universities and tertiary training organizations such as polytechnics. Technical institutions do still exist in the United States' educational environment but have frequently, been replaced by community colleges that provide social service training as well as skills training.

In 1908, Harvard University became one of the first Universities in the United States to authorize the establishment of a School of Business Administration. Other universities and colleges soon followed suit. It was at this point that the role of a business teacher started to shift from that of a journeyman or trainer to that of an academic educator. At the turn of the century, there were a number of breakthrough research articles that lent validity to the academic incorporation of business education. Fredrick Taylor's (1911) observations and innovations led to the Scientific Management movement as the focus of business practice and education. Another academic breakthrough came through the studies of Mayo (1933) and Roethlisberger and Dickson (1939) at the General Electric Hawthorne plant, which concluded that human relations were as essential a part of business operations as the "nuts and bolts" skills are. With these studies, business education started to develop a firm footing in the academic pastures of theory building. Theoretical arguments by researchers such as Maslow (1943), McGregor (1960) and others laid a solid foundation for the argument that the importance of business education was in the construction and elaboration of the underlying theoretical understanding of business processes rather than in the development and refinement of basic business skills. The traditional role of trainer and mentor became less essential to the business educator with this increased focus on the intellectual tenets of business operations.

2.   WINDS OF CHANGE

From the early 1900s through the 1960s, economic conditions in the United States were good and the future looked rosy. With the rapid increases in productivity being experienced in the factories, those who wanted work were almost guaranteed a job with or without a high school diploma. In addition, as the war in Vietnam escalated, a significant percentage of able-bodied workers were conscripted into military service. During this period, due to a variety of alternative opportunities, higher education was reserved for those who were interested in more intellectual or professional education. The United States experienced major economic setbacks in the late 1970s. There was high inflation, high unemployment and productivity levels dropped as international competition began to heat up. The Arab oil producing countries imposed a crushing oil embargo in the late 1970s that further crippled the economy. Companies, fighting for their survival, began seeking drastic means of cost savings. One of the primary ways that American manufacturers cut their production costs was to move assembly line production overseas where they could employ a less expensive labour force. This meant that American workers no longer had the opportunity to make a lifetime career for themselves in low-skilled jobs. In fact, occupations requiring at least an associate's degree are expected to grow faster during 1996 to 2006 than those requiring less education or training (Silvestri, 1997). Furthermore, as production and manufacturing technology became more sophisticated, a high school education became more desirable, even for those entering assembly line work.

The mainstay of those displaced blue-collar workers and those who are entering the workforce with low skill levels is in the service industry. Silvestri (1997) ranks this as the third fastest growing occupational group for the next decade. In fact, he states that professional specialty and service occupations will generate nearly half of the total job growth from 1996 to 2006. While the job market in the service industry has expanded rapidly, the majority of these jobholders earn minimum wages and have had a difficult time supporting a family on service-sector based income.

The 1980s and 1990s have been defined by technology. The United States' recession of the 1980s was lifted on the shoulders of a new generation of "techies" who put their intellectual prowess toward the rapid genesis of technological innovations. This technological emphasis, coupled with the fact that most low skilled jobs had departed for overseas shores, meant that the jobs for the American workforce required high level skills and, therefore, higher education. For example, Silvestri (1997), an economist in the Office of Employment Projects of the Federal Bureau of Labor Statistics, projects that the fastest growing occupations for the 1996-2006 time frame are in the professional specialty group. The second fastest growth rate is expected in the technicians and related support occupations. Of the thirty fastest growing occupations listed in the 1989-99 Occupational Outlook Handbook, put out by the Bureau of Labor Statistics, 18 categories require postsecondary vocational training or higher levels of education.

Recent governmental surveys have revealed that there is a significant relationship between educational attainment and earnings. For example, the Bureau of Labor Statistics reported, in its 1998 Occupational Outlook Quarterly report, that those workers with professional degrees earn a "diploma premium" of 208% over those with a high school degree. A Bachelor's degree will give a worker a 55% premium over a high school diploma. Studies by Pryor and Schaffer (1997), and Frazis and Stewart (1996) have also found support for the economic returns associated with increasing educational attainment.

The pressures, which have erupted from these environmental changes, have forced an increasing number of people to seek higher educational certification. As a consequence, community colleges, four-year colleges and universities have seen a sharp increase in their enrolments. A Bureau of Labor Statistics survey, described in the 1997 Current Population Survey, revealed that 67% of 1997 American high school graduates were enrolled in colleges for the forthcoming academic year. According to the Bureau, this is a 5-percentage point increase over the previous two years. This is a significant jump considering that the enrolment rate had remained steady from 1992 until 1995 at 62%. Of those enrolled, the Bureau reported that two-thirds were planning to attend a 4-year college while the remaining had signed up for 2-year programs. Interestingly, more women graduates (70%) were enrolled in college than men graduates (63.5%).

3.   IMPACT ON EDUCATIONAL INSTITUTIONS

Given the fact that an increasing percentage of people are finding it necessary to complete a higher education program in order to find a profitable career, there has been a change in educational institutions, as well. Many of these alterations have occurred so incrementally, that most business faculty cannot consciously identify the source of these, but do acknowledge that there have been shifts in what their students expect from their higher educational programs.

The most obvious direction of this shift has been from an expectation of mind expanding, horizon developing, general education in the Liberal Arts tradition to employment preparation, job related skills development (albeit "higher order skills" such as management and marketing rather than physical skills like auto repair or bookkeeping) in keeping with the growing demands for increased career preparation by both students and business employers. We would argue that this phenomenon has been most evident in the professional, especially business, programs across the higher education spectrum.

As was discussed at the beginning of this paper, the teaching of business skills has moved from that of on-the-job process training to that of development of an intellectual understanding of business content. This shift in orientation toward business education, as was also mentioned earlier, meant that the role of the business faculty changed from that of a trainer/mentor to that of an educator. The main reason for this transformation was the academic pressure to "intellectualize" business education. As long as students were seeking higher education for intellectual growth, these changes in the business faculty's role were consistent with the needs of the student body and, the faculty who was successful at developing scholars at the graduate level could be equally effective at the undergraduate level since the assumption was that they, too, were seeking scholarship from the educational institutions.

One of the first environmental forces driving the subsequent changes in business education expectations was due to the changing demands of the business needs of the employment community. With the rapid increase in technological adaptations of business processes and the sweeping globalization of the international economy, the business community needed new employees who could quickly transition into this high-paced environment with the necessary skills. It was this need that created the biggest chasm between the type of business taught in academia and the needs of the business employers.

The initial driving force of change created the second and, perhaps most potent, conflict between the traditional academic orientation and the new directions being pushed for business education. As an increasing number of people are finding it necessary to pursue higher education for the primary purpose of securing a financially stable career, the intellectualization of business education has come into direct conflict with students' goals of seeking high level specialized job-related training and skills through their higher education pursuits. Students, particularly at the undergraduate level, seeing the economic benefits associated with higher education attainment, are seeking, at the very least, a certification to enter the workforce, e.g., a college diploma. Or, at the most, they are seeking training on specialized skills that will give them a competitive advantage in the marketplace. The intellectual component of business education, and any general education, is considered to be irrelevant to the current American business undergraduate.

This change in educational expectations has created a clash with the traditional methods of teaching business within an academic environment. Students are pushing business faculty to realign their roles from those principally emphasizing education (questioning/critical thinking development) to those that serve a training function (practical use skills development). Furthermore, an increasing number of students are demanding that faculty serve either as mentors or help the student establish a mentor relationship with a businessperson in his/her chosen career discipline. This student expectation of mentoring and interaction with realistic, business community related programs comes from the perception that the academic world is not the "real" world and, therefore, faculty must provide opportunities for experiences within this arena.

Many business faculty and business schools have proactively responded to these demanded changes. Within the business teaching profession, there has been a shift from a content-based curriculum to an increasing incorporation of process-oriented teaching methods, which seek to blend active learning and participation into the classroom experience. The expanding focus on process-oriented education has been affirmed by accreditation organizations such as the AACSB, which has curriculum standards that require elements of process-based learning within an accredited business program. Evidence of this shift may also be found in the proliferation of process-learning techniques in a variety of disciplines (see Morse & Malik, 1997 for review). The increasing demand for "workplace relevance" has led to the need to "entertain" with case studies, simulations, group "think" sessions, etc. Colleges and universities, particularly at the undergraduate level as well as for many market-centered graduate programs, are instituting wide-ranging real world experiences such as internships, small business development assistance (like the one housed at SUNY at Geneseo) and business community research (like the one semester business sponsored research assignment requirement the University of Waikato imposes for degree completion). These types of programs not only serve the students' demands for "real world" experience but also open up avenues for the institutions to solicit private funding for their programs.

Before the winds of change push the profession too far back on this road of reversal of our professional roles, it behooves us, the business faculty, to examine what this reversal means and whether or not it is truly the future direction that we want for our profession.

4.   SOME DEFINITIONS

Prior to examining where the profession is headed in terms of weighing its roles, it is important that these roles be clearly defined. For this paper, we will focus on three of the principle roles business faculty have performed in the context of passing on knowledge about business to students: educator, trainer and mentor.

Wexley and Latham (1981) make a clear-cut distinction between education and training, although they do acknowledge that there is considerable overlap between the two processes. Specifically, education involves the teaching of facts in order to stimulate the acquisition of knowledge, assimilation of information and cognitive development (Walters & Marks, 1981). Bloom (1987) takes a much broader perspective of education, arguing that the role of the educator, especially those involved in higher education, is to preserve the freedom of the mind by using the content that is taught as the starting point for examining alternative perspectives of thought. The function of an educator, therefore, is to encourage the mind to explore beyond the accepted boundaries. In business education, this involves the development of critical thinking processes that can move the individual beyond the accepted content of the discipline. From an educational framework, there are no right or wrong answers, only better or worse ones.

Training, on the other hand, is the teaching of skills (Wexley & Latham, 1981). Based on this definition, the trainer is concerned with process-based learning because s/he emphasizes the learning of skills that can be applied in a job or some type of work situation. According to this definition, training is a much more narrow method of education because its goal is so specific as is the focus of the material being taught. Training also usually includes high levels of physical involvement (Walters & Marks, 1981). Due to the way most training programs are designed, there are often right or wrong ways to accomplish a task. For example, students are taught that there is one generally accepted way to post sales figures to an Income Statement and they are penalized for not following this approach. In a training situation, there is little room to explore which ways are better or worse for doing a task or performing a skill.

A role that is distinct from, but related to, that of educator and trainer is the role of mentor. Mentors are people who provide newcomers to a profession or career with career-enhancing guidance, support and opportunities (Kram, 1985). Mentorship activities can include sponsorship, coaching, facilitating exposure and visibility and offering challenging work (Kram, 1983). Kram and Isabella (1985) contend that these activities are provided in order to help the newcomer establish an organizational role and learn the ropes while having a senior person as an advisor and friend. Based upon these definitions, mentoring has a lot of components of educating and training but the learning is directed toward getting established in a job or a career. Students, realizing that higher education is needed for a professional career, often do not understand what that education prepares them to do. The fact is that, since the content of their business education provides them with knowledge about so many different disciplines, they have more career options than ever before. Therefore, they turn to their business faculty for ideas and help in identifying and choosing as well as developing in a particular career.

Given this understanding of the three fundamental roles of a business faculty, the next question that we, as members of the profession, have to answer is how should we prioritize them? Based on the explicit needs of the American student of business, the current student body would prefer that the majority of their learning be in a training mode with the residual emphasis on mentoring. The educational function is irrelevant to the American student of today. Anecdotal evidence from Australia strongly indicates that a similar change in student perceptions and requirements is driving a nearly identical change in that part of the world. However, based on scholarly discussions at international conferences, the European, South African and Australian academic systems have dispelled some of the issues facing American academics because of the differentiation between technical training and university education that is inherent in structure of their educational systems. Still, these scholars acknowledge that economic pressures are and will continue to exert a change in the roles of the undergraduate faculty and, to some degree, for graduate-level faculty, too. What are those changes and is the prioritization that the American system is facing what we, the business instructors, desire?

5.   INTO THE NEXT MILLENNIUM

Bloom (1987) makes an eloquent argument that higher education must serve a role that is independent of the demands of society. Specifically, he argues that if institutions of higher education conform to the norms of the social regime of the moment, their basic mission, to preserve the freedom of the mind, will become obscured by the need to constantly adapt to changing social demands. This argument would suggest that business faculty maintain the role of educators as their top priority and continue to focus on the intellectual components of a business education. In addition, if we adopt Bloom's (1987) conception of the role of higher education, business programs need to develop a curriculum that pushes the student to question the existing paradigm in an effort to move beyond those boundaries. In terms of business content, the student needs to be presented with circumstances which require the student to ask "Why not some other way?" or "If this is the only known way, what are other possibilities so far unexplored?" A broad-based business education should also develop an understanding and appreciation of the business world within its larger social context so that the role business has in this context is never assumed but is always being re-evaluated.

It is important to recognize that institutions of higher learning exist in a competitive market that exposes them to the demands of their clientele. In order to survive in a competitive state, institutions must adapt to some of these demands to attract enough constituents to justify their continued existence. As discussed earlier, most business schools have taken conscious, proactive steps to accommodate the changes in their environment. As many examples at this and other conferences have shown, some business schools have embraced the process-based teaching method on an institute-wide basis. Still others are adopting large components of the process as a part of their curriculum. The question becomes how far to make these changes? The answer may lie in teaching techniques such as experiential learning and problem solving. Recent adaptations of these types of methods attempt to blend and balance both the educational and training aspects. This equalization of both content and process teaching components appears to retain the educational agenda supported by Bloom (1987) while fulfilling the student body's demand for skill-specific training.

However, and it is a major mitigating concern, there is a danger that the educational component may get lost if the focus of the experiential learning activity becomes too process-oriented. For this reason, business faculty must highlight and reinforce the intellectual phases of these teaching methods. These methods must remain a part of the entire learning process. In order to fulfill our professional role within institutes of higher learning, the educational component must remain the primary focus of the profession. Only in this way can we faculty create future businessmen/women with the intellectual framework necessary to push the current boundaries of business processes.

REFERENCES

Adams, H. (1998). In M. Albom, *Tuesdays with Morrie: An old man, a young man and life's greatest lesson.* New York: Doubleday press.

Bloom, A. (1987). *The closing of the American mind.* New York: Simon and Schuster.

Bureau of Labor Statistics. (1998). *Earnings of college graduates, 1996.* Occupational Outlook Quarterly. (Fall).

College enrollment and work activity of 1997 high school graduates. (1998). 1997 Current Population Survey, BLS supplement. Washington: U.S. Census Bureau.

Frazis, H., & Stewart, J. (1996). *Tracking the returns to education in the Nineties.* BLS Working Papers. Washington: U.S. Department of Labor: Bureau of Labor Statistics.

Kram, K. (1985). *Mentoring at work: Developmental relationships in organizational life.* Glenview, Ill: Scott-Foresman.

Kram, K. (1983). Phases of the mentor relationship. *The Academy of Management Journal, 26,* 608-625.

Kram, K., & Isabella, L. (1985). Mentoring alternatives: The role of peer relationships in career development. *The Academy of Management Journal, 28,* 110-132.

Morse, K. & Malik, D. (1997). *Problem based learning, experiential learning and lifelong learning: Who's on first?* Paper presented at the 4th EDINEB Conference. Edinburgh, Scotland, Sept.2.

Maslow, A. (1943). A theory of human motivation. *Psychological Review*, 370-393.

Mayo, E. (1933). *The human problems of industrial civilization.* New York: Macmillan.

McGregor, D. (1960). *The human side of enterprise.* New York: McGraw-Hill.

Pryor, F., & Schaffer, D. (1997). Wages and the university educated: a paradox resolved. *Monthly Labor Review*, 3-18.

Roethlisberger, F. ,& Dickson, W. (1939). *Management and the worker.* Cambridge, Mass: Harvard University Press.

Silvestri, G. (1997). Occupational employment projections to 2006. *Monthly Labor Review*, 58-82.

Taylor, F. (1911). *Principles of Scientific Management.* New York: Harper.

Walters, G., & Marks, S. (1981). *Experiential learning and change.* New York: John Wiley & Sons.

Wexley, K. & Latham, G. (1981). *Developing and training human resources in organizations.* Glenview, Ill: Scott-Foresman.

Leadership Development as a Means of Organizational Change

A Collaborative Research Project

Carol Dalglish[1] & Jenifer Frederick[2]

[1]*Brisbane Graduate School of Business, Queensland University of Technology, Brisbane, Australia* [2]*Queensland Audit Office, Brisbane, Australia*

1.   INTRODUCTION AND BACKGROUND

Much has been written concerning the value of learning and education in delivering competitive advantage, particularly in knowledge based service industries (Karpin 1995, p. 189) (Senge 1990, p. 172). There has also been much written about the necessity for real individual behavioral change to underpin effective organizational and cultural change (Quinn 1996, p. 5) In his seminal work 'the fifth discipline' Senge identified Personal mastery as one of the 5 disciplines necessary to effective learning organizations in a changing world environment.

The Department of the Auditor-General was established in Queensland in 1860. Being an organization comprised primarily of auditors, it is not surprising that the culture of the office has been strongly conservative, concerned with detail, and fairly risk averse with a strong focus on centralized control and decision making.

Management as a concept has been well understood in the QAO. As such, training for managers focused on the planning, controlling, and monitoring aspects of management, specifically within the context of managing audits, rather than the organization. "Soft skills", including leadership, were perceived as being less useful for auditors, who were predominantly interested in doing audits and saw other corporate activities and training on matters other than technical accounting and auditing issues as of much lower priority.

T.A. Johannessen, A. Pedersen and K. Petersen (eds.),
Educational Innovation in Economics and Business VI, 283–300.

The QAO is a service knowledge-based organization, which despite having a legislative monopoly recognizes the potential competitive nature of its business. Over the last six years, QAO has undergone significant structural and organizational reform and has focused on changing the people and the culture to align individual behavior with organizational values and direction. QAO has focused on developing competitive advantage through development of its people, and particularly its middle managers.

The QAO has a monopoly on all audits of public sector entities (some 620 in total including departments, local authorities, statutory bodies and controlled entities of these organizations). The large majority of effort is devoted to financial and compliance regularity audits, and in the last two years, QAO has also been auditing performance management systems.

QAO has been running its own in-house leadership programs since 1994. Recognizing the need to institutionalize the leadership program so that it is not dependent on individual sponsorship within the organization, and wanting to provide wider recognition to those who undertake the program, the Queensland Audit Office has entered into partnership with the Brisbane Graduate School of Business at the Queensland University of Technology. Together the QAO and the Graduate School of Business provide a flexible, relevant leadership development program that offers graduate accreditation to those who successfully complete the program.

The nature of the history and role of QAO over a substantial number of years has led to the development of a very specific culture. The explanation and description of culture that is used is provided by Schein (1985, p. 6).

"I will argue that the term culture should be reserved for the deeper level of basic assumptions and beliefs that are shared by members in an organization, that operates unconsciously, and that defines in basic "taken for granted" fashion an organization's view of itself and its environment. These assumptions and beliefs are learned responses to a group's problems of survival in its external environment and its problems of internal integration. They come to be taken for granted because they solve those problems repeatedly and reliably. This deeper level of assumptions is to be distinguished from the "artifacts" and values" that are manifestations or surface levels of the culture but not the essence of the culture."

One of the reasons, it was thought; why previous strategies to bring about change within the QAO was that they did not acknowledge or deal with this culture.

Schein also argues that the unique talent of leaders is their ability to work with culture (Schein, 1985, p. 2). If this is the case, then leadership skills are critical to bringing about the cultural change desired in QAO.

2.   NATURE OF THE PROGRAM

There are traditionally a number of different ways in which leadership training is delivered. Jay Conger (1992) identified 4 categories of leadership training: Personal growth, skill building, conceptual development and feedback. Csoka (1996) provides a simple overview of these strategies, which is used as a framework to understand the development and structure of the QAO program, which drew on all of them.

2.1   Personal growth

Leadership training programs featuring personal growth emphasize the need for managers to become more aware of their inner talents, abilities and limitations. QAO is very supportive of this approach and has included it as a critical element of their leadership program. Because the employing organization recognizes the importance of personal growth as a critical element of leadership training, some of the difficulties identified (Csoka, 1996) when applying this new awareness in the work place are overcome. The support of the Auditor-General, as the CEO of the organization, has been particularly important in ensuring that participants in the program are able to use their newfound self-awareness.

2.2   Conceptual development

This has traditionally been the strength of university leadership programs and works on the premise that if you know the concept you can act on it. The structured program offered to QAO incorporated the thorough conceptual focus that was considered a welcome addition to the in-house leadership program.

2.3   Feedback

Feedback was a critical element in the Leadership Development Program as delivered at QAO. Individuals had to compete for places on the program and were tested against a wide variety of leadership, management and personal style assessment tools.

2.4   Skill building

This is perhaps the most commonly used method for leadership training because it has an intuitive appeal because of the practical approach which organizations need. This element of skill building is integral to the program through the incorporation of real work related projects as part of the course learning activities and assessment.

The Leadership Development Program leads to a Graduate Certificate of Management awarded by the Queensland University of Technology. The program includes existing units from within the MBA program but the possibility exists in the future to include newly created units if required. These units included:

- **Personal Development and Ethics.** This unit as the title suggests focuses on self awareness and the development of ethical decision making skills using a range of conceptual models.
- **Human Resource Management.** This unit responded to the perceived needs of the organization to develop in their leaders a greater awareness of human resource management issues. The unit included not only conceptual development but also a practical in-house project of immediate relevance to both the participants and the organization.
- **Organizational Analysis and Consulting.** This unit included a major practical consulting project which required participants, in teams, to undertake a consulting project within their organization to address an issue of concern to the organization. It provided consulting skills in a situation where the 'power' did not rest with the consultants, contrary to most auditors' previous experience.
- **Leadership I and II.** These units dealt both with the conceptual issues relating to leaders but also with the development of personal leadership skills and focused again on personal awareness and self-knowledge.

The units were chosen because they reflected the areas that the QAO wished to develop, and included the possibility of practical in-house projects as part of the learning experience.

The delivery is in-house at QAO and uses a variety of methods based around learning sets. Information is provided to the learning sets through input sessions and workshops conducted by QUT and other providers and through independent learning and research supported by suggested reading. The learning sets are led by QAO staff that is recognized as tutors of the Brisbane Graduate School. Participants have the opportunity of testing and applying their knowledge through discussion, practical projects, presentations and assignments.

The program commences with significant self-assessment and the use of the Enneagram, 360-degree feedback tools and the development of a personal learning plan. This leads to an individualized learning plan that may require individuals to undertake different activities to ensure meeting the learning outcomes of the program as a whole. The learning sets are the focus of discussion and debate about what is learned. The program will conclude with a second self-assessment and 360 degree feedback process and the completion of a further ongoing leadership development plan.

3.   OBJECTIVES AND METHODOLOGY

The Leadership Development Program was established with clear intentions with regard to organizational change. The underlying assumption was that to bring about effective change to the way QAO did business, the decision makers, as people, needed to change the way they viewed the world and the way they led the organization. Schein (1985) states "leadership is the fundamental process by which organizational cultures are formed and changed." (Schein, 1985, p. ix)

It would clearly be impossible to prove a causal relationship between a program such as the LDP and changes within the organization because of the range of variables that could not be controlled. However, it is hoped to provide evidence of a relationship between the program and the changes that have occurred in the organization over the past year. Understanding the nature of that relationship, which elements of the program have been most effective in facilitating change and other factors in the organization or environment that have been significant in their impact on the organization, is the purpose of this research.

There were some specific changes that the organization was seeking from the design and conducting of the LDP? These included:

- A shift in style from a traditional management focus to leadership focus among participants.
- Increased leadership skills.
- The capacity of the organization to think and act strategically.
- The capacity of the organization to respond flexibly to new issues or demands.
- The ability of the organizational members to work together co-operatively.

4.   EVALUATION METHODOLOGY

To collect the relevant data, a number of strategies were implemented. Eight of the nine members of the Executive Management Group (EMG) were interviewed. Jenifer Frederick, who initiated the program and is a joint writer of this paper, was not interviewed as it was felt that she was too close to the program, had too much invested in it and might therefore bias the results.

Each member of the EMG was interviewed by Dr Carol Dalglish. The interviews took approximately 1 hour each. The questions addressed 4 primary areas:

- Why the organization needed to change and the nature of the required changes.
- The changes that had occurred over the past year in management style, team working, strategic thinking ability and new initiatives. (These are the areas in which the program was designed to bring about change.)
- What contribution, if any, the Leadership Development Program (LDP) had made to the changes, and
- Whether as individuals they would be willing to sponsor and manage the program.

All nine of the first cohorts on the accredited Leadership Development Program (LDP) were interviewed. Each member of the cohort was interviewed by Dr Carol Dalglish. The interviews took approximately 1 hour each. The questions addressed 4 primary areas:

- How the organization had changed over the past year.
- The impact the LDP had on them as individuals and on the organization particularly in terms of management style, team working, strategic thinking ability and new initiatives (These are the areas in which the program was designed to bring about change.), and
- Why the program was perceived to be a success.

There was the potential for an overly positive response as all participants had been taught by Dr Dalglish and were aware of her commitment to the program. It is difficult to assess the extent of the interviewer bias. However, the familiarity with Dr Dalglish, and the openness that was encouraged through the program, may also have lead to more comprehensive answers and a willingness to disclose than might not have been the case with a stranger.

5.   RESPONSES TO THE SENIOR MANAGEMENT QUESTIONNAIRE

Throughout the text I will indicate () the number of people who gave this specific answer. I have changed all answers to the third person although they were all expressed in the first person.

5.1   Reasons why change is necessary

There was remarkable consistency in the answers to these questions. The external environment in which the QAO operates has changed. (2). The Victorian experience suggests that the QAO cannot be sure of their monopoly; to survive they have to be the best. Other Audit Offices have had their mandates significantly reduced.

There are increasing demands for the QAO to do new things and be more flexible. The mandate has broadened (2). To be successful the culture needed to change (2).

- There needs to be greater focus on the organizations that QAO services.
- There needs to be accountability not just compliance and this requires an ability to understand the client (2).
- Expectations from the clients are beyond compliance (3).
- There are greater expectations of professionalism (4) and the QAO needs to be more competitive (3).
- Change is essential to ongoing viability (2).

5.2   Changes in the organization

The Executive Management Group identified a number of ways in which the organization had changed.

Increased devolution has occurred, initiated by the new Auditor General. (4) The new Auditor General has changed the culture with more **delegation of authority**, more participative management style (5). Change of Auditor General brought change from autocratic to more participative management style with greater devolution of responsibility (2). Participants on the Leadership Development Program have demonstrated a willingness to take responsibility, to try new things (4). This delegation is an attempt to create a more flexible and professional organization.

There is a much stronger emphasis on **client focus**, bringing about a significant change in the nature of the relationship with clients, to ensure that work does not depend on current mandate (4). The auditors now work with the client, the policing mindset had to change. Some initiatives in this area include: the appointment of a marketing manager, the development of a speakers kit for auditors: a free newsletter for clients discussing current issues. There is greater focus on communication with client organizations

The Executive Management Group (EMG) has changed to take to more strategic approach (2). The knowledge level about management has increased, as has the awareness of alternative strategies. **Strategic thinking** at the executive level has improved. The LDP is seen as a contributor to this change (2). Strategic planning now involves LDP participants and other staff in development (3). EMG learning sets are being introduced so senior executives have a shared understanding with their subordinates and colleagues on the LDP program and a similar opportunity to discuss contemporary issues. Balancing the operational and strategic is still perceived to be a problem.

There is more collaborative - cross group communication and a sense of shared purpose (3), and a move towards **team work** (3). There is greater focus on people as individuals and as part of a team. Management style has become more people oriented. New leaders (from the program on the executive) not afraid to show they are human.

A **Strategic Development and Performance Unit** was established following a recommendation in an issues paper to the strategic planning workshop by LDP participants. The purpose of the Strategic Development and Performance Unit is to enhance QAO's image, improve client education, increase innovation, find better ways of doing things, and suggest new practices. This Unit is resourced and its existence demonstrates a commitment to innovation and outward focus. One of the LDP participants is a member of this group (2).

The audit staff is beginning to **value disciplines other that auditing** which has led to the Interface between audit and administration improving.

There is greater **professionalism** (2).

These changes are driven by the Auditor General. Participants on the LDP who have modeled the preferred behavior appear to have been rewarded.

5.3   Contribution of the program

It was not easy to separate precisely comments about the contribution of the program from the comments on changes within the organization and it was never the intention to try to establish a causal relationship. The intention in the interviews was to identify what EMG members believed to be the impact on the organization and any relationship there might be between the program and the changes that were occurring.

The most commonly mentioned impact related to the individual participants. Individuals on the program have:

- changed attitudes (4);
- increased confidence (6);
- a broader perspective (5) which the changes require;
- a desire and willingness to contribute, to take responsibility and try new things (2);
- better strategic understanding of issues (3);
- improved interpersonal skills (3);
- a sense of shared purpose (2).

The LDP program has increased **individual self-awareness** and the **increased awareness of individual differences** (2). Those on the program have become used to working together and this has overflowed into the workplace. Individuals on the program promote teamwork in the organization. All would be in one or more teams. The LDP is important because it changes behavior and creates a willingness to challenge ideas

There has been collective improvement creating an impetus that an individual could not achieve. The group has conditioned the organization to expect improvements.

There is much more **lateral communication**, seeking information and advice. Participants are admitting a lack of knowledge that would not have happened before. Other individuals are being drawn into this freer communication.

The LDP has validated the **value of academic study** (3). It filled the gap in leadership training. The accreditation has made this a serious activity and highly credible. Managers are seen to be managers of the organization rather than simply managing audits and the participants are encouraging similar attitudes in their subordinates.

This program appears to be the path to promotion. This supports the message that education is required to get on. This needs to go beyond technical education. Management education is required to get on. LDP participants are rising in the hierarchy - four of the nine receiving **promotion** in one year.

The LDP has created a **learning environment** in which discussion takes place (3).

The 1998 Strategic planning workshop heard issues papers produced as part of the program. This increased the credibility of the papers and the individuals. Recommendations in the issues papers were accepted (4).

The LDP provides knowledge of **alternative ways of doing things** (2) and the ability to substantiate ideas and strategies. The Strategic Development and Performance Unit was established following a recommendation to the strategic planning workshop.

The LDP enables managers to better **respond to devolution**.

The LDP is a **catalyst** in the development of ideas.

The LDP fell on fertile ground because of support of Auditor General who values management studies. Five out of nine members of EMG have some involvement with the program, three have been participants, 1 sponsor, 1 tutor and a very supportive Auditor General means that the learning is transferred to the organization. The Program has speeded up the process of change and increased client focus.

The **combination of supportive leader and the LDP** has changed the organizational climate. The program provides the skills, the Auditor General the necessary climate for them to use the skills. The existence of the program reinforces the importance of leadership in the organization(2). There is pressure on senior executive to be concerned about others and this leads to better performance.

Five of the eight EMG members interviewed indicated a willingness to sponsor the program, should the current sponsor/organizer wish a change. Some thought that this was simply an organizing function now, as the program was well accepted. Two indicated that they would not wish this role but are mentors and/or tutors on the program. The Auditor General indicated an interest in becoming more involved in future years.

6.   RESPONSES TO THE PARTICIPANTS' QUESTIONNAIRE

Throughout the text I will indicate () the number of people who gave this specific answer. I have changed all answers to the third person although they were all expressed in the first person.

6.1   Changes in the organization

The changes to the way QAO is managed and led, as identified by the participants, are remarkably consistent with those expressed by Senior Management. This was not surprising as two of the participants have their views recorded in both surveys. However, the participants appear to be less convinced about the sustainability of the changes than their senior officers.

The organization has become much more client focused (5) and has closer relationships with the contract auditors. The organization has become more outward focused (2). And is engaging in more public relations activities (2) than in the past.

There is an awareness of the potential for change and the introduction of competition (2). A broader approach to accountability is being taken.

The organization is becoming more strategic in its outlook through participative strategic planning workshops, scenario building at Senior Executive level (2) and the setting up of a Strategic Development and Performance Unit which focuses on the future and ways of encouraging continuous improvement.

Communication has improved and hierarchical barriers are being reduced. The new Auditor General has introduced greater devolution of authority and responsibility (3). And is ready to listen to new ideas and act on the ideas (3). This has allowed the LDP to have a more significant impact.

There are some concerns about the real commitment of the organization to the changes and its capacity to stay with them.

6.2 Impact of the program on the participants

There were a number of questions that addressed this aspect of the program which included general questions about personal impact, specific questions about strategic thinking, teamwork and management style, as well as a question asking participants to identify the single most important thing they learned from the program. This was done firstly to focus their answers in the areas of interest to the study i.e. strategic thinking, team work and management/leadership style, but also to pick up other, perhaps serendipitous benefits of the program. This leads to the possibility that the figures in brackets may be enhanced by the same answer being given by a person for two separate questions.

Individuals will obviously learn different things from their experience; however there do appear to be some areas in which the learning was almost universal. Increased self-awareness and understanding of individual difference and the benefits of diversity with resultant improvements in communication and interpersonal interaction appear to be the most acknowledged benefits of the program.

Everyone identified increased self awareness and awareness of individual difference in others (9) as a significant learning. This led on to a number of other attributed benefits such as improved effectiveness in interaction with peers- dealing with each other in the workplace and improved workplace cooperation (6), improved listening skills (2), and communication skills that have changed significantly (4). To take account of personality differences to enable the achievement of desired outcomes(2). From this came a greater understanding of organizations and how people behave within them.

Several participants identified improved presentations skills (3), and an increased ability to think about how to respond to audiences/superiors/subordinates. Several participants commented on their increased confidence (2), an ability to utilize their strengths and an increased willingness to take risks (2). There was less fear of making mistakes and greater flexibility in thinking.

The LDP provided concepts, models and tools including relevant literature to help develop effective strategies (7) for facilitating/managing change and decision-making. Some participants have found it easier to be open about values and are willing to explain themselves to others including subordinates. This personal disclosure has led to increased trust.

A number recognize the ability to think more broadly (6), to include a wider range of issues in decision-making. The LDP opened areas of study and issues not previously considered (2). The participants gained a more comprehensive view of the organization, a systems perspective which caused them to consider the impact of solutions on other parts of the system (2). The LDP provides a challenge to existing mindsets.

Contribution to, and application of strategic thinking, has increased (5). Strategic thinking has been incorporated into personal career planning.

Teamwork has improved because of the recognition of strengths and weaknesses of each person. More aware of diversity of thought which has been positive has brought about the welcoming of new ideas. Communication skills are more effective, and others and their contribution are valued. There is increased openness about values. There is more consciousness of different types of people and the roles they play (2) which has led to increased participation. This doesn't always make it easier managing the differences to achieve outcomes, but there is increased understanding of why it is difficult. There is recognition that teams need to be selected on other criteria than simple hierarchical experience.

Two participants indicated that they had always been team players and that their skills in this area had not changed. However, where this approach was difficult in the past it is much easier now.

The importance of continuous learning to the individual and the organization has become apparent (2), bringing a increased willingness to learn.

The program has brought a feeling of enrichment and sense of self. One participant quoted Martina Navratilova "The better I get, the more I realize how much better I can get".

6.3   Impact of the program on organization

There has been some skepticism from those not on the program and to some it is seen as elitist. The introduction of the 2nd cohort may reduce this. It has sent the message that QAO does care about the development of its people.

The LDP is training more skilled and knowledgeable individuals (2). There appears to be greater self awareness and awareness of others, by participants, in making decisions and taking action. This group is making a contribution to the strategic development of the organization (2). The program provides a relatively free think tank resource for the organization. The group to the Strategic Planning Workshop has established a Strategic Development and Performance Unit following recommendations. Whilst this group is operating under more constraints than originally intended, it is promoting an external focus and proving an incentive to innovate and continuously improve.

The program participants speak a shared language. People on the program have open discussion about issues - within frameworks- so the discussion moves beyond mere opinion. Senior managers get to know each other and transfer their knowledge to the workplace which improves interpersonal interaction (2). The program appears to have contributed to the capacity of people to work together particularly at senior level across areas. There is more sharing of problems.

The accreditation of the LDP gives validity to ideas generated within the group. These ideas are more thought through because of the diversity of the group and the need to submit them to academic scrutiny.

There is an impact on culture and behavior within the organization. This will increase as participants are promoted (as several have been within the past year). Participants believe that change can happen and have a positive attitude to doing something about it. The fact that there is a group, rather than an individual, makes this more powerful.

There appears to be pressure on Senior Management to 'catch up' with those on the program.

6.4   Reasons for the success of the leadership development program

The participants had a range of views as to why the program is regarded as a success. The numbers in brackets indicates the number of respondents who identified this particular reason.

Observable changes in the behavior of participants are bringing benefits to the organization. The program has created optimism. The LDP broadened participants' expertise. In the past being a good auditor was enough for promotion - this is not the case now. This view is supported by senior executive comment.

The program filled a training gap. Previously the organization was very discipline focused (auditing) and task oriented. This program focused on management, leadership and organizational development skills. The LDP was very practical and seen as having direct relevance to the workplace (5) through work related projects. The ideas are shared with colleagues because they are relevant to the work environment. QAO control of the program with the ability to manage the learning to meet organizational needs (2) including the choice of subjects(2), and flexible delivery through both timing and venue, were seen to be important to the success of the program.

Timing - there was already some recognition that things needed to be done differently and that better use could be made of human resources. There had been a 7-year period of talking about change but not a lot happened. There was no obvious connection between talking and outcomes.

The program brought senior people together as teams to find out about themselves. It forced the group to go outside of their expert area and comfort zone. This was supported by their willingness to learn.

A driving force, at senior level to initiate, and keep the program going, was seen as critical (2) as was a supportive CEO and senior management (2). Award recognition enhanced the credibility of the program.

7.   IMPACT OF THE LEADERSHIP DEVELOPMENT PROGRAM

Bringing together the views expressed by both groups there are a number of comments that can be made which answer the specific research questions addressed:

> There is a shared view among the senior management of the need for change. The external environment has changed, with the advent of competition being introduced in Victoria. The mandate of the QAO has been broadened. Change is perceived to be necessary for survival, even though the organization currently has a monopoly position. This perception meets the need for a sense of urgency identified by Kotter (Kotter, 1996). There also appears to be agreement that to meet the challenges ahead, a change of culture is required, i.e. a change in basic assumptions and behaviors.

There is a high level of agreement between senior management and participants about the changes that are occurring within QAO. The new Auditor General has increased the delegation of authority and responsibility. There is an increasingly strategic focus at senior management level, and a Strategic Development and Performance Unit has been established to support a more outward and strategic approach. There is improved cross-group communication and teamwork. The senior management perceives a shared sense of purpose in the organization, whilst the participants articulate this as an increasing awareness of the possibility for change. The most commonly commented change is the increasing client focus and the change in the nature of the relationship between auditor and auditee. This change challenges some of the basic assumptions within public sector auditing and represents a significant cultural change.

There is also considerable commonality in the perception of both senior management and participants with regard to the role that the Leadership Development Program has in these changes. Individual participants have changed their behavior. They have increased confidence, a broader perspective, better strategic understanding and improved interpersonal skills.

Senior Management also sees them as having changed their attitudes and demonstrating an increased willingness to contribute.

For participants the single biggest impact is in their own self-awareness, their awareness of diversity and the impact this has on teamwork and both lateral and vertical communication. They state that they have a shared language which aids them working together, and are sharing that language with their colleagues.

Participants also have new management tools, which many claim to use and which are apparent from the change of language in discussions about organizational issues.

The LDP appears to be acting as a catalyst. Participants of the program contributed effectively to the strategic planning workshop, believe change can happen and are impacting on behavior throughout the organization. Participants believe that the program demonstrates QAO's commitment to the development of its people, and the senior management believes that the program sends a message about the value of academic study and helps generate a learning organization.

So why is the program so successful?

Firstly there are observable changes in the behavior of participants and a supportive Auditor General and Senior management which has allowed the participants to try out their new found skills. The program, and its accreditation, has contributed to the credibility given to participants and their ideas, and has led to increased trust in the implementation of their ideas.

The program itself has a number of characteristics which were seen to contribute to its success.

* The program was practical with direct relevance to the organization.
* QAO had a large measure of control to ensure that the program met the organizational needs in terms of both content and delivery.
* The program focuses on leadership and management, not technical skills.
* It brought managers together to find out about themselves and forced the group to go outside of their area of expertise and comfort zone.
* The manager was a champion within the organization who initiated the program and ensured its continuing relevance.

8.   CONCLUSIONS

The answers to the research questions illustrate the change process within one organization. Much of the change literature (Ashford, 1988; Bridges, 1986; Hockley, 1988; Lorsch, 1986; Schein, 1985) identifies 3 key areas of importance in the change process:

Understanding the reason for change; skills to make the change, and leadership of the change. All three of these elements appear to be present in the LDP at QAO.

According to Kotter (1996) successful change evolves through 8 stages usually in the following order.

- Establish a sense of urgency - find an enemy or a threat.
- Create a guiding coalition.
- Develop a vision and strategy.
- Communicate the vision.
- Empower broad based action.
- Generate short term wins.
- Consolidate gains and produce more change.
- Anchor new approaches in the culture.

There is no doubt that senior management has generated a sense of threat, which is shared.

It would appear possible that the Leadership Development program, with the support of the Auditor General is creating a guiding coalition, who has the skills and commitment to bring about the necessary changes. The credibility of the LDP participants is also enlarging the base, and skills, for action.

There is some attempt to anchor the new approaches in the culture.. The involvement of the university was an attempt to embed the program and give it institutional support. The development of the Strategic Development and Performance Unit also was a conscious effort to embed a strategic perspective into the culture of the organization, and is seen by some to be symbolic of the changes.

There is a recognition that the culture needs to change to allow for the consolidation of gains and the creation of more change. There is still a sense in some quarters that there has been too much change already and that consolidation is required. Much of the consolidation suggested is actually a return to past rather than the embedding of a new cultural approach.

Culture operates as a set of implicit and silent assumptions, which cannot change unless they are brought to the surface and confronted. (Schein, 1985, p. 306) The LDP has begun the process of doing that. This will cause discomfort, not only for the participants on the program, but also for those who are affected by new and different ways of doing business.

The LDP is using a therapeutic change model (Schein, 1985).

"The emphasis is on giving each manager insight into his part in the whole network. Therapeutic change then occurs as each person redefines and monitors his own behavior rather than asking others to change their behavior, and the total system changes without anyone having been specifically asked to change. (Schein, 1985, pp. 307-308)

8.1 Model for change

However for this change model to work effectively there appear to be three key elements to the process.

- Senior Management Support - Willingness to allow change to happen and to commit resources to change. This support allows change to happen rather than directing the change. Setting direction but allowing participants to determine how appears important.
- A Leadership Development Program for key decision makers, and potential decision makers, in the organization. This program must focus on personal awareness and change and leadership skill development rather than organizational change. The program needs to be practical with direct relevance to the organization. Managers are brought together to find out about themselves and their relationship with others and required, as a group, to go outside of their areas of expertise and comfort zone. There needs to be champion within the organization who ensures the continuing relevance of the program.
- A perceived threat which brings a sense of urgency to the change process.

8.2 Questions for the future

QAO is a relatively small organization within the public sector. The Leadership Development Program is bringing them the changes they require currently. A second cohort has begun the program, and it is intended that the program will continue for several years. It will be interesting to see how this therapeutic change model will work over the longer term, with more people exposed to the ideas, and how it might need to change to accommodate that. It is intended that a similar study will be done at the end of 2000, when the 2nd cohort have completed the program.

It will also be interesting to test the 3 key factors in the change model to see if they are equally relevant in other public or private sector organizations.

REFERENCES

Ashford, S.J. (1988). Individual Strategies for Coping with Stress During Organizational Transitions. *The Journal of Applied Behavioural Science, Vol 24* (1).

Bourner, T. (1996). Effective management and the development of self-awareness: a plain manager's guide. *Career Development International,* (1/4).

Bridges, W. (1986). Managing Organizational Transitions *Organizational Dynamics Vol 15* (1), (Summer).

Conger, J. (1992). *Learning to Lead: The Art of Transforming Managers in Leaders.* Jossey Bass.

Csoka, L.S. (1996). The Rush to Leadership Training. *Across the Board Vol 33* (8), 28-32.

Field, L. (1998). The Challenge of Empowered Learning *Asia Pacific Journal of Human Resources, 36* (1).

Fulmer, R.M. (1997). The Evolving Paradigm of Leadership Development. *Organizational Dynamics, Vol 25* (4), 59-72.

Gebelain, S.H. (1994). Multi-rater Performance Appraisal: the Promise, the Pitfalls and the Steps. Paper presented at the American Society of Training and Development Convention Anaheim CA, (May).

Hockley, R. (1988). Organsational Change and Mourning. Australian Institute of Training and Development. (March).

Hughes, R.L., Ginnet, R.C., & Curphy, G.J. (1999). *Leadership - Enhancing the Lessons of Experience.* Irwin McGraw-Hill.

Karpin, D.S. (1995). *Enterprising Nation: Renewing Australia's Managers to meet the Challenges of the Asia-Pacific Century.* Report of the Industry Task Force on Leadership and Management Skills. Commonwealth of Australia.

Kotter, J.P. (1996) *Leading Change.* Boston Mass: Harvard Business School Press.

Lorsch, J.W. (1986). Managing Culture: the Invisible Barrier to Strategic Change. *California Management Review Vol 28* (2), (Winter).

Parry, K. (1996). Transformational leadership: A self-development challenge. *HR Monthly* (June).

Pedlar, M.I. (1997). *Action learning in Practice* (3rd. ed.). Gower Publishing Ltd.

Quinn, R.E. (1996). *Deep Change – Discovering the Leader Within.* Jossey-Bass.

Ruggles, III R.L. (1997). *Knowledge Management Tools.* Butterworth-Heinemann.

Schein, E.H. (1985). *Organizational Culture and Leadership.* San Francisco: Jossey-Bass Publishers.

Scholtes, P.R. (1998). *The Leader's Handbook – Making Things Happen Getting Things Done.* McGraw Hill.

Senge, P.M. (1990). *The Fifth Discipline – The Art and Practice of The Learning Organization.* Australia: Random House.

Teal, T. (1996). The Human Side of Management. *Harvard Business Review Vol 74* (6) (November–December).

Vicere, A.A. (1996). *Executive Education: The Leading Edge Organizational Dynamics. Vol 25* (2), 67-81.

Aspects of Learning Style and Labour Market Entry: an Explorative Study

Judith H. Semeijn & Rolf van der Velden
Research Centre for Education and the Labour Market (ROA), Maastricht University, Maastricht, the Netherlands

1.   INTRODUCTION

Recent demands for people at the workplace are described by modern concepts like flexibility and ability to learn. The capacity of employees to adapt to new skill requirements that result from technological developments and global market dynamics is especially stressed (IRDAC, 1990; WRR, 1995; European Commission, 1996). This implies that important concepts under consideration for research into what makes people successful in labour market functioning are related to learning behavior. In order to become and stay employable, worker's capacity for life-long learning becomes crucial.

In labour market research, educational and skill requirements are considered to be of great importance for successful labour market functioning. However, despite this importance, sociologists and economists have very much considered the educational process as a black box. At best, education has been measured in number of years of education followed, or in terms of educational outcomes by grades, but the actual content of education or learning processes has been left to the domain of educational research. Educational research in turn has neglected the actual outcomes of education in terms of the effect on successful labour market entry and functioning. This research field, however, acknowledged the importance of individual differences in learning for learning outcomes. Already since the sixties and seventies the concept of "learning style" was used. Learning style refers to a set of individual characteristics which are relevant for individual differences i.e. preferences in the learning process (Biggs, 1993). It may be conceived as a relative stable trait of people. This stability stresses the question to what

T.A. Johannessen, A. Pedersen and K. Petersen (eds.),
Educational Innovation in Economics and Business VI, 301–324.
© 2002 *Kluwer Academic Publishers. Printed in the Netherlands.*

extent learning behavior can be developed or changed. However, since growing emphasis is put on the importance of individual skills and differences for labour market functioning (Nijhof, 1997), the existing concept and measurement of "learning style" from within the educational context may be valuable for analyzing differences in labour market functioning. Not only learning outcomes may be affected by differences in learning behavior or preferences, but labour market outcomes as well. And since learning continues after entering the labour market, the concept of learning style may be important during the further stages of working life as well, possibly related to employability.

Interesting research questions in this respect are: To what extent does learning style predict successful labour market entry? Can learning style predict the kind of job people obtain within a certain range of possibilities, matching their preferences related to learning? Does learning style predict employability?

This paper will take a first step by exploring the predictive effect of students' learning style measured during education for labour market entry. Because learning style refers to "preferences" in behavior, both labour market success in quantitative terms and the allocation to different types of jobs will be considered. A sample of graduates in Economics of Maastricht University will be used. The research question we address is: To what extent does learning style predict labour market entry features of graduates?

2.   THEORETICAL BACKGROUND

Traditional labour market research recognizes the importance of education for the labour market. There are mainly two hypotheses: in the human capital theory education is considered to enhance people's productivity directly (Becker, 1964). More education means in this view more productivity. In the screening hypothesis on the other hand, education is considered to reflect desired capacities for employers (Thurow, 1975). In this view people have productive value in tendency for employers, but the real productivity will be developed on the job. Study results traditionally reflect the educational outcomes that are of importance: study results are widely considered to be used as screening devices by employers. However, the emphasis is now put on more individual characteristics in selection practice. And the question rises what these characteristics are exactly and how to measure them.

General skills pertaining to cognitive abilities, personal characteristics and learning skills, are considered as key qualifications for people (e.g. Nijhof, 1997), but it remains unclear in most labour market research how these concepts can be measured. Presland (1994) advocates the use of the learning style concept because of its relevance for continuous development during work. We think the educational concept of learning style has something to offer in this case, although the concept itself still lacks a clear theoretical framework (Rayner & Riding, 1997).

Roughly two views have been developed in learning style research (Biggs, 1993); a narrow view, which emphasizes the cognitive information processing part of learning (for example Kolb, 1976; Kolb, 1984; Schmeck et al., 1977) and a broad view, which implicates several other aspects, in addition to the cognitive processing parts, like motivation and regulation preferences of individuals (for example Entwistle *et al.*, 1979; Nuy, 1991; Vermunt, 1992). In this broad view, an individual's learning style consists of a particular combination of cognitive information processing, regulation aspects and motivational aspects. In general, distinctions in three or four different learning styles are well accepted, as more or less prototypes of learning style. However, the styles are estimated using various composite measurements, depending on the instruments used.

A distinction in three learning style types, that can be described as being reproductive, achievement oriented, and meaning oriented, is rather common though (Entwistle *et al.*, 1979; Nuy, 1991). The meaning oriented style is considered the desirable one; people scoring high on its scales can be characterized by having a large intrinsic motivation, by being disciplined and using cognitive information processing techniques like trying to have an overview, to use concrete examples and elaborate study materials by personal experiences. All in all, the study material is handled to obtain "meaning". The reproductive style is in this way more aimed at trying to remember the material and the achievement style at trying to obtain good study results no matter what.

When considering one learning style as being desirable, the question rises to what extent the learning style can be developed or changed?

From educational research findings the answer seems to be "yes" to a certain extent; several factors affect learning style, such as teaching style (Borg & Shapiro, 1996), kind of tasks (Tsang, 1993), and the educational system or context (Eklund-Myrskog, 1997; Nuy, 1991; Nuy & Moust, 1990). Thus, it should be possible to manipulate students' learning behavior with the "right" tasks, the right teaching style and the right system. It depends on the perspective on "right" and "desirable". Research has been aimed frequently at the effects of learning style on learning outcomes (Crombach et al., 1975; Smit & Van Os, 1985; Vermunt; 1992), but the relationship is not conclusive. Probably, the factors affecting learning style do play a role in this. Gijselaers *et al* (1989) studied the effect of learning style on study outcomes and concluded the educational system had affected students' learning style into an "undesirable" direction.

When learning style is considered rather stable, but on the other hand, can be developed to a certain extent as well, what are the consequences for predicting labour market entry features from learning style measured during education? In this case it seems important to analyze the predictive value of both study results and learning style at the same time to find out whether first of all there are any effects of learning style measured during education on labour market outcomes, and second whether these effects would be merely direct, or indirect, i.e. that the effects are mediated by study results. In the case the effect is independent from study results one could argue the learning style concept has much value for labour market research. When its effects would merely be indirect, meaning study results are stronger indicators for labour market entry features, the concept would not add much value for predicting labour market entry. However, when no effects for learning style could be found, while for study results there could, we should doubt the use of this concept.

It may be possible that learning style is not valuable in predicting a more or less successful labour market entry, but that it regulates the allocation process on the labour market in a more qualitative manner. The question that arizes is whether people with different learning style characteristics end up in different jobs? One could argue that for example "grasping just the main line" during information processing would be positive for a manager, but negative for an accountant, although both graduated in economics. This relates to the matching perspective. In the research field of personnel selection and job analysis, all kinds of individual characteristics have been studied in relation to job characteristics, for example work related values (Judge & Bretz, 1992), cognitive ability (Lancaster et al., 1994) and personality constructs (Raymark *et al.*, 1997). Results show that people tend to choose those jobs that match their abilities, vocational interests and personality (Shrauger & Osberg, 1981; Lancaster *et al.*, 1994). The personal characteristics studied all seem to have a positive effect on job functioning and satisfaction when a match is established. Cognitive ability and specific personality characteristics are considered to be more related to the job, whereas work values are more related to the organization. Despite the argument of its relevance for the working environment (Hayes & Allinson, 1997), the concept of learning style has not been used in this research field. However, it may be possible that the relative stable concept of learning style can tell us something about the kind of job a person chooses.

From different lines of research, learning style seems to potentially have an important effect on differences in labour market position and functioning. Therefore, in this paper, the predictive value of different learning style aspects will be explored with a sample of graduates in Economics of Maastricht University. The research question that will be addressed is: To what extent do learning style aspects predict labour market entry features, when taking the traditional labour market research variables into account?

3.   DATA AND METHODOLOGY

The data in this study consists of a sample of students of Economics of the Maastricht University, for whom data have been gathered in several subsequent waves. In 1986 and 1987 all first year students were asked to give information about their learning behavior (Gijselaers, 1989). Scales have been constructed to measure the different components of students' learning style, each scale consisting of 6 to 10 items. The items are Likert-type. The sum score on a scale is used to reflect the score of an individual for that scale. Most scales turned out to be very reliable with Alpha of .80 or more. The total range of reliability varied from .60 for globalism to .90 for fear of failure.

One and a half year after graduation, all students received a questionnaire relating to the process of labour market entry. These surveys are carried out on a regular basis by the Research Centre for Education and the Labour Market (Dutch shortcut: ROA) and studies are reported every year with cohorts of graduates of the Maastricht University (see Ramaekers, 1993-1996). For this analysis, data were used from the 1991 to 1995 waves. These waves comprise most of the first-year students who were in the original 1986 and 1987 learning style survey. The resulting sample consists of 156 graduates. Six indicators of labour market entry from the labour market survey are used as dependent variables. These indicators pertain to job chances, quality of work and type of job. The dependents are:

- Being employed at the date of the survey (approximately a year and a half after graduation, referring to job chances).
- Having a job within three months after graduation (referring to job chances).
- Having a permanent job (referring to both job chances and quality of work).
- Having a job for which an academic degree is required (quality of work).
- Gross monthly wages (quality of work).
- Having a managing, an accounting, or a research job (referring to kind of job).

Next to the indicators of labor market success, the particular job in which graduates end up is supposed to be related to the learning style. The classification of jobs into particular types is based on theoretical views used in job choice literature and classifications used in labor market research. The classification of jobs for this study will be dealt with in appendix 1. The learning style data used in this paper relate to a number of different aspects. Table 1 presents an overview of the different scales that are used. The scales can be divided into aspects dealing with cognitive information processing or with motivational aspects. It is beyond the scope of this paper to explore their developmental and theoretical background. Rather, we will take their relevance as given and explore these aspects in predicting labor market entry features.

Table 1: Meaning of the scales of learning style as defined by Nuy (1991).

Scales	Description of scale content
Cognitive information processing:	
Holism	Student reacts easily to new study subjects by intuitive knowledge and broad associations; ability to grasp the main point in short time
Globalism	Studying is limited to the most important points, working up to a rough view of the matter, skipping (possibly relevant) details
Extendedness	Broad versus narrow scope in exploring study content; locating answers to study questions within a wider context; taking into account different perspectives to describe the subject
Elaboration	Relating study content to pre-knowledge and own experience; looking for examples and applications
Construction	Active and critical incorporation of concepts and theories into a coherent and interconnected body of knowledge
Memorizing	Learning by hart; concentrating on literal recall
Atomism	Concentration on specific and isolated elements in the subject matter, which prevents reaching an overview
Motivational aspects:	
Intrinsic motivation	Interest in study content; challenged by questions and problems
Extrinsic motivation	Instrumental function of studying
Achievement motivation	Need to excel; high standards of achievement
Fear of failure	Avoidance of stress and uncertainty

For the purpose of this study, relevant covariates were considered for their effect on labor market entry as well. By using administrative data for all students, the following covariates have been taken on board:

- Male (dummy);
- Age;
- Study length;
- Study field business administration, core subjects accounting & finance (dummy);
- Study field business administration, core subjects organization & marketing (dummy);
- Study field international management, core subjects accounting & finance (dummy);
- Study field international management, core subjects organization & marketing (dummy);
- Mean study results during the last two years of the graduate study program;
- Final thesis result; grade for the individual final study project.

Logistic and normal linear regression analyses will be applied with respect to the labor market indicators pertaining to job chances and quality of work for the motivational aspects and the following cognitive information processing aspects: Atomism, Elaboration, Memorizing and Construction.

Multinomial logistic regression analyses will be applied to the type of job graduates obtain with respect to the following cognitive information processing aspects: Holism, Globalism and Extendedness. The reason for including just these three cognitive information processing aspects is the following: when considering the meaning of the scales as described in table 1, the authors interpreted these scales intuitively to be possibly positive for some jobs, but at the same time possibly negative for other jobs. However, the nature of this study is explorative and we therefore do not pretend to have some fundamented reason behind this choice. On the other hand, including all variables into the multinomial logistic regression analyses would not be informative, because of the large number of variables and the modest number of cases. In our opinion, for the other cognitive information processing scales, the different effects for different jobs would be less clear from their content meaning.

Analyses will be applied in a two-step model; in the first step the learning style aspects and covariates age, gender and study length are analyzed for their effect on labor market entry. In the second step, the more traditional labor market research variables are introduced into the model: study field and study results. In this way, the gross effect of learning style will be measured by the first-step model and the net effect in relation to study related independents by the second-step-model.

Table 2a: Descriptive statistics of all variables.

Variables	Mean	SD	N
Indicators of Labour Market Success			
(1) Being employed	0.875	0.332	136
(2) Being unemployed less than three months	0.740	0.440	150
(3) Having a permanent job	0.558	0.499	113
(4) Having a job requiring an academic degree	0.607	0.491	117
(5) Gross monthly wages (log)	8.190	0.300	112
Job Category			
(6) Managers	0.350	0.480	71
(7) Scientists	0.300	0.460	71
(8) Accountants	0.320	0.470	71
(9) Other Jobs	0.028	0.170	71
Learning Style			
Atomism	9.830	4.080	156
Construction	19.050	4.550	156
Elaboration	18.420	3.090	156
Memorizing	8.190	3.920	156
Holism	17.090	3.930	156
Globalism	8.880	3.180	156
Extendedness	11.350	3.590	156
Intrinsic motivation	15.330	3.620	156
Extrinsic motivation	13.010	3.950	156
Achievement motivation	12.760	4.070	156
Fear of failure	8.050	5.120	156
Control Variables			
Male	0.720	0.450	156
Age	25.776	1.509	156
Study length	66.200	11.060	156
Study Field			
Business Adm., accounting/finance	0.310	0.460	154
Business Adm., organization/marketing	0.300	0.460	154
Intern. Man., acc./fin./general economics	0.097	0.300	155
Intern. Man., organization/marketing	0.130	0.340	155
Other Study Fields (reference)	0.157	0.365	153
Study Results			
Mean study results	7.110	0.448	156
Final thesis result	7.342	0.856	155

Table 2b: Pearson's correlations between independent and dependent variables.

Independent variables	Dependent variables					Correlations			
	(1)	(2)	(3)	(4)	(5)	(6)	(7)	(8)	(9)
Learning Style									
Atomism	.151*	-.089	-.152	-.149	.207**	-	-	-	-
Constructions	.042	.159*	-.110	.035	.035	-	-	-	-
Elaboration	.104	.206**	.010	.106	.097	-	-	-	-
Memorizing	.031	.003	-.026	-.189**	-.025	-	-	-	-
Holism	-	-	-	-	-	.310**	-.107	-.163	-.142
Globalism	-	-	-	-	-	-.200*	.162	.080	-.09
Extendedness	-	-	-	-	-	.049	.094	-.013	-.080*
Intrinsic motivation	.071	.188**	-.042	-.006	.158				
Extrinsic motivation	-.033	-.069	.026	.020	-.191*				
Achievement motivation	.068	.217***	.103	.063	.042				
Fear of failure	.060	-.052	-.239*	-.106*	-.271***	-	-	-	-
Control Variables									
Male	-.181**	-.234***	-.074	.114	.033	.134	-.006	-.102	-.083
Age	.017	-.120	.086	-.198	.053	.276**	-.109	-.110	-.185
Study length	-.181**	-.175**	.108	-.125	.113	.237**	-.023	-.145	-.210*
Study field									
Business Adm. acc./fin	.081	.154*	.122	-.046	.059	-.285**	-.369**	.696***	-.114
Business Adm. org./mark	.085	-.005	-.062	-.214	-.180*	.103	.234	-.376**	.110
Interm. Man., acc./fin./gen./ec	-.191**	-.060	.089	.183**	.248**	.162	-.154	.008	-.065
Interm. Man., org./mark.	-.078	-.192**	.033	-.005	-0.128	-.015	.124	-.083	-.065
Other Study Fields (ref.)	-.040	.051	-.179*	.190*	-.137	.086	.215*	-.345**	.128
Study Results									
Mean study results	.151*	.114	-.001	.123	.082	.087	.137	-.200*	-.064
Final thesis result	.296**	.160**	.074	.124	.174*	.209*	-.129	-.088	.001

Note 1: the numbers between parentheses for the dependents refer to the dependent numbers of table 2a.
Note 2: * correlation sign. At the 0.1 level, ** correlation sign. at the 0.05 level and *** correlation sign. at the 0.01 level

4.   RESULTS

4.1   General descriptive statistics

First of all, descriptive results and plots were analyzed to screen for outliers and normality. For learning style aspects, no outliers are present and most interval variables show a near normal distribution. Table 2a presents the descriptives of all variables in the analyses, and Table 2b the Pearson correlations of all variables with the dependents. Table 2c presents the Pearson correlations between learning style aspects and study results.

As can be seen from table 2b, the correlations between the learning style aspects on the one hand and study results on the other hand are rather limited. The only significant results point to negative effects of Extrinsic Motivation and Memorizing on mean study results. With normal linear regression analyses, the effects of learning style aspects on study results have been tested; the negative effect of Extrinsic Motivation can be confirmed for mean study results. No other scales sort any effect. For the final thesis variable, various scales have diverse effects, which are not easy to interpret. The only scale that seems to have an effect from the bivariate correlation, Extendedness, does not have any effect on final thesis result in the regression model.

So far, the learning style scales seem not to have a clear relationship with study results, which makes the possibility that learning style affects labor market entry through affecting study results less convincing.

Table 2c: Pearson's correlation between learning style aspects and covariates.

Variables	Correlations	
Learning style aspects	Mean study results	Final thesis result
Atomism	-0.053	0.084
Construction	0.010	0.013
Elaboration	0.027	0.085
Memorizing	-0.174**	0.006
Holism	0.060	0.119
Globalism	-0.091	-0.081
Extendedness	-0.020	-0.150*
Intrinsic motivation	-0.014	-0.005
Extrinsic motivation	-0.197**	-0.053
Achievement motivation	0.075	0.003
Fear of failure	-0.005	0.050
* significant at 0.10, ** significant at 0.05 and *** significant at 0.01		

Table 3: Regression estimates of the effects of learning style on having a job.

	First-step model		Second-step model	
	B	s.e.	B	s.e.
Constant	-2.438	6.698	-43.804***	15.883
Learning Style Aspects				
Atomism	0.222**	0.105	0.358**	0.156
Construction	-0.034	0.092	-0.059	0.125
Elaborism	0.147	0.134	-0.028	0.241
Memorizing	-0.116	0.087	-0.159	0.119
Intrinsic Motivation	-0.062	0.128	0.132	0.167
Extrinsic Motivation	-0.109	0.094	-0.137	0.151
Achievement Motivation	0.062	0.087	0.044	0.136
Fear of Failure	-0.048	0.069	-0.134	0.101
Control Variables				
Male	-1.884*	1.103	-2.884*	1.494
Age	0.447	0.310	1.208**	0.525
Study Length	-0.096**	0.038	-0.151**	0.068
Study Field				
Business Adm., acc./fin.	-	-	2.851*	1.458
Business Adm., org/mark.	-	-	1.572	1.350
Internat.Man., acc./fin./				
Gen.econ.	-	-	-1.639	1.421
Internat.Man., org./mark.	-	-	0.075	1.223
Study Results				
Mean Study Results	-	-	2.069*	1.122
Final Thesis Result	-	-	1.771***	0.641
Model Statistics				
Number of cases (n)		136		133
Model chi-square		19.573		43.625
Df		11		17
P		0.052		0.000
R^2_L		0.191		0.806

* significant at 0.10, ** significant at 0.05 and *** significant at 0.01.

4.2 Regression results for labor market entry chances

Table 3 presents the results of the logistic regression analysis on the first dependent variable, related to job chances: being employed at the date of the survey. It appears that both models (first- and second-step model) differ significantly from the base model, in which only a constant is included. The learning style aspect Atomism has both in the first and the second-step model a significant positive effect on the odds of being employed a year and a half after graduation. To be precise, a one unit increase in the score on the Atomism scale is related to a multiplicative change in the odds of being employed of 1.25 and 1.43 respectively, which means changes up to 40%. The finding of Atomism being positive related to being employed, is not intuitively clear. Taking the meaning of this cognitive aspect into account (table 1) the effect may be caused by searching behavior in which every vacant job is possibly interesting, ending up in many applications for vacant jobs and (therefore) a larger chance of success. For all other learning style aspects, no effects are found. Study results appear to have strong positive effects on the chance of having a job. And for the control variables, the larger the study length, the more detrimental it is for the chances of having a job, a year and a half after graduation. Men seem to have more difficulties in finding a job than women, and age appears to have a positive effect, although only in the second model. Finally, studying Business Administration, subjects accounting and finance, has a positive effect on the odds of having a job. Table 4 presents the results of the logistic regression on having a job within three months, the next variable related to job chances.

Table 4: Regression estimates of learning style on having a job within three months.

	First-step model		Second-step model	
	B	s.e.	B	s.e.
Constant	6.929	4.233	-0.091	7.305
Learning Style Aspects				
Atomism	-0.052	0.067	-0.045	0.073
Construction	-0.039	0.071	-0.030	0.077
Elaborism	0.081	0.099	0.004	0.113
Memorizing	-0.005	0.058	-0.020	0.065
Intrinsic Motivation	0.078	0.090	0.143	0.097
Extrinsic Motivation	0.005	0.064	0.055	0.075
Achievement Motivation	0.118*	0.062	0.151**	0.073
Fear of Failure	-0.081	0.052	-0.118**	0.059
Control Variables				
Male	-1.645**	0.627	-2.113***	0.695
Age	-0.167	0.160	-0.149	0.182
Study Length	-0.036*	0.021	-0.021	0.023
Study Field				
Business Adm., acc./fin.	-	-	0.552	0.822
Business Adm., org/mark.	-	-	-0.869	0.756
Internat.Man., acc./fin./ Gen.econ.	-	-	-1.422	0.920
Internat.Man., org./mark.	-	-	-1.576*	0.869
Study Results				
Mean Study Results	-	-	0.550	0.600
Final Thesis Result	-	-	0.287	0.276
Model Statistics				
Number of cases (n)	150		147	
Model chi-square	28.194		39.737	
Df	11		17	
P	0.003		0.001	
R^2_L	0.164		0.237	

significant at 0.10, ** significant at 0.05 and *** significant at 0.01

Table 5: Regression estimates of the effects of learning style on having tenure.

	First-step model		Second-step model	
	B	s.e.	B	s.e.
Constant	-1.005	4.213	-12.267	7.564
Learning Style Aspects				
Atomism	-0.059	0.070	-0.053	0.076
Construction	-0.199**	0.087	-0.155*	0.091
Elaborism	0.084	0.094	0.005	0.102
Memorizing	0.014	0.059	-0.004	0.065
Intrinsic Motivation	0.050	0.094	0.116	0.101
Extrinsic Motivation	0.022	0.070	0.054	0.079
Achievement Motivation	0.143**	0.065	0.089	0.070
Fear of Failure	-0.119**	0.052	-0.147**	0.058
Control Variables				
Male	-0.448	0.492	-0.951*	0.571
Age	0.042	0.163	0.138	0.183
Study Length	0.019	0.022	0.034	0.025
Study Field				
Business Adm., acc./fin.	-	-	1.842**	0.812
Business Adm., org/mark.	-	-	0.413	0.773
Internat.Man., acc./fin./ Gen.econ.	-	-	2.008**	1.014
Internat.Man., org./mark.	-	-	0.963	0.888
Study Results				
Mean Study Results	-	-	0.659	0.593
Final Thesis Result	-	-	0.357	0.290
Model Statistics				
Number of cases (n)		113		112
Model chi-square		19.170		29.452
Df		11		17
P		0.058		0.031
R^2_L		0.124		0.237

* significant at 0.10, ** significant at 0.05 and *** significant at 0.01

Table 5 presents the results with respect to the last indicator of labor market chances: having tenure. The results are obtained with logistic regression analyses again. Both the first- and the second-step model differ significantly from the base model. The most striking result is the negative effect of Construction with regard to its meaning. This effect could be explained by the fact that most of the academic research jobs are on a temporary basis. The negative effect of Fear of Failure is more in line with our expectations, taking the content meaning of the scale into account. Achievement Motivation shows a positive effect on this labour market indicator. And being a male seems to be detrimental again. Study field variables in the second model do lead to large differences in the odds of having tenure. Studying Business Administration, subjects accounting and/or finance, or studying International Management with the same subjects, leads to a far larger chance of having tenure, than do the other study programs. Study results, finally, do not show any effect on this labour market indicator.

4.3   Regression results for labour market quality

The next two variables tested in this study pertain to the quality of work. Table 6 presents the results of the effects on having an academic job, the first of these two variables.

Table 6: Regression estimates of the effects of learning style on having an academic job.

	First-step model		Second-step model	
	B	s.e.	B	s.e.
Constant	10.421**	4.080	11.852	7.522
Learning Style Aspects				
Atomism	-0.010	0.066	-0.021	0.071
Construction	-0.078	0.079	-0.137	0.087
Elaborism	0.139	0.091	0.182*	0.099
Memorizing	-0.125**	0.060	-0.096	0.067
Intrinsic Motivation	0.028	0.093	0.004	0.099
Extrinsic Motivation	0.019	0.069	0.013	0.074
Achievement Motivation	0.050	0.062	0.068	0.069
Fear of Failure	-0.047	0.052	-0.040	0.054
Control Variables				
Male	0.685	0.489	0.559	0.541
Age	-0.436***	0.157	-0.409**	0.172
Study Length	-0.001	0.022	0.010	0.025
Study Field				
Business Adm., acc./fin.	-	-	-1.469*	0.850
Business Adm., org/mark.	-	-	-1.727**	0.845
Internat.Man., acc./fin./ Gen.econ.	-	-	0.253	1.314
Internat.Man., org./mark.	-	-	-1.243	0.939
Study Results				
Mean Study Results	-	-	-0.402	0.597
Final Thesis Result	-	-	0.227	0.276
Model Statistics				
Number of cases (n)		117		115
Model chi-square		18.327		27.302
Df		11		17
P		0.074		0.054
R^2_L		0.117		0.214

* significant at 0.10, ** significant at 0.05 and *** significant at 0.01

Both models only differ significantly at the 0.1 significance level from the base model. Memorizing appears to have a negative effect on having an academic job. In the second-step model, Elaborism shows a positive effect. A negative effect of age is present in both models. This effect of age seems rather surprising, but is possibly caused by graduates who finished a study at higher vocational education before entering university. These graduates are in general older and more often inclined to look for a job at higher vocational level. Study fields within the Business Administration course seem to have detrimental effects on this labour market indicator. Study results, finally, appear to have no effects on the odds of having an academic job. The second variable related to the quality of work is (the log of) gross monthly wages, which will be tested in the next analysis. Graduates who are in a Ph. D. program were left out of this analysis, because their wages are fixed at a very low level, more comparable with a student loan than with regular wages. Table 7 presents the results.

Table 7: Regression estimates of the effects of learning style on gross monthly wages (log).

	First-step model		Second-step model	
	B	s.e.	B	s.e.
Constant	8.445***	0.049	7.624***	0.740
Learning Style Aspects				
Atomism	-0.002	0.008	-0.006	0.008
Construction	-0.018*	0.009	-0.019**	0.009
Elaborism	0.001	0.011	0.001	0.011
Memorizing	0.001	0.006	0.005	0.007
Intrinsic Motivation	0.023**	0.010	0.022**	0.010
Extrinsic Motivation	-0.009	0.008	-0.008	0.008
Achievement Motivation	0.005	0.007	0.005	0.007
Fear of Failure	-0.014**	0.006	-0.012**	0.006
Control Variables				
Male	0.029	0.054	-0.009	0.056
Age	-0.001	0.017	0.010	0.018
Study Length	-0.001	0.002	0.001	0.002
Study Field				
Business Adm., acc./fin.	-	-	0.025	0.085
Business Adm., org/mark.	-	-	-0.106	0.083
Internat.Man., acc./fin./ Gen.econ.	-	-	0.175	0.105
Internat.Man., org./mark.	-	-	-0.071	0.096
Study Results				
Mean Study Results	-	-	0.024	0.059
Final Thesis Result	-	-	0.041	0.033
Model Statistics				
Number of cases (n)		105		103
Model chi-square		0.065		0.139
Df		1.662		1.973
P		0.095		0.022
R^2_L				

- significant at 0.10, ** significant at 0.05 and *** significant at 0.01

Only the second-step model differs significantly from the base model at the 0.05 level. Intrinsic Motivation shows a stable positive effect on wages. Fear of failure shows a negative effect on wages in both models. Construction shows a negative effect on wages as well, for which no clear argumentation can be given. No effects of study results and control variables are found.

5.   REGRESSION RESULTS FOR OBTAINING DIFFERENT JOBS

To test the effect of the remaining three cognitive learning style aspects on labor market position, a different perspective is used. To see whether high scores on these different aspects would lead to (preference for) a different type of job, multinomial logistic regression is applied, again following the two step method of all other analyses, with exception of the inclusion of the variable study field. Study field is considered to be related to the type of job people obtain, because of relevance of the content. It is considered to be an important selection device for employers. In this way a match between study field and type of job is obvious. Table 8a shows the relation between study field and type of job.

Table 8a: Cross tabulation of study field with job category.

Study field	Job category			Total
	Managing job	Accounting job	Research job	
Business Adm., acc/finance	3	17	1	21
Business Adm., org./marketing	7	0	8	15
Int.Man.,acc./fin./gen.econ.	5	3	1	9
Int. Man.,org./marketing	3	2	4	9
Total	18	22	14	54

As can be seen from table 8a, accountants and other employees from the accountant job category are recruited almost exclusively from the study field accounting and finance. Researchers are in general recruited from the study fields organization and marketing. Only in the case of management jobs recruitment takes place from all possible study fields. Considering the high correlation between study field and type of job we expect that any effect of learning style on the type of job will be mediated through the choice of a specific study field. As we are interested merely in the gross effect of learning style on type of job, we decided to leave the study field variable out of the analyses altogether. Table 8b presents the results of the analysis.

Table 8b: Estimates of the effects of learning style on having an accounting job and a research job compared to having a managing job.

	First-step model				Second-step model			
	accounting		**research**		**accounting**		**research**	
	estimate	s.e.	estimate	s.e.	estimate	s.e.	estimate	s.e.
Constant	-9.957	6.724	0.217	6.446	-12.050	10.193	14.725	9.835
Learning style aspects								
Holism	0.186*	0.102	0.001	0.101	0.167	0.104	0.032	0.107
Globalism	-0.216**	0.105	-0.065	0.100	-0.210*	0.107	-0.063	0.105
Extendedness	-0.152	0.102	-0.079	0.100	-0.184*	0.105	-0.108	0.106
Control Variables								
Male	-0.122	0.392	0.139	0.340	-0.139	0.398	0.087	0.359
Age	0.384	0.275	0.130	0.273	0.380	0.276	0.025	0.277
Study length	0.008	0.036	-0.029	0.035	0.012	0.038	-0.059	0.041
Study Results								
Mean Study Results	-	-	-	-	-0.233	0.811	-1.775**	0.828
Final Thesis Result	-	-	-	-	0.575	0.457	0.345	0.441
Model Statistics								
Number of cases (n)	69				69			
-2 Log Likelihood	133.309				125.548			

* significant at 0.10, ** significant at 0.05 and *** significant at 0.01.

As can be seen from table 8b, in both models effects of learning style aspects are present. In the analysis managing jobs are the reference category. The analysis tests the effects of the independents on the chance to obtain a job from the accounting job category or the research job category, in comparison with the managing job category (for more information about the job categories see appendix 1). The effect of Holism in the first model points to a positive effect of a high score on the Holism scale on entering an accounting job. No effect appears for entering a research job (in comparison with a manager's job). The effect of Holism is only significant at the 0.1 level and disappears in the second model, however. Globalism shows a negative effect on entering an accounting job in both models. This would mean that scoring high on the Globalism scale would decrease the chances for entering an accounting job, in comparison with a manager's job, which is consistent with our expectation based on the content meaning of the scale; being accurate and precise is extremely important in accountant jobs. Globalism would not be convenient in such jobs.

For managing jobs, however, Globalism is (sometimes) inevitable and therefore much more useful. Extendedness shows a negative effect on entering an accounting job in comparison with a manager's job in the second model at the 0.1 level. Again, no effect for entering a research job is found. With respect to the covariates, no effects are found. Higher mean study results, however, seem to be detrimental for entering a research job in the second-step model. This seems rather surprising. Apparently, people with better study results do enter more managing and accounting jobs than research jobs.

To summarize the most important results of this paper, table 9 presents the significant outcomes for the learning style and study results variables.

As can be seen from table 9, learning style aspects affect both labour market entry success and type of job. Study results in fact only affect the indicator of having a job in general and obtaining a research job in this study. The effect of study results on having a job seems independent from the effect of the learning style aspect Atomism; the effect of Atomism does not disappear when the study related variables are introduced into the model. However, for the other dependents no profound effects of study results are found at all. The only learning style aspect that appeared to correlate with study results was Memorizing. However, for obtaining an academic job, Memorizing shows a stable negative effect, while study results do not show any effect at all.

Based on the content meaning of the scales, the effects of the motivational aspects of learning style seem rather straightforward, while the effects of the cognitive information processing aspects are far more difficult to explain. In the following and last section, the results of this explorative study will be considered for some conclusive remarks.

Table 9: Results of the analyses.

Independents	Being employed	Being un-employed < 3 mths	Having tenure	Having an academic job	Gross monthly wages	Accounting job category	Research job category
Learning Style Aspects							
Atomism	X+	X	X	X	X		
Construction	X	X	X-	X	X-		
Elaboration	X	X	X	X+	X		
Memorizing	X	X	X	X-	X		
Holism						X+	X
Globalism						X-	X
Extendedness						X-	X
Intrinsic motivation	X	X	X	X	X+		
Extrinsic motivation	X	X	X	X	X		
Achievement motivation	X	X+	X+	X	X		
Fear of failure	X	X-	X-	X	X-		
Study Results							
Mean study results	X+	X	X	X	X	X	X-
Final thesis result	X+	X	X	X	X	X	X

X = the independent variable is included in the analysis.
+ = effect of the independent variable is positive.
- = effect of the independent variable is negative.

6.   CONCLUSION

In this explorative study the effects of learning style aspects on labour market entry success and type of job have been explored. The following conclusions can be drawn.

Aspects of cognitive information processing appear to affect both labour market chances and quality. Getting an academic job is the one indicator affected by only cognitive learning style aspects; a negative effect of Memorizing and a positive effect of Elaboration appeared. Since Memorizing correlates with study results within our sample, the effect of this aspect seems all the more important. Introducing the study results variables into the model did not diminish the effect of Memorizing, nor revealed an effect of study results variables themselves. For the other indicators of labour market success the effects of information processing aspects were less easy to interpret.

Motivation seems important for both job chances and quality of work. We found positive effects of Intrinsic and Achievement Motivation and negative effects of Fear of Failure, all reasonable to explain. Extrinsic Motivation shows no effect, which in fact means that it has no detrimental effect for labour market entry success.

With respect to the relation between learning style and type of job, the results were not conclusive. Globalism appears to have a negative effect on entering an accounting job in comparison with a managing job, for which we could give some reasonable explanation. On the other hand, we also found a positive effect of Holism and a negative effect of Extendedness on entering an accountant job, in comparison with a managing job. Both effects are not intuitively clear.

Study results only show an effect on the chance of being employed at the time of the survey. On the other indicators of labour market entry success no significant effects were found. This striking outcome seems to suggest that the effects of learning style aspects are more important for explaining labour market entry success than the more traditional labour market research variables.

However, careful choice of the instrument to measure learning style is warranted. Recent findings indicate relevant aspects of learning style as meta-cognition or self-regulating activities. These aspects seem to be very important in learning outcomes (Schouwenburg, 1996; Simons, 1997). Possibly, they will be important in labour market functioning as well. These aspects were not incorporated in the measurement of learning style used in this study.

Further, aspects of the learning style concept can be considered fundamental individual characteristics themselves, like personality traits and differences in brain functioning. The value added by using the learning style concept should therefore be clearly distinguished from these other concepts and possible measurements in further research.

Despite the limitations of the study, we think the results are promising. The findings indicate the importance of individual differences in cognitive information processing and motivational aspects for labour market research. However, we found only an effect on one of the indicators of labour market success. We think that linking the educational concept of learning style with labour market research reveals promising possibilities in extending both research fields. This is extremely important for both fields, now arriving at the point of integration, forced by the recent developments in the working environment.

APPENDIX 1:

Job classification

The classification of jobs used in this paper was designed to distinguish a limited number of meaningful categories. To make the categories of jobs as meaningful as possible, an approach is used, which combines ideas of Holland (1985), the division used by Spenner (1985), and the knowledge of job experts working at the Research Centre for Education and the Labour Market (Dutch shortcut ROA).

Based on the findings of Holland (1985) a distinction can be made in six personality types and their preferences for six different environments. Consequently, the work environment type can also be translated in terms of jobs or functions. Holland distinguishes the artistic, the realistic, the intellectual, the social, the entrepreneurial and the conventional type (of personality, environment, job). Being dominantly characterized by one type, persons, environments and jobs do also have characteristics of the other types, to a certain extent. In fact, the typology represents a framework: a hexagram. Persons, environments and jobs can be described by their position on this figure. The characteristics determine the position and some characteristics do relate easier than others, which means they are more consistent than others. In this hexagram there are three 'opposite' characteristics: conventional with artistic, realistic with social and intellectual with entrepreneurial. In formulating a classification of three different groups of jobs, it seems plausible to avoid to cluster these opposite, or inconsistent types. More related types are found more often empirically (Hogerheide, 1994).

In this way, it is defendable to cluster conventional with realistic, intellectual with artistic, and social with entrepreneurial, or conventional with entrepreneurial, social with artistic and intellectual with realistic. In both situations these combinations do have the least distance, which means the largest consistency. However, the first classification appeals more to our approach with respect to differentiating jobs, than the second. Spenner (1985) is talking about "working with people, data, and things" in a study with respect to complexity in work. Working with people can be related to the entrepreneurial/social cluster, working with data to the intellectual/artistic cluster, and working with things to the conventional/realistic cluster. When using the other cluster possibility of Holland's hexagram, the difficulties arise obviously in the intellectual/realistic cluster, where data and things mix. However, in this study a sample of graduates in economics is at hand, for whom possible jobs are by definition of a higher degree in complexity than just dividing them in working with people, things or data. But, when trying to classify the jobs, which are hold by our graduates in economics, we can define jobs in which these categories could be reflected by accountants-jobs or computer-jobs (things, conventional/realistic), research-jobs, or didactic jobs (data, intellectual/artistic), and managers-jobs or policy maker/advisory jobs (people, social/entrepreneurial). This classification was double checked by a panel of job experts from ROA.

APPENDIX 2:

Detailed information on table 2a
As can be seen from table 2a, 87.5% of the graduates were employed at the time of the labour market survey. The other 12.5% were unemployed. Some 75% of the graduates did find a job very soon after graduation, and were unemployed less than three months. The other 25% were unemployed for more than three months. Of all employed graduates more than a half (56%) had tenure at the moment of the survey. Additionally, 60% of the graduates held a job for which an academic degree was required, whereas the other 40% were working in a job for which higher vocational education or less was sufficient. The mean gross monthly wages amounted to 3790 Dutch guilders. Of all academically employed graduates, 35% was working in a managing job, 30% in a research or teaching job, and another 32% in an accounting job. A small group of graduates of about 3% was employed in another kind of job, which wasn't defined by the former three categories. The largest part of our sample consists of men (72%), and the mean age at the moment of the labour market survey was nearly 26 years. Most respondents graduated in Business Administration (61%), with equal shares of the core subjects accounting/financing and organization/marketing. The other 39% consists of graduates in International Management (about 23%), also divided over the two core subjects, and graduates in other subjects, which aren't defined further (the remaining 16%). The mean study length of the graduates in our sample is approximately 66 months, or 5.5 years.

REFERENCES

Becker, G.S. (1994). *Human Capital*. New York: NBER.

Biggs, J. (1993). What do inventories of student's learning processes really measure? A theoretical review and clarification. *British Journal of Educational Psychology, Vol. 63*, 3-19.

Borg, M.O., & Shapiro, S.L. (1996). Personality type and student performance in principles of Economics. *Journal of Economic Education, Vol. 27*, 3-25.

Crombag, H.F., Gaff, J.F., & Chang, T.M. (1975). Study behavior and academic performance. *Tijdschrift voor Onderwijsresearch, Vol. 1*, 3-14.

Eklund-Myrskog, G. (1997). The influence of the educational context on student nurses' conceptions of learning and approaches to learning. *British Journal of Educational Psychology, Vol. 67*, 371-381.

Entwistle, N., Hanley, M., & Hounsell, D. (1979). Identifying distinctive approaches to studying. *Higher Education, Vol. 8*, 365-380.

European Commission (1996). Teaching and Learning, Towards the Learning Society, White Paper, Luxembourg.

Gijselaers, W.H., Nuy, H., & Mullink, J.P.M. (1989). *Studie-aanpak en studierendement: deelrapport 1 van studies naar het propedeuserendement van de FdEWB*. Vakgroep Onderwijsontwikkeling en Onderwijsresearch.

Hayes, J., & Allison, C.W. (1997). Learning styles and training and development in work settings: lessons from educational research. *Educational Psychology, Vol. 17*, 1&2, 185-193.

Hogerheide, R.P. (1994). De beroepskeuzetheorie van John L. Holland. In R.M.H. Spijkerman, A.J. Vincken, & M.J. Weekenborg, (Eds.), *Handboek Studie- en Beroepskeuzebegeleiding*, Samsom, H.D., Willink, T. Alphen aan den Rijn.

Holland, J.L. (1985). *Making Vocational Choices: a theory of vocational personalities and work environments*. Odessa, Florida: Psychological Assessment Resources.

Industrial Research and Development Advisory Committee (1991). *Skill Shortages in Europe*. Brussels.

Judge, T.A., & Bretz, R.D. (1992). Effects of work values on job choice decisions. *Journal of Applied Psychology, Vol 77* (3), 261-271.

Kolb, D.A. (1976). *Learning Style Inventory, technical manual*. New York, Englewood Cliffs: Prentice-Hall.

Kolb, D.A. (1984). *Experiential Learning, experience as a source of learning and development*. New York Englewood Cliffs: Prentice-Hall,.

Lancaster, S.J., Colarelli, S.M., King, D.W., & Beehr, T.A. (1994). Job applicant similarity on cognitive ability, vocational interests, and personality characteristics: do similiar persons choose similiar jobs? *Educational and Psychological Measurement, Vol. 54* (2), 299-316.

Nijhof, W.J. (1997). Qualifying for the future. In W.J. Nijhof, & J.N. Streumer, (Eds.), *Key Qualifications in Work and Education*. Dordrecht: Kluwer Academic Press.

Nuy, H.P.J. (1991). Interactions of study orientation and student's appreciation of structure in their educational environment. *Higher Education, Vol. 22*, 267-274.

Nuy, H.P.J., & Moust, J.H.C. (1990). Students and problem-based learning: how well do they fit in? *Journal of Professional Legal Education, Vol. 8* (2), 97-114.

Presland, J. (1994). Learning styles and CPD. *Educational Psychology in Practice, Vol. 10* (3), 179-184.

Ramaekers, G.W.M. (1996). WO-scanner economie 1995. Basismeting cohort '94, ROA-R-1996/15, Research Centrum voor Onderwijs en Arbeidsmarkt, Maastricht.

Ramaekers, G.W.M. (1996). WO-scanner economie 1994. Basismeting cohort '93, ROA-R-1996/1, Research Centrum voor Onderwijs en Arbeidsmarkt, Maastricht.

Ramaekers, G.W.M. (1994). Arbeidsmarktscanner Rijksuniversiteit Limburg: Basismeting cohort '92, ROA-R-1994/7, Research Centrum voor Onderwijs en Arbeidsmarkt, Maastricht.

Ramaekers, G.W.M., & Heijke, J.A.M. (1993). Arbeidsmarktscanner Rijksuniversiteit Limburg: Basismeting cohort '91, ROA-R-1993/13, Research Centrum voor Onderwijs en Arbeidsmarkt, Maastricht.

Ramaekers, G.W.M., & Heijke, J.A.M. (1993). Arbeidsmarktscanner Rijksuniversiteit Limburg: Basismeting cohort '90, ROA-R-1993/1, Research Centrum voor Onderwijs en Arbeidsmarkt, Maastricht.

Raymark, P.H., Schmit, M.J., & Guion, R.M. (1997). Identifying potentially useful personality constructs for employee selection. *Personnel Psychology, Vol. 50*, 723-736.

Rayner, S., & Riding, R. (1997). Towards a categorisation of cognitive styles and learning styles. *Educational Psychology, Vol. 17*, 5-27.

Schmeck, R.R., Ribick, R., & Ramanaiah, N. (1977). Development of a self report inventory for assessing individual differences in learning processes. *Applied Psychological Measurement, Vol.1*, 413-431.

Schouwenburg, H.C. (1996). Een onderzoek naar leerstijlen. *Tijdschrift voor Onderwijsresearch, Vol. 21* (2), 151-161.

Shrauger, J.S., & Osberg, T.M. (1981). The relative accuracy of self-predictions and judgement by others in psychological assessment. *Psychological Bulletin, Vol. 90* (2), 322-351.

Simons, P.R.J. (1997). Ontwikkeling van leercompetenties. *Opleiding en Ontwikkeling, Vol. 6*, 17-20.

Smit, W., & Van Os, W. (1985). Van studeergedrag naar studieresultaat. In J.G. Lodewijks, & P.J. Simons, (Eds.), *Zelfstandig Leren (bijdragen aan de ORD'84)*. Lisse: Swets & Zeitlinger.

Spenner, K.I. (1985). The upgrading and downgrading of occupations: issues, evidence, and implications for education. *Review of Educational Research, Vol. 55*, 125-154.

Thurow, L.C. (1975). *Generating Inequality*. New York: Basic Books.

Tsang, N.M. (1993). Shifts of students' learning styles on a social work course. *Social Work Education, Vol. 12* (1), 62-76.

Vermunt, J.D.H.M. (1992). *Leerstijlen en sturen van leerprocessen in het hoger onderwijs: naar een procesgerichte instructie in zelfstandig denken*. Amsterdam/Lisse: Swets & Zeitlinger.

Wetenschappelijke Raad voor het Regeringsbeleid (1995). Hoger onderwijs in fasen. *Rapporten aan de Regering, 47*, SDU, Den Haag.

Index

Educational Innovation in Economics and Business

KLUWER ACADEMIC PUBLISHERS – DORDRECHT / BOSTON / LONDON